Revision WorkBook

Land Law

EDITED BY
Gordon Henry LLB

THIRD EDITION REVISED AND UPDATED BY
P. Bridges BA, Barrister

HLT Publications

HLT PUBLICATIONS
200 Greyhound Road, London W14 9RY

First Edition 1990
Reprinted 1991
Second Edition 1992
Reprinted 1992
Third Edition 1994

© The HLT Group Ltd 1994

All HLT publications enjoy copyright protection and the
copyright belongs to The HLT Group Ltd.

All rights reserved. No part of this publication may be reproduced
or transmitted in any form or by any means, electronic,
mechanical, photocopying, recording or otherwise, or stored in
any retrieval system of any nature without either the written
permission of the copyright holder, application for which should
be made to The HLT Group Ltd, or a licence permitting restricted
copying in the United Kingdom issued by the Copyright Licensing
Agency.

Any person who infringes the above in relation to this publication
may be liable to criminal prosecution and civil claims for damages.

ISBN 0 7510 0451 0

British Library Cataloguing-in-Publication.

A CIP Catalogue record for this book is available from the
British Library.

Printed and bound in Great Britain.

CONTENTS

ACKNOWLEDGEMENT

Some questions used are taken or adapted from past University of London LLB (External) Degree examination papers and our thanks are extended to the University of London for their kind permission to use and publish the questions.

Caveat

The answers given are not approved or sanctioned by the University of London and are entirely our responsibility.

They are not intended as 'Model Answers', but rather as Suggested Solutions.

The answers have two fundamental purposes, namely:

a) To provide a detailed example of a suggested solution to an examination question, and

b) To assist students with their research into the subject and to further their understanding and appreciation of the subject of Laws.

INTRODUCTION

This Revision WorkBook has been designed specifically for those studying Land Law to undergraduate level or its equivalent. Its coverage is not restricted to any one syllabus but embraces all the core land law topics which can be found in university and polytechnic and institutional examinations.

Each chapter contains an introduction explaining the scope and general content of the topic covered. This is followed by detailed 'key points' which direct students to the material they must know if they are to fully understand the topic. Recent cases and statutes are explained where necessary.

A valuable feature of the Revision WorkBook are the examination questions which enable the student to focus on the examinable issues within each topic. These questions have been selected to cover as far as possible all the question variations that an examiner may set in each topic. Each question has a skeleton answer followed by a full suggested solution. Although students are not expected to produce a skeleton answer in the examination it can be a useful examination technique to adopt, and ensures a well planned, full and logical answer.

In this revised 1994 edition the final chapter contains the complete June 1993 University of London LLB (External) Land Law question paper, followed by suggested solutions to each question. Thus the student will have the opportunity to review a recent examination paper in its entirety, and can, if desired, use this chapter as a mock examination - referring to the suggested solutions only after first having attempted the questions.

HOW TO STUDY LAND LAW

The study of Land Law should be directed to answering the two types of question found in the examinations - the essay question and the problem question.

The essay-type of question may be either purely factual in asking you to explain the meaning of a certain doctrine or principle, or it may ask you to discuss a certain proposition usually derived from a quotation. In either of these cases, the approach to the answer is the same in that a clear programme must be devised to give the examiner the meaning or significance of the doctrine, principle or proposition; its origin in common law, equity or statute and cases which illustrate its application in Land Law. In anticipation of such questions, a card index of leading cases and statutory references could be prepared as part of your own revision process, using the Revision Schedule as a basis.

The problem-type question requires a different approach. You may well be asked to advise a client or merely discuss the problems raised in the question. In either case, the most important factor is to take great care in reading the question. By its nature, the question will be longer than the essay-type question and you will have a number of facts to digest. Time spent in analysing the question may well save time later and time must always be watched in the Land Law examination where the very size of the syllabus means you must already have considerable basic legal knowledge which you feel you must impress on the examiner. The quantity of knowledge is itself a trap and you must always keep within the boundaries of the question in hand. It is very tempting to show the examiner the extent of your knowledge of Land Law, but if this is outside the question, it is time lost and no marks earned. It is inevitable that some areas which you have studied and revised will not be the subject of questions, but under no circumstances attempt to adapt a question to a stronger area of knowledge at the expense of relevance.

When you are satisfied that you have grasped the full significance of the problem-type question, set out the fundamental principles involved. You may well be asked to advise one party, but there is no reason why you should not introduce your answer by:

'I would advise A on the following matters...'

and then continue the answer in a normal impersonal form. This is a much better technique than answering the question as an imaginary conversation.

You will then go on to identify the fundamental problem, or problems, posed by the question. This should be followed by a consideration of the law which is relevant to the problem. The source of the law, together with the cases which will be of assistance in solving the problem must then be considered in detail. The very good problem questions may well have alternative answers and in advising A you should be aware that alternative arguments may be available. If, however, you only identify one fundamental problem, do not waste time worrying that you cannot think of an alternative - there may very well only be that one answer.

The examiner will then wish to see how you use your legal knowledge to formulate a case and then how you apply that formula to the problem(s) within the question. It is this positive approach which can make answering a problem question a high mark earner for the student who has fully understood the question and clearly argued his case on the established law.

Always try to prepare a rough outline before embarking upon the formal answer. This will give you time to assemble your thoughts and organise your material. It may also help to ensure that you answer all the points you believe the examiner has raised. In developing a particular theme within the answer, it is very easy to overlook a matter which you had remembered in the initial review of the question. The Suggested Solutions in this Revision WorkBook use this technique by way of Skeleton Answer which precedes the full Suggested Solution.

Finally, always leave sufficient time in the examination to enable you to read your answers. Such a final revision can often bring a real bonus in terms of marks awarded.

The key to this approach is knowledge and the requirement to read the subject as often as time permits will bring the benefits when the examination is faced. The reading of the compulsory textbook is, therefore, an essential pre-requisite to a satisfactory result in the examination and is equally essential if full advantage is to be taken of the Revision WorkBook.

There are various ways of assembling Land Law for revision purposes. One method would be to divide the subject into four parts and devote revision time, in that order, to:

Revision WorkBook

Part	Chapter	Chapter No.
1	1925 legislation	1
	Settlements and trusts for sale	3
	Co-ownership	4
2	Registration	10
	Adverse possession	11
3	Leases	5
	Licences	6
4	Covenants	7
	Easements and profits à prendre	8
	Mortgages	9

REVISION AND EXAMINATION TECHNIQUE

(A)   REVISION TECHNIQUE

Planning a revision timetable

In planning your revision timetable make sure you don't finish the syllabus too early. You should avoid leaving revision so late that you have to 'cram' - but constant revision of the same topic leads to stagnation.

Plan ahead, however, and try to make your plans increasingly detailed as you approach the examination date.

Allocate enough time for each topic to be studied. But note that it is better to devise a realistic timetable, to which you have a reasonable chance of keeping, rather than a wildly optimistic schedule which you will probably abandon at the first opportunity!

The syllabus and its topics

One of your first tasks when you began your course was to ensure that you thoroughly understood your **syllabus**. Check now to see if you can write down the **topics** it comprises from memory. You will see that the chapters of this WorkBook are each devoted to a syllabus topic. This will help you decide which are the key chapters relative to your revision programme. Though you should allow some time for glancing through the other chapters.

The topic and its key points

Again working from memory, analyse what you consider to be the key points of any topic that you have selected for particular revision. Seeing what you can recall, unaided, will help you to understand and firmly memorise the concepts involved.

Using the WorkBook

Relevant questions are provided for each topic in this book. Naturally, as typical examples of examination questions, they do not normally relate to one topic only. But the questions in each chapter *will* relate to the subject matter of the chapter to a degree. You can choose your method of consulting the questions and solutions, but here are some suggestions (strategies 1-3). Each of them pre-supposes that you have read through the author's notes on key points and question analysis, and any other preliminary matter, at the beginning of the chapter. Once again, you now need to practise working from *memory*, for that is the challenge you are preparing yourself for. As a rule of procedure constantly test yourself once revision starts, both orally and in writing.

Strategy 1

Strategy 1 is planned for the purpose of *quick revision*. First read your chosen question carefully and then jot down in abbreviated notes what you consider to be the main points at issue. Similarly, note the cases and statutes that occur to you as being relevant for citation purposes. Allow yourself sufficient time to cover what you feel to be relevant. Then study the author's *skeleton solution* and skim-read the *suggested solution* to see how they compare with your notes. When comparing consider carefully what the author has included (and concluded) and see whether that agrees with what you have written. Consider the points of variation also. Have you recognised the key issues? How relevant have you been? It is possible, of course, that you have referred to a recent case that *is* relevant, but which had not been reported when the WorkBook was prepared.

Strategy 2

Strategy 2 requires a nucleus of *three hours* in which to practise writing a set of examination answers in a limited time-span.

Select a number of questions (as many as are normally set in your subject in the examination you are studying for), each from a different chapter in the WorkBook, without consulting the solutions. Find a place to write where you will not be disturbed and try to arrange not to be interrupted for three hours. Write your solutions in the time allowed, noting any time needed to make up if you *are* interrupted.

After a rest, compare your answers with the *suggested solutions* in the WorkBook. There will be considerable variation in style, of course, but the bare facts should not be too dissimilar. Evaluate your answer critically. Be 'searching', but develop a positive approach to deciding how you would tackle each question on another occasion.

Strategy 3

You are unlikely to be able to do more than one three hour examination, but occasionally set yourself a single question. Vary the 'time allowed' by imagining it to be one of the questions that you must answer in three hours and allow yourself a limited preparation and writing time. Try one question that you feel to be difficult and an easier question on another occasion, for example.

Mis-use of suggested solutions

Don't try to learn by rote. In particular, don't try to reproduce the *suggested solutions* by heart. Learn to express the basic concepts in your own words.

Keeping up-to-date

Keep up-to-date. While examiners do not require familiarity with changes in the law during the three months prior to the examination, it obviously creates a good impression if you can show you are acquainted with any recent changes. Make a habit of looking through one of the leading journals - *Modern Law Review, Law Quarterly Review* or the *New Law Journal,* for example - and cumulative indices to law reports, such as the *All England Law Reports* or *Weekly Law Reports,* or indeed the daily law reports in *The Times.* The *Law Society's Gazette* and the *Legal Executive Journal* are helpful sources, plus any specialist journal(s) for the subject you are studying.

(B)   EXAMINATION SKILLS

Examiners are human too!

The process of answering an examination question involves a *communication* between you and the person who set it. If you were speaking face to face with the person, you would choose your verbal points and arguments carefully in your reply. When writing, it is all too easy to forget *the human being who is awaiting the reply* and simply write out what one knows in the area of the subject! Bear in mind it is a person whose question you are responding to, throughout your essay. This will help you to avoid being irrelevant or long-winded.

The essay question

Candidates are sometimes tempted to choose to answer essay questions because they 'seem' easier. But the examiner is looking for thoughtful work and will not give good marks for superficial answers.

The essay-type of question may be either purely factual, in asking you to *explain the meaning* of a certain doctrine or principle, or it may ask you to *discuss* a certain proposition, usually derived from a quotation. In either case, the approach to the answer is the same. A clear programme must be devised to give the examiner the meaning or significance of the doctrine, principle or proposition and its origin in common law, equity or statute, and cases which illustrate its application to the branch of law concerned.

The problem question

The problem-type question requires a different approach. You may well be asked to advise a client or merely discuss the problems raised in the question. In either case, the most important factor is to take great care in reading the question. By its nature, the question will be longer than the essay-type question and you will have a number of facts to digest. Time spent in analysing the question may well save time later, when you are endeavouring to impress on the examiner the considerable extent of your basic legal knowledge. The quantity of knowledge is itself a trap and you must always keep within the boundaries of the question in hand. It is very tempting to show the examiner the extent of your knowledge of your subject, but if this is outside the question, it is time lost and no marks earned. It it inevitable that some areas which you have studied and revised will not be the subject of questions, but under no circumstances attempt to adapt a question to a stronger area of knowledge at the expense of relevance.

When you are satisfied that you have grasped the full significance of the problem-type question, set out the fundamental principles involved. You may well be asked to advise one party, but there is no reason why you should not introduce your answer by:

'I would advise A on the following matters ...'

and then continue the answer in a normal impersonal form. This is a much better technique than answering the question as an imaginary conversation.

You will then go on to identify the fundamental problem, or problems posed by the question. This should be followed by a consideration of the law which is relevant to the problem. The source of the law, together with the cases which will be of assistance in solving the problem, must then be considered in detail.

Very good problem questions are quite likely to have alternative answers, and in advising A you should be aware that alternative arguments may be available. Each stage of your answer, in this case, will be based on the argument or arguments considered in the previous stage, forming a conditional sequence.

If, however, you only identify one fundamental problem, do not waste time worrying that you cannot think of an alternative - there may very well be only that one answer.

The examiner will then wish to see how you use your legal knowledge to formulate a case and how you apply that formula to the problem which is the subject of the question. It is this positive approach which can make answering a problem question a high mark earner for the student who has fully understood the question and clearly argued his case on the established law.

Examination checklist

1 Read the instructions at the head of the examination carefully. While last-minute changes are unlikely - such as the introduction of a *compulsory question* or *an increase in the number of questions asked* - it has been known to happen.

2 Read the questions carefully. Analyse problem questions - work out what the examiner wants.

3 Plan your answer *before* you start to write. You can divide your time as follows:

   (a) working out the question (5 per cent of time)

   (b) working out how to answer the question (5 to 10 per cent of time)

   (c) writing your answer

Do not overlook (a) and (b)

4 Check that you understand the rubric *before* you start to write. Do not 'discuss', for example, if you are specifically asked to 'compare and contrast'.

5 Answer the correct number of questions. If you fail to answer one out of four questions set you lose 25 per cent of your marks!

Style and structure

Try to be clear and concise. Basically this amounts to using paragraphs to denote the sections of your essay, and writing simple, straightforward sentences as much as possible. The sentence you have just read has 22 words - when a sentence reaches 50 words it becomes difficult for a reader to follow.

Do not be inhibited by the word 'structure' (traditionally defined as giving an essay a beginning, a middle and an end). A good structure will be the natural consequence of setting out your arguments and the supporting evidence in a logical order. Set the scene briefly in your opening paragraph. Provide a clear conclusion in your final paragraph.

TABLE OF CASES

TABLE OF STATUTES

TABLE OF STATUTES

1   BASIS OF LAND LAW

1.1   Introduction

Although many examiners neglect this area of Land Law it remains important to understand these fundamental principles. In particular no candidates should go into a Land Law examination without a working knowledge of s1 of the Law of Property Act 1925. The ability to give definitions to the two legal estates will be particularly useful as, also, is a knowledge of the contents of s205(1) LPA 1925.

1.2   Key points

Introductory

Nature of land - s205(1)(ix) LPA 1925

History

Definitions of 'land' and 'real property' ('land' wider to include leaseholds as 'chattels real')

Tenures and estates

a) *Doctrine of tenure - quality of the holding - the terms on which the land is held*

    i) Lay tenures

        • Miscellaneous

        • Knight service

          (note the 'incidents' of tenure)

        • Grand serjeanty

        • Petty serjeanty

        • Common socage

    ii) Spiritual tenures

        • Frankalmoign

1

- Divine service

iii) Unfree tenure - copyhold: s128 and 12th Schedule LPA 1922

iv) Effect of 1925 legislation - Cheshire states 'A conception of merely academic interest it no longer restricts the tenant in his free enjoyment of the land.' Of little practical importance today.

b) *Doctrine of estates - quantity of the holding - describes for how long the land is held*

   i) Original freehold estates

   - Fee simple

   - Fee tail

   - Life estate

   - Estate - pur autre vie

   ii) Original estates less than freehold

   iii) Estates and interests since 1925 - continues to be of importance and retains the flexibility as a characteristic of English Land Law.

   - It is important to study in detail the reduction in legal estates and interests made by

     LPA 1925 s1(1), (2) and (3)

   - Fee simple absolute in possession - see s205(1)(xix) LPA 1925) ('possession')

   - Terms of years absolute - see s205(1)(xxvii) LPA 1925

   - Modified fees - compare the determinable fee simple with the conditional fee simple

   - Note the Reverter of Sites Act 1987. Land is now held on trust for sale for the revertee as a beneficiary under a statutory trust for sale - there is no automatic revesting and trustees cannot gain a title by adverse possession.

   iv) The estate in fee simple

   Method of creation

   - At common law

   - Wills

   - s60(1) LPA 1925 - will pass the fee simple or whatever estate is presently held of the vendor

   - Corporations

   - Registered land

s19(1) LRA 1925 - title must be completed by registration

s123 LRA 1925 - title is void if not submitted for registration within two months.

c) *Extent of ownership*

i) Cujus est solum ejus est usque ad coelum et ad inferos (whosoever has the soil also owns to the heavens above and to the centre beneath)

Cheshire - 'The common law principle is that a tenant in fee simple is owner of everything in, on and above his land.'

Commissioner for Railways v *Valuer-General* [1974] AC 328, Lord Wilberforce: 'At most the maxim is used as a statement, imprecise enough, of the extent of the rights, prima facie, of owners of land.'

Megarry and Wade - 'The absolute freedom of the owner is qualified in many ways.'

Limitations

*   Overhanging objects

*   Treasure trove

*   Chattels under or attached to land - fixtures - see below

*   Wild animals

*   Minerals

*   Flights over land - s76(1) Civil Aviation Act 1982 and *Bernstein* v *Skyviews & General Ltd* [1977] 3 WLR 136, Griffiths J:

    'the balance was best struck by restricting the rights of an owner in the airspace above his land to such heights as was necessary for the ordinary use and enjoyment of his land and the structures upon it, and declaring that above that height he had no greater rights in the airspace than any other member of the public.'

*   Fishing rights in non-tidal parts of rivers

*   Water rights

*   Bed of non-tidal river

*   Effects of legislation including security of tenure provisions

ii) More particularly, limitations should be noted as follows:

*   Rights over the land of another - rights *in alieno solo*

*   Rights in airspace:

    Woollerton and Wilson Ltd v *Richard Costain Ltd* [1970] 1 WLR 411

    Kelsen v *Imperial Tobacco Co Ltd* [1957] 2 QB 334

Bernstein v *Skyviews & General Ltd* [1977] 3 WLR 136 and s76 Civil Aviation Act 1982

Anchor Brewhouse Developments Ltd v *Berkley House (Docklands) Developments Ltd* (1987) 284 EG 625

- Minerals - gold and silver - petroleum - coal

- Treasure trove - gold/silver - found hidden in/on land - owner not known

Attorney-General of the Duchy of Lancaster v *G E Overton (Farms) Ltd* [1982] Ch 277

Wild animals - res nullius - things without an owner

- Water
  - Common law

    Own land or flowing past - riparian rights.

    River - abstraction for ordinary purposes or extraordinary purposes.

    Swindon Waterworks Co v *Wilts & Berks Canal Navigation Co* (1875) LR 7 HL 697

    Percolating water - unlimited amounts regardless of damage.

    Stephens v *Anglian Water Authority* [1987] 1 WLR 1381

    Langbrook Properties Ltd v *Surrey County Council* [1970] 1 WLR 101

  - Statute - Water Resources Act 1963 - licence required

- Liability in tort - trespass - nuisance - negligence. Duty of care on landlord - s4 Defective Premises Act 1972

- Statute - Megarry and Wade - 'Much legislation imposing on landowners restrictions and liabilities in the public interest.'

  Town and Country Planning Acts - Housing Acts - Public Health Acts - security of tenure provisions

iii) Fixtures

- Definition - goods annexed to land in such circumstances that the law assumes that they are now to be treated as land.

- Why is the question of fixtures important? Who now owns the goods?

- Explain the two tests applied to fixtures: (a) degree of annexation; (b) purpose of annexation.

- Is test (a) conclusive? No, rebut by showing intention of person who affixed.

- Evidence of rebuttal? Object merely resting on land or better enjoyment of object. What benefits - the land or the object?

- Why was test (b) required? Limitations of test (a).

- Which areas of Land Law are affected by 'fixtures'?

  Landlord and tenant: trade: domestic: agricultural (s10 AHA 1986)

  Tenant for life - remainderman: *D'Eyncourt* v *Gregory* (1866) LR 3 Eq 382, *Leigh* v *Taylor* [1902] AC 157

  Mortgagor - mortgagee: *Hobson* v *Gorringe* [1897] 1 Ch 182, *Reynolds* v *Ashby* [1904] AC 466

  Vendor - purchaser: *Berkley* v *Poulett* (1976) *The Times* 3 November, *Dean* v *Andrews* (1985) *The Times* 25 May

- Problems of reconciling some cases: seats in a cinema/theatre.

  Fixtures: *Vaudeville Electric Cinema Ltd* v *Muriset* [1923] 2 Ch 74 (tip-up seats bolted to cinema floor).

  Not fixtures: *Lyon & Co* v *London, City and Midland Bank* [1903] 2 KB 235 (chairs temporarily fixed to floor of a theatre) or walling stones used as illustration in *Holland* v *Hodgson* (1872) LR 7 CP 328 (blocks of stones stacked on top of each other in a builders' yard, chattels; same stones arranged on top of each other as a wall, fixtures).

1.3   Recent cases and statutes

Anchor Brewhouse Developments Ltd v *Berkley House (Docklands) Developments Ltd* (1987) 284 EG 625 - trespass by jib of crane.

Stephens v *Anglian Water Authority* [1987] 1 WLR 1381 - percolating water - abstract unlimited amount regardless of damage.

Reverter of Sites Act 1987

This Act excludes from s7(1) LPA 1925 certain statutes, including the School Sites Acts, which allowed for sites to be made available for schools, churches, libraries or museums.

The effect is to replace the right of reverter, in such cases, with a statutory trust for sale. Upon the particular use coming to an end the land will be held on trust for sale for the revertee who becomes the beneficiary under this statutory trust for sale.

This ends the automatic revesting of the land and will, in the cases where the 1987 Act applies, prevent the trustees obtaining a title by adverse possession, as occurred in *Re Rowhook Mission Hall, Horsham* [1985] Ch 62.

The consequence is that the trustees can now sell the property without fear of the title being challenged by the purchaser because of the potential existence of some beneficiary who, initially, could not be traced. Equally there is no longer a need for the trustees to wait a further twelve years in order to adopt the solution in *Re Rowhook Mission Hall, Horsham* (1985) of establishing a title by adverse possession.

Once the use had ended and it is established that any potential beneficiary cannot be traced, the trustees may sell the land. At this time the trustees should also apply to the Charity Commissioners for a scheme to be set up for the administration of the proceeds of sale. This scheme may not be the exact purpose of the original trust, but should have similar objectives. If the beneficiary can be traced the commissioners will not set up a scheme without the consent of that beneficiary.

If the beneficiary cannot be traced there are requirements for advertising the proposals in order to establish that every effort has been made to discover any beneficiary. If a beneficiary does come forward within five years of the above scheme being approved, compensation may be paid equivalent to that beneficiary's right at the date the interest was extinguished by these provisions.

1.4 Analysis of questions

As indicated in the Introduction, a working knowledge of s1 LPA 1925 is essential. The other examinable feature of the estate is to know and identify the modified fees simple. One method of doing this is to use the 'clue words' by which a determinable fee simple is identified by the use of words such as 'until', 'during', 'while' or 'as long as' whilst the conditional fee simple is identified by phrases such as 'on condition that', 'provided that' or 'but if'. The consequences of the identification must be known and in particular the effect of s7(1) LPA 1925, as amended by the Law of Property (Amendment) Act 1926, on the conditional fee simple. This effect is clearly to reduce the quality of the word 'absolute', but only in the context of the fee simple absolute in possession.

A further area for questions could be the 'cujus' maxim. Of these the problems of air space, rights over water and fixtures are of importance.

1.5 Questions

Question 1

Explain the effect of the following dispositions taking effect today:

a) a lease to A for life at a rent of £500 per annum;

b) a yearly tenancy to B, with a provision that the lessor will not give notice to quit during B's lifetime;

c) a lease of Blackacre to C for 50 years, or until C shall cease to reside at Blackacre;

d) a lease to D for 7 years at a rent of £400 per annum, with an option to renew, on identical terms and conditions.

University of London LLB Examination
(for External Students) Land Law June 1986 Q1

General comment

Many see this type of question as the 'traditional' introductory question to a Land Law paper. The question is heavily weighted towards leases, which may distort an examination paper which already has separate Landlord and Tenant questions.

Skeleton solution

a) *Lease for life at a rent*

Consider: s149(6) LPA 1925

If no rent paid: see s20(1)(iv) SLA 1925

b) *Yearly tenancy*

Effect of proviso - lessor will not give notice during tenant's lifetime

Re Midland Railway Co's Agreement [1971] Ch 725

Centaploy Ltd v *Matlodge Ltd* [1974] Ch 1

c) *Term certain*

50 years or *until* C shall cease to reside there

Lace v *Chantler* [1944] 1 All ER 305

d) *Option to renew 'on identical terms and conditions'*

Consider: s145 and 15th Schedule LPA 1922:

Consider and compare: *Northchurch Estates Ltd* v *Daniels* [1947] Ch 117, *Caerphilly Concrete Products Ltd* v *Owen* [1972] 1 All ER 248 and *Marjorie Burnett Ltd* v *Barclay* (1980) 258 EG 642

Suggested solution

a) A has been granted a lease for life at a rent of £500 per annum. This clearly comes within the provisions of s149(6) of the Law of Property Act 1925 which provides: 'Any lease or underlease, at a rent, or in consideration of a fine, for life or lives or for any term of years determinable with life or lives ... shall take effect as a lease ... for a term of 90 years determinable after the death ... of the original lessee ... by at least one month's notice in writing ...'

The effect is that A has a term of 90 years which will continue after his death for the residue of the 90 year period. Once A has died the lease can be brought to an end by notice in writing of at least one month given to expire 'on one of the quarter days applicable to the tenancy'.

(It may be mentioned, in passing, that if A had not been under an obligation to pay rent he would have become a tenant for life under s20(1)(iv) of the Settled Land Act 1925. But such a grant must clearly refer to no rent whatever: *Re Catling* (1931).)

b) This is expressed as a yearly tenancy but the proviso contradicts this expression. Any provision which is repugnant to the nature of any periodic tenancy, such as the yearly tenancy in the question, is void and unenforceable. The problem is to decide whether the proviso is an attempt to prevent the landlord giving notice for an extended period of time. It could be argued that the literal effect of the proviso is to give A a lease for life rather than a yearly tenancy. On the other hand, if it can be said that the landlord is not permanently deprived from giving notice to quit then the proviso may be valid as in *Re Midland Railway Co's Agreement* (1971).

In this problem it may be argued that the proviso is not compatible with a yearly tenancy and, if so, that the proviso is void leaving B with a yearly tenancy subject to the normal common law period of six months' notice to terminate the tenancy: see Whitford J in *Centaploy Ltd* v *Matlodge Ltd* (1974).

c) Every lease must be for a certain period: *Lace* v *Chantler* (1944). In this problem we have a certain period of 50 years: then a condition has been added which will bring the lease to an end if C ceases to reside in the property. This introduces an element of uncertainty and we must decide whether this is a fundamental flaw in the lease. If the maximum period of the lease is fixed and certain then it is possible to make it determinable by some uncertain event within the period. Megarry and Wade quote the example of a valid lease 'for 21 years determinable if the tenant ceases to live on the premises'. The authors conclude: 'It is therefore perfectly possible to make a lease determinable upon some future uncertain event, provided that the device of a determinable fixed term is employed.'

Thus C will have a lease for 50 years but if he does cease to reside at Blackacre the lease will come to an end. This is a condition subsequent and may cause the lease to be ended when the future uncertain event takes place.

d) The lease to D is for a basic period of seven years and the intention was to give, presumably, one option to renew, on identical terms and conditions. The fundamental question is whether the phrase 'on identical terms and conditions' creates a perpetually renewable lease. The law is to be found in s145 of and the 15th Schedule to the Law of Property Act 1922 which came into force on the 1st January 1926 as part of the so-called 1925 property legislation. The effect of creating a perpetually renewable lease is that it becomes a term of 2000 years calculated from the date fixed for the term to commence. The 15th Schedule LPA 1922 contains the detailed provisions as to this term. These include that the tenant, but not the landlord, may terminate the lease on any date upon which, but for the conversion, the lease would have expired if it had not been renewed. The landlord has no right to determine the lease at the renewal dates.

The phrase 'on identical terms and conditions' was used in *Northchurch Estates Ltd* v *Daniels* (1947). A tenancy agreement of a cottage provided that 'the term shall be for a period of one year certain from March 25 1938, the tenant having the option to renew the tenancy from year to year on identical terms and conditions as hereinafter stated notice of such intention to renew the tenancy to be given in writing on or before December 25 in each year'. It was held that even though the court may lean against perpetually renewable leases, this must give way to the language used by the parties and, in this case, there was no real doubt that they had intended to create such a leasehold. The consequence was that by virtue of s145 and the 15th Schedule LPA 1922 the agreement was converted into a contract to create a term of 2000 years.

It would appear that this decision is conclusive. The fact is that the courts do lean against perpetual renewability, and the lease should be scrutinised with care to ensure that there is no possible way to distinguish this lease from that in *Northchurch Estates Ltd* v *Daniels* (1947). In more recent cases the courts have emphasised the need for more specific reference to the renewal clause before they would find perpetual renewability: see, eg, *Caerphilly Concrete Products Ltd* v *Owen* (1972). The most recent statement against perpetual renewability was by Nourse J in *Marjorie Burnett Ltd* v *Barclay* (1980). The statement in the question may not be totally unequivocably expressed as being perpetually renewable but it would appear to be caught by the decision in *Northchurch Estates Ltd* v *Daniels* converting a lease in those terms into a lease for 2000 years within the LPA 1922.

Tutorial comments

Consider:

a)   i)   s149(6) LPA 1925

     ii) s145 LPA 1922

     iii) the decision in *Northchurch Estates Ltd* v *Daniels* [1947] Ch 117

Compare the decisions in:

b)   i)   *Caerphilly Concrete Products Ltd* v *Owen* [1972] 1 All ER 248; and

     ii) *Marjorie Burnett Ltd* v *Barclay* (1980) 258 EG 642

Question 2

Consider the effect of the following dispositions made by an owner in fee simple absolute in possession:

a) A conveyance of land to trustees in fee simple 'for as long as the premises are used as a public library'.

b) A conveyance of land to trustees in fee simple 'provided that it shall always be used exclusively for the purposes of a hospital'.

c)   i)   A conveyance of Blackacre to Percy, subject to and with the benefit of an existing lease to Terry who is in possession:

     ii) A yearly tenancy of Whiteacre which either party may determine by notice and which contains a forfeiture clause giving the landlord a right to re-enter the premises in the event of breach of covenant by the tenant.

d) A lease giving the tenant a right of renewal 'on identical terms and conditions'.

University of London, LLB Examination
(for External Students) Land Law 1980 Q1

General comment

The usual style of introductory question associated with many Land Law examinations. A good question to attempt early in the examination in order to sharpen the recall faculties, even if part has to be left in order to return later. Beware of time because it is a long question and the good candidate may even have to be selective as to the amount of information he can express in the answer. The emphasis on the 'clue words' which identify the type of modified fee simple is important.

Skeleton solution

a) *Clue words*: 'for as long as' indicate a determinable fee simple. Ends automatically if cease to use as a public library. But if the trustees remain in possession then grantor/successors must resume possession within 12 years or risk losing the right under the Limitation Act 1980 - *Re Rowhook Mission Hall, Horsham* [1984] 3 All ER 179. Effect: a strict settlement within s1(1)(ii)(c) SLA 1925.

b) *Clue words*: 'provided that' indicate a conditional fee simple. Gives A right to re-enter if hospital use ends - must re-enter. Effect: a fee simple absolute within s7(1) LPA 1925 (as amended) - 'a fee simple subject to a ... right of entry or re-entry is ... a fee simple absolute' (added by LP(A)A 1926).

c) i) 'Possession' defined in s205(1)(xix) LPA 1925 to include 'receipt of rents and profits' so Percy acquires 'fee simple absolute in possession' (see diagram in suggested solution).

   ii) 'Term of years absolute' defined in s205(1)(xxvii) LPA 1925 as a 'term of years ... either certain or liable to determination by notice, re-entry ...' The yearly tenancy is a term of years absolute ('includes a term ... for a year') which is absolute even though the landlord may re-enter in the event of a breach of covenant.

d) *Renewal on 'identical terms and conditions'*. Normally should go on to say 'including this right of renewal' to create a perpetually renewable lease within s145 LPA 1922, but such a phrase was held to create a perpetually renewable lease in *Northchurch Estates Ltd* v *Daniels* [1947] Ch 117.

   The court does lean against this interpretation but the *effect* here is to create a term of 2000 years which the tenant (only) may terminate on any date lease would expire by at least 10 days' written notice: 15th Schedule LPA 1922.

Suggested solution

Parts (a) and (b) of the question require the student to identify and distinguish between the conditional fee simple and the determinable fee simple. It is a question of locating the limiting words and then deciding upon the effect of those words.

a) The conveyance to the trustees in fee simple is 'for as long as' a particular use as a public library continues. A conditional fee simple is identified by phrases such as 'on condition that' or 'provided that' and has the effect of imposing a condition which may bring the grant to an end. On the other hand, a determinable fee simple is identified by the use of such words as 'until' or 'as long as'. The effect of a determinable fee simple is much different in that it will end automatically on the happening of the determining event, although this may never occur.

In the problem, the premises may continue to be used as a public library for all time and the determining event only occurs when they cease to be so used. In the event the conveyance has created a determinable fee simple which will continue 'as long as' the use as a public library continues. If that use ceases, then the grant automatically comes to an end. Whilst the use as a public library continues, there is a possibility of reverter in the grantor. This means there would be a possibility of the land reverting to the grantor if the use as a public library ceases.

b) A conditional fee simple is identified by the use of phrases such as 'on condition that' or 'provided that'. The effect is to create a separate condition which may bring the grant to an end. This event is a condition subsequent and, unlike the determinable fee simple, it does not automatically bring the grant to an end. The effect of the conveyance is to create a conditional fee simple which means the trustees hold the land subject to the condition that the land is 'used exclusively for the purposes of a hospital'.

If the grant had been a determinable fee simple, the interest would cease immediately its hospital use ceased. In this problem, however, we have a conditional fee simple which merely sets out the circumstances under which the condition will operate. If the hospital use ends, the condition gives a right to enter and determine the interest, but it will continue until such right of re-entry has been exercised. As a condition subsequent operates as a forfeiture clause, it will be construed strictly and if for any reason it is void, it will be struck out, leaving the conveyance free from the condition.

In part (a) the grantor has a possibility of reverter whereas in this case the conditional fee simple means that the grantor has a right of re-entry if the condition operates. The distinction between the two grants is summarised by Megarry and Wade in *The Law of Real Property* in these words:

'The essential distinction is that the determining event in a determinable fee itself sets the limit for the estate first granted. A condition subsequent, on the other hand, is an independent clause added to a limitation of a complete fee simple absolute which operates so as to defeat it.'

A conditional fee simple is construed strictly and may be held void if it is contrary to public policy. In the problem, it would be a pre-requisite to the grant that the acceptable use of the land for the purposes of the Town and Country Planning legislation was for hospital purposes otherwise this would render the condition void and so make the grant a fee simple absolute.

c) i) Section 1(1) of the Law of Property Act 1925 provides that:

'1) the only estates in land which are capable of subsisting or of being conveyed or created at law are -

a) An estate in fee simple absolute in possession;

b) A term of years absolute.'

The question to be considered here is whether the 'conveyance of Blackacre to Percy, subject to and with the benefit of an existing lease to Terry' vests a fee simple absolute in possession in Percy. He is clearly not in physical possession during the currency of the lease to Terry.

Assistance is provided by s205(1)(xix) of the 1925 Act where 'possession' is defined to include 'receipt of rents and profits or the right to receive the same'. Thus, possession not only includes physical possession, but also the receipt of rents from, for example, a tenant for years who will be in actual physical possession of property. A fee simple absolute will still be 'in possession' even though the owner is only entitled to receive the rent reserved in the lease. Percy will therefore acquire a fee simple absolute in possession in Blackacre. This will be represented by the rent paid by Terry during the course of the lease and when this ends, Percy will be able to assume possession of Blackacre.

This answer is based on the general law of property without specific reference to such specialised legislation as the Rent Acts.

For ease of reference, the above problem could be demonstrated by the following diagram:

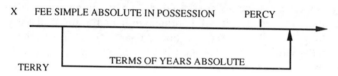

ii) Is a 'yearly tenancy of Whiteacre which either party may determine by notice and which contains a forfeiture clause giving the landlord a right to re-enter the premises in the event of breach of convenant by the tenant' a 'term of years absolute' within s1(1)(b) of the Law of Property Act 1925? On the face of it, such conditions must raise a question as to the 'absolute' nature of the yearly tenancy in Whiteacre. The question is again resolved by s205 of the Law of Property Act 1925. Section 205(1)(xxvii) gives a comprehensive definition of 'terms of years absolute' in these terms:

'a term of years ... either certain or liable to determination by notice, re-entry, operation of law, or by a provision for cesser on redemption, or in any other event ... and in this definition the expression "term of years" includes a term for less than a year, or for a year or years and a fraction of a year or from year to year'.

The effect of this is clearly explained by Megarry and Wade:

'This means that a term of years may be absolute even if it contains a clause enabling either party to determine it by giving notice or if it provides (as is almost always the case) that the landlord may recover the land if the rent is not paid or a covenant is broken.'

Thus, the yearly tenancy of Whiteacre is a 'term of years absolute' within s1(1)(b) of the Law of Property Act 1925 even though the 'absolute' quality may be defeated by the operation of the conditions for determination or forfeiture by the landlord in the event of a breach of covenant.

d) The subject of perpetually renewable leases was covered by s145 of and the 15th Schedule to the Law of Property Act 1922 which came into force on 1st January, 1926 as part of the 1925 property legislation. A perpetually renewable lease gives the tenant the right to renew the lease each time it expires. If the renewal clause is in the terms of the question as a right of renewal 'on identical terms and conditions', then it is held to be perpetually renewable, even though that was not the intention of the parties.

The phrase in question was used in *Northchurch Estates Ltd* v *Daniels* (1947) where a tenancy agreement of a cottage provided that 'the term shall be for a period of one year certain from 25 March 1938, the tenant having the option to renew the tenancy from year to year on identical terms and conditions as hereinafter stated notice of such intention to renew the tenancy to be given in writing on or before 25 December in each year'. It was held that even though the court may lean against perpetually renewable leases, this must give way to the language used by the parties and, in this case, there was no real doubt that they had intended to create such a leasehold.

The consequence was that by virtue of s145 of and the 15th Schedule para 7(1) to the Law of Property Act 1922, the agreement was converted into a contract to create a term of two thousand years.

Thus the effect of creating a perpetually renewable lease after 1925 is, in fact, to create a term of 2,000 years calculated from the date fixed for the term to commence. The 15th Schedule to the Law of Property Act 1922 contains detailed provisions as to this 2,000 year term which include that the tenant, but not the landlord, may terminate the lease on any date upon which, but for the conversion, the lease would have expired if it had not been renewed, provided he gives at least ten days' written notice to the landlord. The landlord has no right to determine the lease at the renewal dates.

Paragraph 7(1) of the 15th Schedule to the Law of Property Act 1922 states:

'(1) Any contract entered into after the commencement of this Act, for the grant of a lease, subterm, or other leasehold interest with a covenant or obligation for perpetual renewal shall ... operate as an agreement for a demise for a term of two thousand years ... to commence from the date agreed for the commencement of the term ... and in every case free from the obligation for renewal ...'

The courts do lean against perpetual renewability and any renewal clause in a lease should be examined carefully to ensure that there is no possible way to distinguish the lease from existing decisions such as *Northchurch Estates Ltd* v *Daniels* (1947). In more recent cases the courts have emphasised the need for more specific reference to the renewal clause before they would hold the lease to be perpetually renewable: see, eg, *Caerphilly Concrete Products Ltd* v *Owen* (1972). Another statement against perpetual renewability was by Nourse J in *Marjorie Burnett Ltd* v *Barclay*

(1980) in which he emphasised '... that the court must bear in mind the leaning against perpetually renewable leases, and must find expressed in the lease an express covenant or obligation for perpetual renewal.'

Tutorial comments

a) Compare the determinable fee simple with the conditional fee simple.

b) Note the definition of 'term of years absolute' in s205(1)(xxvii) LPA 1925.

Question 3

a) 'There are thus two fundamental doctrines in the law of real property ... tenure answers the question "upon what terms is it (land) held"?: estates answers the question "for how long"?' (Megarry and Wade, *The Law of Real Property*).

   Explain this statement.

b) What interests, if any, are created by each of the following transactions?

   i) A conveys Blackacre to B in fee simple, imposing covenants and reserving a right of re-entry on breach of convenant.

   ii) C, lessee of Whiteacre, sublets to D for the remainder of the term without asking for the consent of L, the landlord, as provided in the lease.

University of London LLB Examination
(for External Students) Land Law June 1985 Q1

General comment

A question to remind the candidate that all examinations are based on a syllabus and the examiner is entitled to select questions from any part of that syllabus. Part (a) emerges from the first substantive paragraph of the syllabus and is a welcome encouragement to those tutors who advise students that an understanding of Land Law is always helped by an appreciation of fundamental areas such as this.

Part (b) reminds candidates that leases effectively feature twice in the syllabus being part of the general debate on s1 LPA 1925 and subsequently as a separate area of study in their own right.

Skeleton solution

a) *Describe tenure*

   quality of holding;

   feudal pyramid - diagram;

   forms of tenure - diagram;

   tenures today.

   Describe estate

   quantity of the holding;

types of estate before 1926 - diagram;

the legal estate today (s1(1) LPA 1925) - diagram;

conclusion - the estate today.

b) i) 'Conveys':

indicates fee simple absolute in possession;

'absolute' where a right of re-entry exists;

effect of s7(1) LPA 1925 of Law of Property (Amendment) Act 1926.

ii) Is this a sub-lease or an assignment? Illustrate distinction. Qualified covenant applies, depending on terms, to both sub-lease and assignment. Effect of s19(1)(a) Landlord and Tenant Act 1927 on such a qualified covenant. Response of C (s53 Landlord and Tenant Act 1954): interpretation of reasonableness in this context.

Suggested solution

a) This statement of Megarry and Wade summarises the rules which formed the basis of Land Law.

Tenure answered the question 'upon what terms' was the land held. This described the quality of the holding and, in particular, referred to the early rules of subinfeudation by which the grantee held 'land' in return for services. This concept of subinfeudation emerged after the Norman Conquest and represented the rewards given by the King to those who had supported him. This created a form of holding which acquired the title of the feudal pyramid because all 'land' was held either directly, or indirectly through intermediaries, from the King himself. This may be represented by the following diagram of freehold tenures:

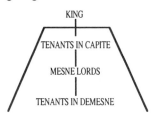

KING

TENANTS IN CAPITE

MESNE LORDS

TENANTS IN DEMESNE

Thus each intermediary would grant an interest in land in return for some service and in this way the fabric of feudalism was created. It did not last for many years in that it became much easier to pay for services than provide them directly. As a consequence the doctrine of subinfeudation was brought to an end by the statute Quia Emptores in 1290. The major effect of the statute was to replace subinfeudation by substitution. This is described in Megarry and Wade as follows: 'Quia Emptores marked the victory of the modern concept of land as alienable property over the more restrictive principles of feudalism. For no new tenures in fee simple could thenceforth be created except by the Crown.' This is followed by a suitable epitaph to the feudal pyramid: 'After 1290 the feudal pyramid began to crumble. The number of mesne lordships could not be increased, evidence of existing mesne lordships gradually disappeared with the passing of time, and so most land came to be held directly from the Crown.' In the words of the statute itself:

'Our Lord the King ... at the instance of the great men of the realm... ordained, that from henceforth it shall be lawful to every freeman to sell at his own pleasure his lands and tenements, or part of them; so that the feoffee shall hold the same ... fee, by such service and customs as his feoffor held before.'

The forms of tenure may be described as the quality of the holding. This quality was varied by the nature of the services to be provided by the grantee. A popular diagram of the forms of tenure is as follows:

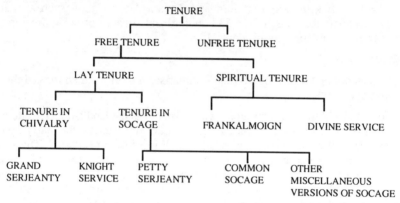

Of these forms of tenure the most significant was, probably, knight service. This contained many 'incidents' which formed the basis of the tenure and included relief, escheat, wardship and marriage. Most of the forms of tenure had ended before they were abolished by the Tenures Abolition Act 1660: some, including frankalmoign and the services incident to grand and petty serjeanty, survived until 1925. From the 1st January 1926 the only surviving form of tenure is socage now known as freehold tenure. The consequence is neatly summarised by Cheshire: 'The result is that though the general theory of tenure is still a part of English law in the sense that all land is held by a superior and is incapable of absolute ownership, yet the law of tenure is both simpler and of less significance than it was before 1926. It is simpler because there is now only one form of tenure: namely socage. It is of less significance because all the tenurial incidents (including escheat) which might in exceptional cases have brought profit to a mesne lord have been abolished ... We can, in fact, now describe the theory of tenure, despite the great part that it had played in the history of English law, as a conception of merely academic interest. It no longer restricts the tenant in his free enjoyment of the land.'

Estate deals with the duration of interest and describes the quantity of the holdings. It is, again, possible to demonstrate this by way of a diagram in which it will be noted there are two major categories of estate - the freehold and the less than freehold estate. Unlike tenures, the concept of estates remains with us today and formed the essential part of s1(1) of the Law of Property Act 1925. The types of estate that existed before 1926 may be shown diagrammatically as follows:

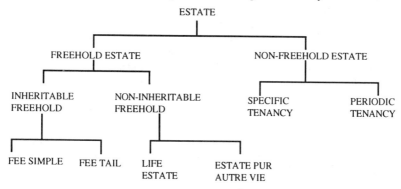

Of these estates the fee simple and the non-freehold estate remain as legal estates under s1(1) LPA 1925. They are now, respectively, the 'fee simple absolute in possession' and the 'term of years absolute'. The fee tail and the life estate also continue but are now equitable interests known, respectively, as the entailed interest and the life interest. A feature of the estate is that several could exist concurrently and this is retained by s1(5) LPA 1925 which provides: 'A legal estate may subsist concurrently with or subject to any other legal estate in the same land ...' The effect today is the possibility of the fee simple, leases and sub-leases all being separate estates in the same land.

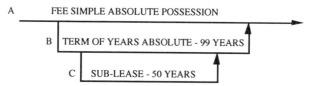

It will be seen that 'estate' is not the land itself. The estate is a conceptual matter which has been separated from the land. It is the estate that is the subject of conveyance, lease or assignment whilst the land itself remains in the ownership of the Crown as a further reminder of the feudal origins. Cheshire defines 'estate' as '... the right to possess and use the land for the period of time for which it has been granted'.

Most authors recognise the unique quality of the estate and the right of seisin which represents the present right to enjoy the possession of the land by an owner of the freehold estate holding for freehold tenure. A fitting conclusion is provided by Cheshire:

'In conclusion, it may be said that this doctrine of the estate has given an elasticity to the English law of the land that is not found in countries outside the area of the common law.'

17

b)   i)   The use of the word 'conveys' indicates that A holds the fee simple absolute in possession in Blackacre and he conveys the freehold estate to B. The conveyance includes covenants which mean that A will retain an interest as covenantee and will be able to enforce the covenants, whether they are positive or negative, as a matter of contract against B. The question which arises is whether B has an 'absolute' fee simple when A may re-enter if any of the covenants are broken. This clearly is a restriction on the 'absolute' nature of the estate as the word 'absolute' is defined in general usage. This problem was recognised, belatedly, by the draftsmen of the 1925 legislation and the following words were added to s7(1) LPA 1925 by the Law of Property (Amendment) Act 1926. '... and a fee simple subject to a legal or equitable right of entry or re-entry is for the purposes of this Act a fee simple absolute'. The effect of this addition to s7(1) is that B does hold a 'fee simple absolute in possession', a legal estate, even though A has a right of re-entry if any of the covenants are broken.

ii) Every sub-lease requires the sub-lessor to retain a reversion even if it is just for one day. The effect of this transaction may be seen:

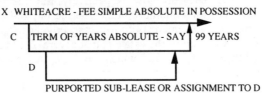

X WHITEACRE - FEE SIMPLE ABSOLUTE IN POSSESSION

C   TERM OF YEARS ABSOLUTE - SAY 99 YEARS

D

PURPORTED SUB-LEASE OR ASSIGNMENT TO D

The effect of this transaction will be to assign to D the residue of the term of years presently vested in C. D will become the tenant of X and C will cease to have any interest whatsoever in Whiteacre except that he will continue to be bound to X by privity of contract if X and C were the original landlord and tenant respectively.

The original lease contains a requirement that C should obtain the consent of X before parting with possession of Whiteacre. The clause would presumably express the restriction in words such as:

'C shall not assign, underlet or part with possession of Whiteacre without the consent of X.'

If the covenant is expressed in these terms it is a qualified covenant and C will be liable to X.

The assignment itself will still be effective and any notice to quit would have to be served on the assignee D: see *Old Grovebury Manor Farm Ltd v W Seymour Plant Sales & Hire Ltd (No 2)* (1979).

Because the covenant is qualified by requiring the consent of X reference must also be made to s19(1)(a) of the Landlord and Tenant Act 1927 which provides:

'1) In all leases whether made before or after the commencement of this Act containing a covenant condition or agreement against assigning, underletting, charging or parting with the possession of demised premises or any part thereof without licence or consent, such covenant condition or agreement shall, notwithstanding any express provision to the contrary, be deemed to be subject:

a) to a proviso to the effect that such licence or consent is not to be unreasonably withheld ...'

If C does not apply to X for consent he will be liable in damages. The risk to D is that the lease would also become liable to forfeiture for breach of covenant. If X unreasonably refuses consent C may apply to court for a declaration that the consent has been unreasonably withheld, in which case C could then assign the residue of the term to D. The jurisdiction is in the county court: s53 of the Landlord and Tenant Act 1954. The burden of proof is placed on the landlord by ss1 and 2 of the Landlord and Tenant Act 1988.

There are problems over the nature of the test of reasonableness. Cheshire states: 'It is submitted that the question must be approached objectively, and that, as it has been aptly put, the landlord's mental processes and uttered words are irrelevant.' The question was further discussed by Balcombe LJ in *International Drilling Fluids Ltd* v *Louisville Investments (Uxbridge) Ltd* (1986), although the matter must now be further considered in the light of ss1 and 2 of the 1988 Act.

Megarry and Wade conclude: 'The test, however, is not subjective but objective, and so depends on what a reasonable landlord would think.'

Tutorial comments

a) Consider the roles of

i) tenures and

ii) estates, today.

It is the estate which remains important.

b) Note the contents and meaning of s1(1) LPA 1925.

c) Note the significance of the amendment to s7(1) LPA 1925 by the Law of Property (Amendment) Act 1926.

d) Always understand the distinction between 'assignment' and 'sub-lease' by reference to what is left with the vendor.

2 ACQUISITION OF A BENEFICIAL INTEREST IN LAND

2.1 Introduction

2.2 Key points

2.3 Recent cases and statutes

2.4 Analysis of questions

2.5 Questions

2.1 Introduction

A very important subject which underpins much of land law. Two types of question can arise. Firstly, a question which is concerned solely with acquisition of a beneficial interest in land, and which could either be an essay or problem question. Secondly, a question which has an acquistion element, but which goes on to deal with protection of that interest against third parties, or the alienation of it.

2.2 Key points

a) *Introduction and definitions* - four methods of acquiring an interest; express trust, resulting trust, constructive trust and proprietary estoppel.

b) *Express trust*

    i) Where stated? - in conveyance or will.

    ii) Effect? - conclusive of the party's beneficial interests: *Goodman* v *Gallant* [1986] Fam 106.

c) *Resulting trusts*

    i) Elements - common intention and contribution.

    ii) Common intention:

        • Purchase by two or more and conveyance not into all their names.

        • Inferred from contributions: *Gissing* v *Gissing* [1971] AC 886; *Pettitt* v *Pettitt* [1970] AC 777

        • Not inferred from gift or loan: *Re Sharpe* [1980] 1 WLR 219; *Risch* v *McFee* (1990) 61 P & CR 42.

    iii) Contribution:

        • to deposit.

- to mortgage instalments.
- indirect contribution to mortgage: *Burns* v *Burns* [1984] Ch 317.

iv) Effect - beneficial interest proportionate to contribution.

d) *Constructive trusts*

i) Basis - express informal agreement and detriment OR imputed agreement based on conduct.

ii) Express informal agreement and detriment:

- At time of acquisiton or exceptionally later: *Lloyds Bank* v *Rosset* [1990] 2 WLR 867.
- Cogent evidence: *Eves* v *Eves* [1975] 1 WLR 1338; *Cooke* v *Head* [1972] 1 WLR 518; *Hammond* v *Mitchell* [1992] 2 All ER 109.
- Detriment: *Hammond* v *Mitchell* [1992] 2 All ER 109.
- Effect - size of share determined by agreement.

iii) Imputed agreement based on conduct:

- Direct financial contributions: *Lloyds Bank* v *Rosset* [1990] 2 WLR 867.
- Other contributions: *Lloyds Bank* v *Rosset* [1990] 2 WLR 867; *Hammond* v *Mitchell* [1992] 2 All ER 109.
- Effect - size of shcare determined by contribution.

e) *Proprietary estoppel*

i) Elements: *Willmott* v *Barber* (1880) 15 Ch D 96; *Taylor Fashions* v *Liverpool Victoria Trustees* [1982] QB 133; *Grant* v *Edwards* [1986] Ch 638; *Hammond* v *Mitchell* [1992] 2 All ER 109.

ii) Detriment:

- Expenditure: *Inwards* v *Baker* [1965] 2 QB 29.
- Other: *Greasley* v *Cooke* [1980] 1 WLR 1306.

iii) Expectation

Present or future interest: *Re Basham* [1986] 1 WLR 1498.

iv) Reliance

Detriment as evidence of reliance: *Coombes* v *Smith* [1986] 1 WLR 808.

v) Satisfying the equity:

Determination of remedy: *Crabb* v *Arun DC* [1976] Ch 179; *Pascoe* v *Turner* [1979] 1 WLR 431; *Inwards* v *Baker* [1965] 2 QB 29; *Dillwyn* v *Llewellyn* (1862) 4 De GF & J 517.

2.3 Recent cases and statutes

Lloyds Bank v Rosset [1990] 2 WLR 867

Facts

Husband and wife decided to buy a semi-derelict property which was to be renovated and occupied as the family home. The purchase money came from the husband's family trust and the house was conveyed into the husband's sole name. With agreement of the vendors, builders acting for the purchasers began renovation work prior to completion. The wife carried out some work herself and directed the renovation work as a whole. Without the knowledge of the wife the husband took out an overdraft to meet the cost of the renovations and signed a legal charge in favour of the bank. When arrears mounted up the bank sought possession of the property. The wife claimed a beneficial interest in the house.

Held

The wife's activities in relation to the renovation of the property were insufficient to justify a finding that she had a beneficial interest in the house based on an inference of common intention.

Lord Bridge:

'The first and fundamental question which must always be resolved is whether, independently of any inference to be drawn from the conduct of the parties in the course of sharing the house as their home and managing their joint affairs, there has at any time prior to acquisition, or exceptionally at some later date, been any agreement, arrangement or understanding reached between them that the property is to be shared beneficially. The finding of an agreement or arrangement to share in this sense can only, I think, be based on evidence of express discussions between the partners, however imperfectly remembered and however imprecise their terms may have been. Once a finding to this effect is made it will only be necessary for the partner asserting a claim to a beneficial interest against the partner entitled to the legal estate to show that he or she has acted to his or her detriment or significantly altered his or her position in reliance on the agreement in order to give rise to a constructive trust or a proprietary estoppel.

In sharp contrast with this situation is the very different one where there is no evidence to support a finding of an agreement or arrangement to share, however reasonable it might have been for the parties to reach such an arrangement if they had applied their minds to the question, and where the court must rely entirely on the conduct of the parties both as the basis from which to infer a common intention to share the property beneficially and as the conduct relied on to give rise to a constructive trust. In this situation direct contributions to the purchase price by the partner who is not the legal owner, whether initially or by payment of mortgage instalments, will readily justify the inference necessary to the creation of a constructive trust. But, as I read the authorities, it is at least extremely doubtful whether anything less will do.

Hammond v *Mitchell* [1992] 2 All ER 109

Facts

M and H began living together. A bungalow was purchased with the aid of a mortgage in H's sole name. H assured M that her name did not appear on the conveyance for tax reasons and that when they got married he would look after her. At H's insistence M gave up her job and assisted H in certain business ventures, as well as developing her own commercial activities. During an 11-year period the bungalow was extended, the finance being provided by way of overdraft secured by a charge on the property.

In 1984 H entered into a series of risky ventures including one in Spain with some assistance from M. In consequence a property was purchased in Spain and H and M went to live there. M continued her own businesses in Spain after H had returned to England. When the relationship broke down M claimed an interest in the bungalow and Spanish property.

Held

In determining beneficial interests it was necessary to see whether the parties had reached any sort of agreement in respect of the property, and secondly, to see whether the party claiming an interest has acted to his detriment or significantly altered his position in reliance on that agreement thereby giving rise to a constructive trust or proprietary estoppel. On the facts, M's participation in the commercial ventures was consistent with the view that she had a beneficial interest in the bungalow. Moreover, she had acted to her detriment in giving full support to the risky ventures which had they failed would have involved the sale of the bungalow to repay the bank. She therefore was entitled to a 1/2 half in the bungalow. However, her contributions in Spain, although useful, fell short of justifying an inference that she had an interest in the Spanish property.

Waite J:

'The template for that analysis has recently been restated by the House of Lords and the Court of Appeal in *Lloyds Bank plc* v *Rosset* [1990] 2 WLR 867, [1991] 1 AC 107 and *Grant* v *Edwards* [1986] 2 All ER 426, [1986] Ch 638. The court first has to ask itself whether there have at any time prior to acquisition of the disputed property, or exceptionally at some later date, been discussions between the parties leading to any agreement, arrangement or understanding reached between them that the property is to be shared beneficially. Any further investigation carried out by the court will vary in depth according to whether the answer to that initial inquiry is Yes or No. If there have been discussions of that kind and the answer is therefore Yes, the court then proceeds to examine the subsequent course of dealing between parties for evidence of conduct detrimental to the party without legal title referable to a reliance upon the arrangement in question. If there have been no such discussions and the answer to that initial inquiry is therefore No, the investigation of subsequent events has to take the form of an inferential analysis involving a scrutiny of all events potentially capable of throwing evidential light on the question whether, in the absence of express discussion, a presumed intention can be spelt out of the parties' past course of dealing.'

2.4 Analysis of questions

Questions which are solely on the acquisition of a beneficial interest in land require an application of the four methods outlined above. In particular, the overlap between constructive trusts and proprietary estoppel is usually apparent.

Other questions involve a brief and preliminary discussion of the acquisition of an interest, for instance, trust for sale questions (Chapter 3), co-ownership questions (Chapter 4) and registration questions (Chapter 10).

2.5 Questions

Question 1

In 1984 John and Karen met and became lovers. At the time they were both married and living with their spouses, but they both hoped to obtain divorces and then to marry each other. In 1985 Karen became pregnant by John and John purchased a flat for her to live in. Karen gave up her job, left her husband and moved into the flat. Shortly afterwards she gave birth to a daughter, Clare. The flat was conveyed into John's sole name and he paid both the deposit on the purchase price, all the bills and all the repayments. For three years John provided Karen with the financial support for herself and Clare. In 1988 Karen found a good job and thereafter supported herself and her daughter as well as spending some money on maintaining and decorating the flat. On one or two occasions Karen asked John why he did not put the flat in their joint names, and he replied that it was because of his tax position, but that she had no reason to worry because she could stay in the flat for as long as she wished and because he was leaving her the flat in his will.

In 1991 John was killed in a car crash. In his will he left his entire estate to his wife, Wilma. His executors now seek possession of the flat with a view to selling it.

Advise Karen.

University of London LLB Examination
(for External Students) Land Law June 1991 Q5

General comment

Another topical question on the area of licences and proprietary estoppel which demanded a good knowledge of case law for a satisfactory answer. Students need to be careful with this type of question that they do not spend time setting out their views on how this type of situation should be dealt with and not spending sufficient time on the law as it stands today.

Skeleton solution

Legal title passes to executors and Wilma entitled to estate under will - What claims does Karen have? - Constructive trust: was there an agreement between the parties? - Has Karen acted to her detriment in reliance? - Contractual licence? - Proprietary estoppel: consider *Coombes* v *Smith* (1986), *Re Basham* (1986) - Has Karen relied on any promise? - Flexibility of doctrine - Conclusion: looks unpromising but perhaps has a right to stay until daughter is older.

Suggested solution

Legal title in the flat has passed to John's executors and Wilma is entitled to John's estate under his will. Karen must try to establish some claim which will be binding on the executors. There are a number of possible claims. She could argue that she is entitled to some form of equitable proprietary interest in the flat, that she has some form of licence entitling her to remain there and that she is entitled to some remedy under the doctrine of proprietary estoppel. There is no indication that John ever gave her the deeds of the flat and no possibility on the facts as set out in the question of making a claim of a valid donatio mortis causa under *Sen* v *Headley* (1990). The various possible claims will be examined in turn.

John had sole legal title to the flat and in order for Karen to claim a property interest in it, she must show that she is entitled under some form of trust and a constructive trust is the most appropriate here. The recent decision of the House of Lords in *Lloyds Bank* v *Rosset* (1990) attempted to clarify the law relating to the circumstances in which the court will impose a constructive trust. If there has been an express agreement between the parties, either prior to acquisition or exceptionally at some later date, the court will impose a constructive trust if the party claiming an equitable interest has acted to his detriment or changed his position in reliance on that agreement. If there has been no such agreement, the court relies on conduct to infer the existence of a common intention to share and Lord Bridge doubted whether anything other than a direct contribution to the purchase price would be sufficient to justify the inference. There does not seem to be any express agreement between the parties prior to the acquisition that it would be shared beneficially and Karen has not made any direct contribution to the purchase price, either initially or by contributing to the mortgage repayments. The work which she did in decorating the flat would surely be disregarded as in *Rosset* itself and *Burns* v *Burns* (1984).

There is some evidence that at a later stage, John led Karen to believe that she would have a share in the flat as he said to her that he did not put the flat into joint names because of his tax position. This sounds like *Eves* v *Eves* (1975) where the man said that the only reason the property was being put in his name alone was that his female partner was under 21, and *Grant* v *Edwards* (1986), where the man told his female partner that the only reason the property was not being acquired in joint names was her divorce proceedings. Both ladies acted to their detriment in reliance on this promise and a constructive trust was imposed in their favour. The difficulty for Karen is that John's statement to her was made sometime after the actual acquisition, but Lord Bridge did indicate that in exceptional circumstances a later agreement might be sufficient. He did not give any guidance as to what would constitute exceptional circumstances were. In any event, has Karen acted to her detriment or changed her position in reliance? She has merely continued to live in the flat, although she might argue as in *Greasely* v *Cooke* (1980) that she forewent opportunities of moving elsewhere. This does not sound convincing as the period is not so long that it would now be impossible for her to find other accommodation and she has not foregone employment opportunities as in *Greasely* v *Cooke*. She has spent her own money in maintaining and decorating the flat. This might possibly count as acting to her detriment, if done after John's statement to her, but it could be argued that she did this simply in order to be more comfortable. The more money she spent, the more convincing the argument will sound.

On the whole, a claim based on constructive trust to a share in the property does not look very strong. Karen could claim to have a licence to remain in the flat, but the disadvantage of this claim is that it can only give her a right to remain as opposed to a right in the property itself. In *Coombes* v *Smith* (1986) the facts were quite similar. The plaintiff claimed a contractual licence on the basis that the defendant had offered to provide a roof over her head if she moved in with him. It was held that there was no enforceable contract. A more attractive claim is one based on proprietary estoppel. Has Karen acted to her detriment in reliance on a mistaken belief in her legal rights? In *Coombes* v *Smith* it was held that the plaintiff had not had a mistaken belief in her legal rights, even though she probably had believed that the defendant would always provide for her. Whenever she had asked for the house to be put into joint names, the defendant had refused and there was no evidence of any discussions about what would happen if the relationship broke down. Karen's case is stronger as John had assured her that she could stay in the flat as long as she wished and that he had left her the flat in his will. It was held in *Re Basham* (1986) that proprietary estoppel includes cases where the plaintiff is led to believe that he will have a right in the future.

It is still necessary for Karen to show that she acted to her detriment or altered her position on the faith of her belief. In *Coombes* v *Smith* it was held that having a child, moving away from her husband, redecorating and not trying to provide otherwise for herself did not show acting to one's detriment. The actions were either due simply to a desire to live with the defendant, or done as occupier of the property. By contrast, in *Re Basham*, a long history of working without pay, foregoing opportunities to move, caring for the deceased and spending her own money to resolve a boundary dispute were sufficient for a claim based on proprietary estoppel when coupled with frequent promises by the deceased that his property would pass to the plaintiff on his death. Karen's situation looks closer to that in *Coombes* v *Smith*. Although John did promise to leave her the flat in his will, it is difficult to see that Karen has changed her position in reliance on that.

In conclusion therefore Karen could try to claim an interest under a constructive trust or base a claim on proprietary estoppel. The difficulty with the trust claim is that she made no contribution to the acquisition and the only evidence of a common intention that there would be sharing is John's statement made after the purchase. Even if that is enough, Karen must still show that she significantly changed her position as a result and she seems merely to have continued as before. There is no real evidence of contract to found a claim based on contractual licence and the remaining possibility is that of proprietary estoppel. Again Karen's difficulty is that although she was mistaken about her future legal rights, it is not easy to see that she acted to her detriment in reliance. Such acts as looking after a child, failing to provide for herself otherwise and redecorating were held insufficient in *Coombes* v *Smith*. However Karen's claim is not hopeless. In *Coombes* v *Smith* the defendant had already conceded that the plaintiff could stay in the house until the child was 17 and that he would pay the mortgage for that period. It might be that the court would use the flexibility of the doctrine of proprietary estoppel to grant Karen some lesser remedy than a transfer of or share in the flat itself and allow her to remain living there for a limited time until her daughter Clare is, say, 17. There was a clear promise made to her and it is a matter of how flexible the court will be about what constituted acting in reliance on that promise.

Question 2

Old Mr Jones, feeling that he would not be able to look after himself for very many more years, wrote to Mary, his unmarried daughter, suggesting that she come and live near him. He offered to buy her a flat to live in. Mary accepted the offer; she gave up her job and her council flat and moved into the flat her father had bought for her. The flat was conveyed into her father's name and he paid the whole of the purchase price. When Mary suggested that she would like the flat to be in her name, he dismissed the idea as absurd because, as he said, 'I am leaving everything to you in my will anyway'. Mr Jones paid all the outgoings on the flat and Mary paid nothing for the use of the flat. Mary found a part-time job and visited her father daily. This arrangement continued happily for two years when Mr Jones died, leaving all his estate to charity. Now his executors seek possession of the flat.

Advise Mary.

Would your advice be any different if Mary had provided one-tenth of the purchase price of the flat?

University of London LLB Examination
(for External Students) Land Law June 1992 Q6

General comment

A question involving the acquisition of a beneficial interest in land. A good knowledge of resulting and constructive trusts and the principles of proprietary estoppel is needed. Candidates attempting this question should be able to demonstrate a good grasp of the relevant principles and authorities, and the ability to apply them to the facts. It is important to structure the answer in a logical and coherent fashion.

Skeleton solution

* Declaration of trust in conveyance - *Goodman* v *Gallant* (1986).

* Constructive or resulting trusts - express informal agreement - *Eves* v *Eves* (1975) and *Cooke* v *Head* (1972) - direct financial contributions.

* Proprietary estoppel - *Lloyds Bank* v *Rosset* (1990); *Re Basham* (1968) and *Grant* v *Edwards* (1986).

Suggested solution

In order for Mary to claim an interest in the flat she will have to look to equity for assistance. Mary is not on the title deeds so no trust arises in her favour as in *Goodman* v *Gallant* (1986). Consequently, the law relating to resulting and constructive trusts and proprietary estoppel must be considered.

27

In the first place it is notable that Mary has not made any direct financial contributions to the purchase of the flat, whether by way of deposit or instalments. Her father provided all the purchase monies and therefore Mary cannot claim an interest based on an imputed intention that she should have an interest: see Lord Bridge in *Lloyds Bank* v *Rosset* (1990).

Mary could seek to argue that she has an interest by virtue of express informal agreement at the date of acquisition (or exceptionally later) with her father, which she has acted upon to her detriment (see Lord Bridge in *Rosset*). It is unclear whether the father made the statement at the time of buying the flat or later, but it may be possible to assert that his response to Mary's request to put the property into her name ('I'm leaving everything to you anyway') is evidence of such an agreement as was recognised in *Cooke* v *Head* (1972) and *Eves* v *Eves* (1975). In the former case the man said that the woman's name should not appear on the title deeds as it might prejudice her pending divorce, and in the latter because she was too young. In both cases the Court of Appeal took the view that the statements were evidence of an intention that the women should have an interest. If *Cooke* and *Eves* are followed, Mary will have an interest which is determined according to the agreement and not in proportion to any contribution she may have made.

In order to succeed in such a plea Mary would have to establish not only the existence of the agreement but also that she acted to her detriment on it. The most common form of detriment is a material sacrifice in the nature of financial contributions or improvements to property. On the facts Mary has not acted to her detriment in either of these ways and it is a moot point whether she has acted to her detriment in giving up her job and council flat, so as to raise a constructive trust in her favour. It could be argued that the giving up of the council flat is connected with the alleged agreement (*Grant* v *Edwards* (1986)) but, the giving up of the job may not be related to the agreement at all but may have been the result of Mary's love and affection for her father.

Should Mary fail to establish an interest under a constructive trust she may be able to rely on a proprietary estoppel - a point which was specifically recognised by Lord Bridge in *Rosset* where he approved *Grant* and *Re Basham* (1986). Mary would have to show that there was a representation that she would receive an interest, then or in the future: *Re Basham*. For these purposes her father's statement would suffice. Additionally, Mary would have to show that she acted to her detriment in reliance on that statement. Therefore, the date when the statement was made is all important. Assuming that the statement preceded Mary leaving her flat and job, those acts could be seen as acts of detriment: see *Jones* v *Jones* (1977). Mary's acts of visiting her father are likely to be seen as the acts of a loving and caring daughter and not acts of detriment. Should the father's statement have come after Mary gave up her job and flat, those acts cannot be seen as acts *in reliance on* that statement, and an estoppel will not arise.

On balance, it seems unlikely that Mary can plead that a resulting or constructive trust has arisen in her favour, but it may be possible for her to show that an estoppel has arisen which binds everyone except the bona fide purchaser: *Inwards* v *Baker* (1965).

If Mary had provided one-tenth of the purchase price

If Mary had provided one-tenth of the purchase price, in the absence of evidence to show that it was a gift to her father, she would acquire an interest in the property, proportionate to her contribution, by virtue of a resulting trust by way of direct financial contribution referable to acquisition.

3 SETTLEMENTS AND TRUSTS FOR SALE

3.1 Introduction

3.2 Key points

3.3 Recent cases and statutes

3.4 Analysis of questions

3.5 Questions

3.1 Introduction

This topic is often denigrated as being out of touch with modern society. Who creates a settlement today? Many people fail to realise exactly how many new settlements are created each year by way of trust for sale. If the student is asked to consider these settlements it may well be by way of comparison with the original form of family settlement using a strict settlement. In addition there is a need to understand the trust for sale by way of introduction to the rules of co-ownership. The moral is: understand both forms of settlement but emphasise the trust for sale today. The proposals of the Law Commission on the reforms to trusts for sale should be understood.

3.2 Key points

a) *Introductory and definitions* - s1 SLA 1925 - to provide for two or more persons in *succession.*

b) *Settlements under Settled Land Act 1925*

    i) General effect - originally to keep land in the family and prevent it from being sold.

    ii) How it works - by re-settlement at each generation.

    iii) Where is the legal estate? In the tenant for life.

    iv) Definition of 'settlement' now in SLA s1 - emphasis on succession.

    v) Creation of a strict settlement under the SLA 1925 ss4 and 5. Need for two documents - a vesting deed and a trust instrument.

    vi) The tenant for life and his powers.

       • Definition of tenant for life - ss19 and 20 SLA 1925

       • Definition of trustees of settlement - s30 SLA 1925

- Legal estate is vested in the tenant for life
- Statutory powers of tenant for life.
  - Power of sale - s38(1) SLA 1925
  - Power of exchange
  - Power to lease - ss41 - 48 SLA 1925
  - Power to accept surrenders of leases
  - Power to take leases of other lands
  - Power to grant options
  - Power to mortgage or charge - s71 SLA 1925
  - Power to effect improvements - s84 and 3rd Schedule, SLA 1925
  - Power to sell timber ripe for cutting (and 'waste') - s66 SLA 1925
  - Power to sell heirlooms
  - Any transaction for benefit of settled land - s64 SLA 1925
- Purported limitations of tenant for life's powers - s106 SLA 1925
- Non-assignability of powers - remain in tenant for life, but note s24 SLA 1925.
- Exercise of powers of disposition to the tenant for life
- Effect of failure to use correct machinery to create a strict settlement: see (vii), below
- Faulty conveyances: ss18(1) and 110 SLA 1925 - compare *Weston v Henshaw* [1950] Ch 510 and *Re Morgan's Lease* [1972] Ch 1

vii) Failure to use correct machinery to create a strict settlement. Section 13 SLA 1925 - paralysing section. Megarry and Wade: 'The policy of the Act is ... to make it impossible to deal with the land in any case where a vesting instrument ought to exist but does not.'

Where a tenant for life has become entitled to have a vesting deed/instrument executed no disposition of a legal estate can be made until a vesting instrument has been executed. Any purported disposition of the land inter vivos operates only as a contract to carry out the transaction after the necessary vesting instrument has been executed. Exceptions - where a sale may be effected without a vesting instrument:

- Personal representatives in course of administration of estate.
- Section 13 does not apply if disposition made to a purchaser of the legal estate without notice of tenant for life entitled to vesting deed. After 1925 must register as land charge Class C(iv) - void if not registered (s4 LCA 1972).

- If settlement at an end before vesting deed made then no settlement still in existence: *Re Alefounders' Will Trusts* [1927] 1 Ch 360. Megarry and Wade: 'When the land ceases to be settled, the fetters of s13 drop off.'

- Where s1 of the Law of Property (Amendment) Act 1926 applies. This enables owners of land subject to family charges to sell land as if it was not settled with indemnity given by vendor. But purchaser is still subject to such charges with only the protection of this personal indemnity by vendor.

  NOTE: It is the trustees of the settlement who must execute the vesting deed - the settlor cannot rectify his own mistake by executing the vesting deed himself: s9(2) SLA 1925. Megarry and Wade: 'The section ... does not prevent the tenant for life from disposing of his equitable interest (eg his beneficial life interest) or exercising any equitable powers given to him by the trust instrument.'

viii) Determination of a settlement - need for a deed of discharge?

ix) Functions of Settled Land Act trustees.

c) *Trusts for sale*

i) Introductory - consider the doctrine of conversion.

ii) Definition s205(1)(xxix) LPA 1925 - 'an immediate binding trust for sale, whether or not exercisable at the request or with the consent of any person, and with or without a power at discretion to postpone the sale'.

iii) Creation of trusts for sale

iv) Position of trustees - s25 postpone sale

v) Powers and duties of trustees

vi) Rights of beneficiaries - s29 delegation. Note s30 LPA 1925 - where trustees for sale refuse to exercise their powers, any person interested may apply to the court for an order and the court may make such order as it thinks fit.

d) *Overreaching provisions in settlement or trust for sale*

i) Definition - see also s2 LPA 1925.

ii) Effect - Megarry and Wade - '... allows land held upon trust to be sold to a purchaser free from the trust, even though he has notice of it ... if an interest is overreached, it is transferred from the land to money in the hands of trustees ...'

  - Trust for sale - no overreaching? But conversion applies.

  - Settlement - s72 SLA 1925 - this effect may be demonstrated in the following diagramatic form:

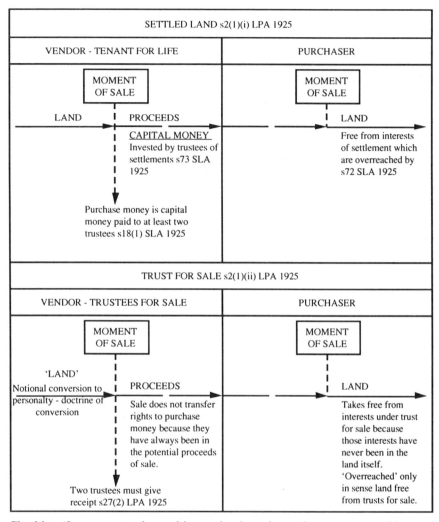

Cheshire: 'In contrast to the position under the strict settlement, overreaching under the trust for sale is automatic: no statutory intervention is necessary.'

3.3 Recent cases and statutes

Ahmed v *Kendrick* (1987) *The Times* 12 November

Perry v *Phoenix Assurance plc* [1988] 3 All ER 60

3.4 Analysis of questions

There has been a temptation to invite candidates to compare the two forms of settlement. This is becoming less significant and the good candidate should now be prepared to look to the future and be in a position to discuss the effect of the proposals of the Law Commission.

In addition the effect of the trust for sale on co-ownership should not be overlooked. Another recent feature has been to introduce elements of registered land into the discussion on settlements. The candidate should know how the settlements are dealt with in the context of the Land Registration Act 1925.

3.5   Questions

Question 1

Victor, a rich and elderly bachelor, consults you. He wants to settle his country estate Blackacre (which includes an ancient manor house) on his unmarried nephew William for life and thereafter on William's first and other sons successively in tail male. Victor also wants to ensure:

i) that William shall have the management of Blackacre unless and until he goes bankrupt; and

ii) that neither Blackacre as a whole nor any part thereof shall be sold without the consent of the trustees of the settlement who, Victor proposes, should be his sisters Yvonne and Zoe.

Advise Victor how far his wishes may be achieved:

a) by a settlement made under the Settled Land Act 1925; and

b) by a settlement made by way of trust for sale.

University of London LLB Examination
(for External Students) Land Law June 1986 Q9

General comment

It is not always easy to keep settlement questions relevant without resorting to the matrimonial home. Credit is due to the examiner for providing a question which does avoid the limiting aspects of the family home problem and yet is pertinent to events of today. In particular the question highlights some of the criticisms presently expressed against having two forms of settlement available today, and the drawbacks to some of the proposed solutions.

Skeleton solution

a) *Settlement under SLA 1925*

   Principal mansion house, s65 SLA 1925

   Two documents required, s4 SLA 1925

   Definition of 'settlement', s1(1)(i) SLA 1925

   Form of such a strict settlement including the entailed interests

   Tenant for life, s19(1) SLA 1925

Trustees of the settlement, s30 SLA 1925

Must not derogate from powers, s106 SLA 1925

Effect of bankruptcy, s24 SLA 1925 and *Re Thornhill's Settlement* (1941)

Consent - principal mansion house, s65 SLA 1925 - otherwise no effect because of s106 SLA 1925

b) *Settlement by way of trust for sale*

Definition, s25(1)(xxix) LPA 1925 - immediate binding trust for sale

Re Parker's Settled Estates (1928)

No requirement for two documents - two often used

Powers of trustees for sale, s28(1) - tenant for life and trustees of settlement under SLA

But problems where intend to create successive interests

Delegation, s29(1) LPA 1925, power to postpone sale, s25(1) - power to postpone but duty to sell, *Re Mayo* (1943)

Use of s30 LPA 1925 - purpose of the trust, *Re Buchanan-Wollaston's Conveyance* (1939)

Consents, s28(1) LPA 1925

Use of incentives to postpone sale - *Re Inns* [1947] Ch 576

Is there a need for two forms of settlement today? Victor's problems provide both a negative and a positive answer to this question.

Suggested solution

Victor has very precise wishes and these illustrate one of the major problems of settling land today in that some of his proposals may be achieved under one system whereas other proposals may be achieved under the alternative system. The problem is that neither system can completely satisfy all Victor's wishes and the element of compromise within either system is strictly limited by the legislation which is relevant to that particular system. We will look at the effect of each system in turn.

a) *Settlement under the Settled Land Act 1925*

Victor owns a country estate which includes an ancient manor house. Whether this is a principal mansion house is determined by s65(2) SLA 1925. The provision operates negatively in that if a house is usually occupied as a farm house, or if the site of a house and the pleasure grounds and park and lands usually occupied therewith do not together exceed 25 acres, the house will NOT be a principal mansion house. Whether it is or not has little bearing on our advice to Victor except that if it is a principal mansion house then under s65(1) SLA 1925 the settlement must expressly require consent of the trustees or order of the court to be obtained before any disposition of the principal mansion house is made. If no such provision is included in the settlement then the ordinary rules of notice, mentioned hereafter, will apply. Victor seeks to establish the traditional form of family settlement. He will need to use two documents: s4(1) SLA 1925. The public document, the principal vesting deed, will vest the legal fee simple in the tenant for life, William. It will also describe the property and name Yvonne and Zoe as the trustees of the settlement. In order to achieve privacy for the family trusts the second document, the trust instrument, will declare the beneficial interests of William and the other successive interests required under the family settlement. These trusts will take effect 'behind the curtain' and will not be readily available to any potential purchaser.

Victor requires Blackacre to be settled on William for life then to William's first and other sons successively in tail male. In seeking this objective Victor places his proposals squarely within the definition of a settlement in s1(1)(i) SLA 1925. In drafting the settlement Victor must be advised of two potential problems: William is unmarried, and he may never marry nor have any sons. The settlement should take account of these facts. The strict settlement should begin by providing an interest for Victor until William marries. Provision should also be made for William's wife by way of a pin money rentcharge and also for her widowhood if William should die first. In addition provision should be made for portions terms in order to provide for the younger children of William's marriage. Victor has proposed an entailed interest and this will be achieved within his directions by making William the tenant for life then providing for William's first and other sons successively in tail male. This is a rather unambitious proposal and may not cover every eventuality. Victor may be persuaded to extend the entail by going on to provide for the sons in tail general and then to the daughters as tenants in common in tail general with cross-remainders between them.

As indicated above, at the moment William is unmarried and it would be sensible to include a remainder to Victor in fee simple. Thus if William does not marry the entails must fail and the land would then revert to Victor or his successors.

The fact that William becomes the tenant for life under this form of settlement is recognised by s19(1) SLA 1925: 'The person of full age who is for the time being beneficially entitled under a settlement to possession of settled land for his life is for the purposes of this Act the tenant for life of that land and the tenant for life under that settlement.'

Section 30 SLA 1925 explains who are the trustees of the settlement. Provided Victor does not give an ineffective power of sale to some other person, s30(1)(ii) confirms that Yvonne and Zoe will be the trustees of the settlement provided they are expressly declared to be the trustees for the purposes of the Settled Land Act 1925.

Having established the strict settlement Victor now has two precise requirements to consider. Can a provision be inserted whereby William is to have the management of Blackacre unless and until he goes bankrupt? The SLA 1925 gives William general power of management of the settled land including powers to sell, lease and mortgage the settled land. In addition these powers cannot be limited by any provision which prohibits or prevents him exercising these powers: s106(1) SLA 1925. On the other hand if William does become bankrupt the court may 'on the application of any person interested in the settled land' make an order authorising Yvonne and Zoe as the trustees of the settlement to exercise in William's name and on his behalf 'any of the powers of a tenant for life under this Act': see s24(1) SLA 1925 and *Re Thornhill's Settlement* (1940). Whilst such an order is in force s24(2) prevents William from exercising any of those powers himself. The order must be registered under the Land Charges Act 1972 as an order affecting land: s6(1) LCA 1972.

The second restriction proposed by Victor reflects the concern of many settlors. He requires that neither Blackacre as a whole nor any part thereof should be sold without the consent of the trustees of the settlement. If Blackacre is large enough to come within s65 SLA 1925 as a principal mansion house then s65(1) SLA 1925 will allow such a restriction to require the consent of the trustees of the settlement to be obtained before 'any disposition of the principal mansion house itself' or 'the pleasure grounds and park and lands, if any, usually occupied therewith'. If Blackacre does not come within the negative definition of 'principal mansion house' mentioned earlier, no such requirement for consent may be imposed. The only rule which then applies is that before any disposition by way of sale, lease exchange or mortgage of the settled land notice of such intention must be given to the trustees of the settlement: s101 SLA 1925. Any attempt by Victor to impose heavier requirements such as consent would be void under s106(1) SLA 1925 as being a restriction on the exercise by William of his tenant for life's powers.

b) *Settlement made by way of trust for sale*

Settlements by way of trust for sale are governed by the Law of Property Act 1925 and through this by some of the provisions of the SLA 1925. The LPA 1925 is, however, the predominant legislation covering trusts for sale. The first point to be made is that it will not matter whether Blackacre is a principal mansion house or not; the same rules will apply in either event.

In order to come within these provisions there must be 'an immediate binding trust for sale': s205(1)(xxix) LPA 1925. Although the meaning of this provision is not entirely free from doubt, there must be a clear duty to sell. A failure to make this duty clear may create a strict settlement as in *Re Newbould* (1913). Although the definition does itself recognise the possibility of a power to postpone sale, the duty to sell must be immediately effective. Finally the definition requires the trust for sale to be 'binding'. It has been suggested that this means the trust for sale will only be binding if it applies to the whole legal and equitable interest in the land. Romer J in *Re Parker's Settled Estates* (1928) held that land cannot be described as held on trust for sale so as to take it out of the Settled Land Act unless the whole legal estate is vested in the trustees. In many respects the best summary of the present position is set out in Megarry and Wade: 'A "binding" trust for sale is thus one which is capable of binding the whole legal estate that has been settled, and not merely part of it.'

In executing the settlement by way of trust for sale, Victor must ensure that he imposes on William this immediate, binding duty to sell the whole of Blackacre. Unlike s4(1) SLA 1925 there is no statutory requirement that the trust for sale must be in two documents. It is true, however, that for exactly the same reasons of the curtain principle, keeping private affairs away from the public eye, a trust for sale does use two documents. The effect is to keep the family affairs off the title to Blackacre. Yvonne and Zoe will become the trustees for sale of this settlement. Their powers are set out in s28(1) LPA 1925 including all the powers of a tenant for life and the trustees of the settlement under the SLA 1925. On the other hand there is no way that the successive interests can be seen to pass as land because this would create a settlement under the SLA 1925. In using the trust for sale, Victor would, to some extent, lose control of the situation once he had created an immediate binding trust for sale.

Victor now needs to know whether his particular requirements can be met within the trust for sale provisions. William will not have the powers of management initially because these are given to Yvonne and Zoe as the trustees for sale, having the powers of both the tenant for life and the trustees of the settlement under the SLA 1925.

Section 29(1) LPA 1925 does provide that Yvonne and Zoe may in writing delegate to William (provided he is of full age), as the person for the time being beneficially entitled in possession to the net rents and profits of the land for his life, the powers of leasing, accepting surrenders of leases and management. There is however no express provision for revocation on bankruptcy. However, if the bankruptcy inhibits William to the extent that he refuses to exercise any of the delegated powers, 'any person interested' may apply to the court for an 'order directing the trustees for sale to give effect' to any proposed transaction: s30 LPA 1925. It is suggested that such an order would then prevail over the written delegation effected under s29(1) LPA 1925 above.

Victor's second requirement is that Blackacre should not be sold without the consent of the trustees of the settlement. As Yvonne and Zoe are the trustees for sale such as proposition becomes something of a non sequitur. A more relevant question is whether any restrictions are possible on the apparent unrestricted duty of Yvonne and Zoe to sell the land. The definition in s205(1)(xxix) gives the initial clue by direct reference to consent and the power to postpone sale. Unless a contrary intention was inserted by Victor, there is a power to postpone sale implied in the trust for sale by s25(1) LPA 1925. There is, apparently, nothing to prevent this postponement lasting indefinitely provided both Yvonne and Zoe agree. If, however, they cannot agree then the duty to sell must prevail over this power to postpone sale: *Re Mayo* (1943).

William does have a safeguard in that he qualifies as a 'person interested' under s30 LPA 125 and if the trustees for sale refuse to sell he may apply to the court for an order of sale. The court will not automatically grant such an order but will take into account factors such as the reason why the trust was created before exercising their discretion to 'make such order as it thinks fit': *Re Buchanan-Wollaston's Conveyance* (1939).

In addition to the power to postpone sale, s28(1) LPA 1925 recognises that the general powers of the trustees for sale may be made subject to the requirement of consent of specified persons. As indicated above, the consent of Yvonne and Zoe is not relevant for our purposes but Victor could provide for William to give his consent and thereby give William some element of management.

It is true that the combination of these powers to postpone sale and obtaining the consent of the remainderman or beneficiary may well result in the sale not being effected. This is especially true if some 'incentive' is offered to the person whose consent is required which may deter the giving of the consent. This was seen in *Re Inns* (1947). On the other hand the provisions of s30 would still prevail to give the court the last word on the application of any person interested in the land.

Thus Victor could achieve some of his objectives by the use of the trust for sale although the results are not as clear cut as in the case of the Settled Land Act 1925.

Tutorial comments

a) Formalities for settlements.

b) Powers of the tenant for life and the trustees for sale.

c) Respective controls on the use of these powers.

d) The need for reform: see Law Commission Report No 181 'Trusts of Land', 15th June 1989.

Question 2

Samuel is consulting the family solicitor, and writes to him as follows:

'Ever since my wife and two dear boys died in that horrible accident, my two sisters, Eva - who's ten years older than me - and Florence - two years younger - have lived at Oddstone Manor with me. I want them both to be able to stay there, and then it can be divided between all my nieces and nephews. I was talking to one of them, Timothy, the other day and he said there are two ways to tie up property that way. It sounded a bit technical so I want you to explain that. My two sisters are not very business-like, but young Tim and his sister Una are both very good and they can keep an eye on things if you advise that.'

To which two methods of 'settling' land was Samuel referring? Describe each of them and indicate which you would recommend in the circumstances of this case.

University of London LLB Examination
(for External Students) Land Law June 1987 Q5

General comment

The search for realism in a question is to be commended and the idea of the letter is sound. Why not quote the letter itself by referring to 'two ways to tie up property that way' rather than using the word 'settling', between inverted commas, when it does not appear in the text itself? I wonder how many candidates wasted valuable time looking, unnecessarily as it transpires, for the non-existent source of the quotation. Apart from this, the question does have the air of realism sought by the examiner. As with many problem questions a simple diagram will help candidates keep the various names in their appropriate family groups.

Skeleton solution

(See diagram in suggested solution.)

'Two ways to tie up property that way' - SETTLEMENTS

STRICT SETTLEMENT - SLA 1925

s1	Land limited in trust for persons 'by way of succession'
ss4/5	Two deeds - principal vesting deed (public)
	trust instrument (private)
ss19/20	Tenant for life
s30	Trustees of the settlement
	Wide powers given to the tenant for life. Sale, lease, mortgage.
s106	Cannot deprive the tenant for life of these powers.

TRUST FOR SALE - LPA 1925

s205(1)(xxix)	Definition - 'immediate binding trust for sale'.
s25	Power to postpone sale
s26	May include need for consents.

Keeping land in the family today: *Re Inns* (1947)

Which to recommend in these circumstances?

(Problems with sisters who 'are not very business-like')

If create STRICT SETTLEMENT: Samuel - tenant for life - then sisters - then Timothy and Una.

Risk of any tenant for life dissipating the assets - which cannot be prevented - s106 SLA 1925.

If create TRUST FOR SALE: as well as the duty to sell use the power to postpone sale (s25) and the need for consents. May give Timothy and Una this power to consent, perhaps also a capital sum in respect of Oddstone Manor if it remains unsold as an incentive to keep it unsold. In this way Timothy and Una can play a significant part in the administration.

RECOMMENDATION: USE A TRUST FOR SALE PLUS power to postpone and require consents of Timothy and Una to sell.

Quote: Cheshire

Megarry and Wade

Suggested solution

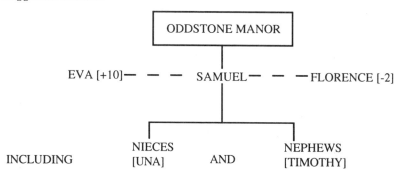

Samuel has correctly identified that 'there are two ways to tie up property that way'. These two methods of settling land are the strict settlement controlled by the Settled Land Act 1925 and the trust for sale controlled generally by the Law of Property Act 1925.

The strict settlement is the traditional family settlement and was seen as the method by which land could be tied up for successive generations. This satisfied the acquisitive tendencies of such settlors but was seen to have a detrimental effect on the quality of the land itself. The strict settlement was subject to statutory intervention during the nineteenth century, particularly by the Settled Land Act 1882, and is now controlled by the provisions of the Settled Land Act 1925. The major objective of these statutory reforms was to identify a person in control of the settled land and then vest all the powers of management of the land in that person.

Section 1 SLA 1925 explains what constitutes a settlement and the predominant feature is land limited in trust for persons 'by way of succession'. Thus any attempt to create successive interests by Samuel will, prima facie, create a strict settlement. Sections 4 and 5 deal with the machinery of the strict settlement and require every settlement to 'be affected by two deeds, namely a vesting deed and a trust instrument': s4(1) SLA 1925. The Act sets out the contents of each. Suffice it to say that the principal vesting deed (s5(1) SLA 1925) is the public document which describes the settled land, declares the land is vested in the tenant for life and names the trustees of the settlement. The trust instrument declares the trusts of the settlement, but as these are private matters it is left off the title to the land and is said to be 'behind the curtain'.

The person who controls the settled land, with considerable powers given by the SLA 1925, is the tenant for life. Sections 19 and 20 SLA 1925 identify the tenant for life as 'the person of full age who is for the time being beneficially entitled under a settlement to possession of settled land for his life': s19(1) SLA 1925. If no such person exists, s20 SLA 1925 identifies a list of people who can have the powers of the tenant for life in the given circumstances. The tenant for life is given wide powers including sale, lease and mortgage of the land. There are some restraints imposed, but for the above powers all the tenant for life has to do is give notice to the trustees of the settlement of his intention to exercise the respective powers. These trustees of the settlement are identified, in descending order, in s30 SLA 1925. The effect is that in most cases the trustees appointed by the settlor in the trust instrument will officiate as the trustees of the settlement. They have functions of a supervisory nature and ensure no problems are created by the tenant for life. In spite of this the tenant for life has a very free hand and this is reinforced by s106 SLA 1925 which prevents the powers of the tenant for life from being restricted either directly or indirectly. The picture of the strict settlement is of a strong manager of the land and the fact that Samuel's sisters 'are not very business-like' may have an effect on the final recommendations.

The trust for sale is controlled by the Law of Property Act 1925 and is, somewhat inadequately, defined in s205(1)(xxix) LPA 1925 as 'an immediate binding trust for sale, whether or not exercisable at the request or with the consent of any person, and with or without a power at discretion to postpone the sale'. The latter part of the explanation is helpful, but trouble has arisen over the meaning of 'immediate binding trust for sale'. If Samuel is recommended to adopt the trust for sale he must ensure there is a clear duty to sell.

Re Newbould (1913) shows the danger of over generalisations. An instruction to sell 'as and when they think proper' was held not to be a duty in the trustees but only a power of sale. There is no need to sell immediately because s25(1) LPA 1925 implies a power to postpone sale unless a contrary intention appears. The courts have been particularly troubled by the meaning of the word 'binding'. The better view is that the trust binds the whole legal estate the subject of the trust for sale: *Re Parker's Settled Estates* (1928). Thus land cannot be made subject to a trust for sale if it is still subject to any outstanding interests created by an earlier settlement.

As indicated in the statutory definition, there is a power to postpone sale: s25(1) LPA 1925. In general sale can only be postponed if all the trustees agree to postpone; otherwise the duty to sell will prevail: *Re Mayo* (1943).

The definition also refers to the consent of any person and there is a further obligation under s26(3) LPA 1925 in the case of a statutory trust for sale to consult the person of full age 'beneficially interested in possession in the rents and profits of the land' and give effect to their wishes or the wishes of the majority in value if there is any dispute between them. It is the question of consent which provides most interest today for the authors of any proposed settlement. Following the effect of the decision in *Re Inns* (1947), it may be possible to use the trust for sale to keep the land unsold. This is achieved by giving the consent powers to the ultimate remaindermen who are known to wish to enjoy the land rather than have it sold. In this way there will be a reluctance to give consent and the land will continue to remain unsold. In *Re Inns* the testator devised his house on trust for sale (but with the consent of his widow and Stevenage Urban District Council) on trust if the house was unsold to allow his widow to reside there, subject to her keeping the house in good repair and condition and insured. After the widow's death or remarriage the house was to be offered to the UDC for use as a hospital and, if accepted, the testator bequeathed £10,000 to the council as an endowment. If not accepted the house fell into residue. Although this aspect of the decision was secondary to the claim by the widow for further funds to help with the upkeep of the premises, at no stage was any doubt cast on the validity of the requirement of the consent of the widow and Stevenage UDC. Thus it is unlikely that the house would be sold during the widow's lifetime because if the UDC did consent to a sale there would be no house to be offered at the widow's death and both house and endowment would be lost.

It may be, therefore, that the objective of the settlors of the early family settlements to keep the land in the family may still be achieved today.

It is now necessary to advise Samuel as to the most appropriate settlement to be used in the given circumstances. He appears to have problems because his two sisters, Eva and Florence, are 'not very business-like'. On the other hand there is a risk they could inherit the property and there is an equal need for sound trustees who can administer the property or some other way must be found to neutralise the risk from their lack of business skills.

If Samuel uses a strict settlement he would, probably, become the tenant for life, then his sisters in succession followed by Timothy and Una. Any tenant for life has the power to sell the settled land and this power cannot be taken away: s106 SLA 1925. There is no safeguard against any member of the family who has become a tenant for life from dissipating the assets.

If Samuel uses a trust for sale he would impose a duty to sell the land including Oddstone Manor. He could also rely on the statutory power to postpone sale by not putting any contrary intention in the trust deed: s25(1) LPA 1925. To give a further reassurance he could require consents before the sale took place. He would be advised to give these consent provisions to Timothy and Una on the basis that they will probably wish to enjoy the land in its existing state. A further 'encouragement' could be a capital sum in respect of Oddstone Manor left to them as remaindermen in the event of the property not being sold. This would mirror the trust for sale used in *Re Inns* (1947) to which Wynn-Parry J took no exception in principle. This would also ensure that Timothy and Una play a significant role in the administration of the family trust. Cheshire could be said to confirm this conclusion:

'Thus, today, a settlement, the object of which is to keep the land or the capital money representing it in the family, may be achieved through a trust for sale. Paradoxically, it is easier to prevent the land from being sold if it is settled by way of trust for sale. Not only may the trustees retain the land under their power to postpone sale indefinitely, but they may be restrained from selling it unless they obtain the consent of certain persons, and the settlor may choose as one of these the person beneficially entitled to the income for his life.'

A similar point of view is expressed by Megarry and Wade:

'For most purposes a trust for sale is simpler, cheaper and more suitable generally. It may even offer better prospects of keeping the land in the family, since sale may be made subject to consent in a way which cannot be done with settled land. In this respect settlements and trusts for sale have changed places since the middle of the last century.'

Tutorial comments

a) Keeping land in the family, the old and the modern methods.

b) Apply the facts and decision in *Re Inns* [1947] Ch 576.

Question 3

Herbert died in 1987 and by his will after appointing Roe and Doe as executors and trustees, settled his Meadows estate on his wife Wilma for life, then on his son Stephen for life on condition he always lives in England, then the fee simple to his grandchildren Jack and Jill in equal shares. Wilma died in 1989.

a) What legal formalities were required on the deaths of Herbert and Wilma:

    i)   if the title is unregistered;

    ii)   if the title is registered under the Land Registration Act 1925?

b) Advise Stephen, who wishes to emigrate to Australia.

University of London LLB Examination
(for External Students) Land Law June 1983 Q9

General comment

It is becoming increasingly difficult to create new questions on settlements. This is no longer a subject of much litigation and there is always the feeling of treading the path of previous generations of examiners. To this end the examiner should be congratulated for part (a) in that he has introduced a novelty which may well have confounded some candidates. There is certainly nothing wrong in this because the well prepared student should be able to draw on the general knowledge of Land Law to work through to an answer. The only people at a disadvantage will be those ill-advised candidates who believe that the Land Law examiner's lightning does strike twice and have only revised a set number of topics based on previous examination papers. Questions of this nature are always welcome as an added incentive to those who believe in learning the subject as a whole rather than certain pre-digested aspects of a subject. One cannot over-emphasise the danger of such a policy in Land Law examinations. This question is best approached precisely in the manner in which it was set, apart from prefacing the answer by an introductory paragraph before going on to part (a). The will creates a strict settlement and following the death of Herbert in 1987 Wilma will become the first tenant for life with Roe and Doe as the trustees of the settlement. When Wilma dies in 1989 Stephen will probably become the tenant for life.

Skeleton solution

Settled land - interests in succession: s1(1)(i) SLA 1925.

Title is unregistered: death of Herbert.

Will creates strict settlement. Two documents required: s4(1) SLA. Roe/Doe execute (1) vesting assent to Wilma as tenant for life. (2) Will: trust instrument. Roe/Doe: trustees of the settlement - s30(3) SLA.

Death of Wilma - remains settled land. Roe/Doe: special personal representatives - Stephen becomes tenant for life (if of full age) (vesting assent) - s19(1) SLA.

Title is registered - legal estate registered in Wilma's name as registered proprietor - beneficial interests under settlement are minor interests: s3(xv)(b) LRA 1925 - protect by restriction on proprietorship register: Form 9, Schedule to LR Rules 1925.

Death of Wilma - special personal representatives (Roe/Doe) execute vesting assent in favour of Stephen who becomes registered proprietor. (Any transaction overrides these interests just as overreached in unregistered land.) Advice same whether unregistered or registered. Advise Stephen - resolve problem before emigrating - otherwise practical management problem. Section 104(1) SLA - cannot assign or release powers of tenant for life - remain exercisable by Stephen. But s105(1) SLA - can assign his interest, with intent to extinguish it, to persons next entitled under the settlement. Jack/Jill - then exercisable as if Stephen dead.

Jack/Jill have fee simple in equal shares (words of severance) - end of strict settlement, becomes a trust for sale settlement with Jack/Jill holding legal estate as joint tenants for themselves on statutory trusts as tenants in common in equity: ss34(2), 35 LPA 1925. Under s36(1) SLA - Megarry and Wade - 'The land cannot be settled land and the statutory trust for sale takes effect' - the same point is made by Cheshire - 'The settlement within the meaning of the SLA 1925 comes to an end and is replaced by a trust for sale'.

Suggested solution

a)   i)   If the title is unregistered - death of Herbert

Herbert's will creates a strict settlement and will be covered by the provisions of the Settled Land Act 1925. The major provision as to formalities is set out in s4(1) of the SLA 1925 which provides:

'(1) Every settlement of a legal estate in land inter vivos shall ... be effected by two deeds, namely, a vesting deed and a trust instrument ...'

Where a settlement is created by will the legal estate will devolve upon Roe and Doe as the personal representatives, who hold it upon trust to convey the legal estate to Wilma as the person first entitled to the tenancy for life under the will.

This conveyance will be made by a vesting assent which need not be under seal but which corresponds to the vesting deed used in the corresponding inter vivos settlement.

The will is then considered to be the trust instrument.

The contents of the vesting deed are described in s5(1) SLA 1925 and it should be noted that this is the public document which provides merely sufficient information to a purchaser that there is a settlement and details of the trustees of the settlement to whom any purchase money must be paid. The contents of the trust instrument are described in s4(3) SLA 1925. This is, essentially, a private document in which the trusts of the settlement are set out. It is assumed that Roe and Doe will be made the trustees of the settlement but, for the purposes of s30(1) SLA 1925, they must be specifically declared by the settlement to be the trustees for the purposes of the Settled Land Act. In this case the vesting assent must make such a specific appointment of Roe and Doe as the trustees of the settlement in addition to their function as the executors and trustees of the will and estate of Herbert. Until such appointment is made the fact that Roe and Doe are the personal representatives of Herbert is sufficient to make them trustees of the settlement: s30(3) SLA 1925.

Death of Wilma

The land will remain settled and will vest in the trustees of the settlement as 'special personal representatives'. It will, of course, be necessary to inspect Herbert's will as the trust instrument to confirm this fact that the land continues to be settled land. The special personal representatives will administer the settled land separate from her own estate and it may be that a distinct grant of probate is made to ordinary personal representatives in respect of her non-settled land interests. Following the granting of probate Stephen will become tenant for life provided he is not an infant. If he is an infant the settled land will vest in the trustees of the settlement as statutory owners until Stephen attains his majority. On the basis that Stephen has attained his majority he will become the tenant for life.

ii)   If the title is registered under the Land Registration Act 1925

Basically there is still a strict settlement because the Settled Land Act 1925 applies whether the title to the land is registered or not.

Death of Herbert

The legal estate in the settled land will be registered in Wilma's name. The beneficial interests under the settlement are included in the definition of 'minor interests' in s3(xv)(b) LRA 1925:

'in the case of settled land, all interests and powers which are under the Settled Land Act 1925 ... capable of being overriden by the tenant for life or statutory owner ...'

These interests must be protected by restrictions entered on the proprietorship register. These warn persons dealing with the settled land of the limitations on the powers of the registered proprietor under the Settled Land Act or the settlement itself.

The form of the restriction is set out in Form 9 of the Schedule to the Land Registration Rules 1925.

'No disposition under which capital money arises is to be registered unless the money is paid to AB of ... etc and CD of ... etc ... (the trustees of the settlement, of which there must be not less than two or more than four individuals, or a trust corporation), or into court.

Except under an order of the Registrar, no disposition is to be registered unless authorised by the Settled Land Act 1925.'

This restriction will be entered in the proprietorship register to Wilma's title. This protects the beneficial interests of the settlement without any details being brought onto the register.

In other ways the procedure remains as in the case of unregistered land with the personal representatives, Roe and Doe, executing a vesting assent in favour of Wilma.

Death of Wilma

Again the procedure is based on that described earlier. The special personal representatives will execute a vesting assent in favour of Stephen. If Stephen is an infant the vesting assent will be in favour of the statutory owners with a restriction entered on the proprietorship register in the form set out in the Schedule to the Land Registration Rules 1925 (Form 10).

If Stephen has attained his majority he will be entered as the proprietor in the register, and the restriction in Form 9 (above) will continue as an entry in the proprietorship register.

Any purchaser from the tenant for life, Wilma or Stephen, respectively, who complies with the restriction in Form 9 will override the beneficial interests just as they would be overreached in the case of unregistered land.

b) The advice to Stephen will be the same whether the title to the land is unregistered or registered under the Land Registration Act 1925. The most important advice is that he must resolve the problem before emigrating. If he fails to do so he will continue as tenant for life with all the problems of administrating the settlement from the other side of the world. The basic statement on his powers is contained in s104(1) SLA 1925:

'The powers under this Act of a tenant for life are not capable of assignment or release, and do not pass to a person as being, by operation of law or otherwise, an assignee of a tenant for life, and remain exercisable by the tenant for life after and notwithstanding any assignment, by operation of law or otherwise, of his estate or interest under the settlement.'

To this should be added the provisions of s105(1) SLA 1925. If Stephen wishes to emigrate he can assign his interest, with intent to extinguish that interest, to the person next entitled under the settlement, in this case Jack and Jill. If he does this his statutory powers cease to be exercisable by Stephen and become exercisable as if he were dead.

The original settlement created by Herbert's will vested the fee simple in his grandchildren Jack and Jill in equal shares. This marks the end of the settlement so Stephen will, in fact, convey the legal estate to Jack and Jill by an ordinary conveyance as the land will cease to be settled land. As Jack and Jill will hold the land in 'equal shares' there will in fact be a trust for sale. These words of severance create a tenancy in common in equity and Jack and Jill will hold the legal estate as joint tenants upon the statutory trusts referred to in ss34(2) and 35 of the Law of Property Act 1925.

If Stephen conveys his interest to Jack and Jill with this intent to extinguish his interest, he can then emigrate without any further worry as to the settlement created by Herbert's will. For the purposes of the Settled Land Act 1925 the provisions of the will will operate as if Stephen 'were dead.'

Tutorial comments

a) Definition of settlement.

b) Settlement in unregistered land.

c) Any difference where the title to the land is registered? Consider the form of the restriction which is entered on the proprietorship register in the case of both a strict settlement and a trust for sale.

d) Effect when the settlement comes to an end.

Question 4

'There is no justification today for retaining two methods of creating settlements of land.'

Discuss. If a single method is to be adopted, what form should it take?

University of London LLB Examination
(for External Students) Land Law June 1991 Q1

General comment

Although this is not a difficult question for a reasonably well-prepared student, it is probably one which most students would have been better advised not to attempt. Essay questions are deceptively difficult to answer well in examination conditions and it is all too easy to spend a lot of time and words in saying very little of real significance. Certainly anyone who had not read the Law Commission paper on Trusts of Land should have chosen another question.

Skeleton solution

What was the historical justification for two systems? - Do these reasons apply today? - Main characteristics of the SLA settlement - What are the main problems of the SLA? - Is there still a need to retain the SLA? - Is the trust for sale always appropriate? - What alterations should be made to the trust for sale? - Conclusion: suggest single system based on the trust for sale but with some modifications.

Suggested solution

The reason for the present dual system of creating settlements of land is historical. The original idea behind a settlement under the SLA 1925 (and its predecessors) was to retain land in the family, in circumstances where the life tenant would be residing on the property and would require wide powers of management in order to deal with the settled land to the best advantage of all interested persons. The land was likely to be a large estate. By contrast, the idea behind the trust for sale was to create a mechanism for holding land as an investment pending a sale of the land. Considerable differences remain between the two systems but it is by no means clear whether the existence of these differences justifies the retention of both systems.

The legal estate under an SLA settlement is held by the tenant for life and he will make all the management decisions concerning the property, including the decision whether or not to sell. It is impossible by s106 SLA to interfere with his exercise of these powers in any way. Under a trust for sale the legal estate is held by the trustees and they will make all the management decisions, although they may delegate the powers of leasing and management to the beneficiary. The legislation still gives priority to the SLA so that if no proper advice is taken, it is possible to have an SLA settlement by mistake - this is because if successive interests in land are created, there will be a settlement under the SLA unless an 'immediate binding trust for sale' is created, so that a home-made will which leaves a house to the widow for life and then to the children will create an SLA settlement with its attendant expense and complexity. It seems that a grant of a right of residence for life will also create an SLA settlement: see *Bannister* v *Bannister* (1948), *Binions* v *Evans* (1972).

The Law Commission identified several problems with the working of the SLA in their report on Trusts of Land. The system is complicated and expensive to administer with the requirement for two documents, a vesting deed and a trust instrument, and the need to take out a special grant of probate when the tenant for life dies. Further problems arise with settlements created accidentally under the SLA as these are bound to be improperly created without the required two documents. Conveyancing difficulties arise if it is not clear whether the settlement is under the SLA or a trust for sale as it is unclear whether the tenant for life of trustees should execute the relevant documents. There may well be a conflict of interest between the personal wishes of the tenant for life and the interests of the other beneficiaries and the latter are in a very weak position with no real right to object to the exercise of his powers by the tenant for life.

The conclusion of the Law Commission was that strict settlement under the SLA be abolished. The recommendation was made on the basis that there was no longer sufficient justification in retaining two parallel systems. The historical reasons for two systems no longer applied and research undertaken by the Commission showed that hardly any new settlements were created under the SLA in any event. The mechanism was cumbersome and expensive and its only advantage was that in some cases it was more appropriate for the tenant for life than the trustees to manage the settled property. The Commission suggested granting an enhanced power of delegation to trustees instead. The old reason for a settlement under the SLA was to keep land in the family and this is easier to achieve with a trust for sale by requiring consents to be obtained before sale.

However the Commission did not simply recommend that the trust for sale become the single possible system for creating trusts of land. The trust for sale is used in settlements with successive interests and when concurrent interests exist. In the latter case the trust for sale is an artificial concept. The Law Commission suggested that the type of co-ownership envisaged in 1925 would have been the situation of land being left to children in a will, when a sale would have resulted. In modern cases of co-ownership the land is purchased for occupation primarily rather than as an investment. The doctrine of conversion which applies to trusts for sale is incomprehensible to non-lawyers.

The recommendation was that the strict settlement and trust for sale should both be replaced by a new single system which would apply to all trusts of land, including bare trusts and concurrent interests. The land would be held by trustees with a power to retain and a power to sell. The doctrine of conversion would not apply. The powers of the trustees would be based on those of the absolute owner. The advantages of the new single system would be that it would remove the complexities inherent in a dual system and many conveyancing difficulties would disappear. In most cases it is more appropriate for the trustees to exercise the powers of management, but there would be improved delegation powers if it was wished that the life tenant should manage the property. The new system would be more in accord with the expectations and understanding of the lay person as it applied to co-ownership.

In conclusion, it is difficult to find any real justification for retaining the two systems of settling land and the scarcity of new SLA settlements in practice seems to confirm this view. The historical reasons for the two systems no longer apply. Therefore in the interests of simplicity a single system is preferable. If a single system is to be adopted, the trust for sale is certainly a more appropriate choice than the strict settlement, which is really of little practical relevance today, but there are significant problems with the trust for sale itself. Therefore a new system based on the trust for sale with certain changes is suggested. The emphasis on the duty to sell and the doctrine of conversion would be abolished and the trustees given power both to retain the land and sell it. This system, as put forward by the Law Commission, would be closer to the layman's understanding of the position.

4   CO-OWNERSHIP

4.1   Introduction

4.2   Key points

4.3   Recent cases and statutes

4.4   Analysis of questions

4.5   Questions

4.1   Introduction

This subject is frequently the most popular with examination candidates. There are few obvious problems but one type of question should be approached with some care. This is the chronological question where annual changes to the facts are provided. In itself a familiar-looking question, if you do not make the correct diagnosis the answer starts to go wrong and may never give the you the opportunity to rectify your mistake. The following diagram will help to overcome this problem of identification.

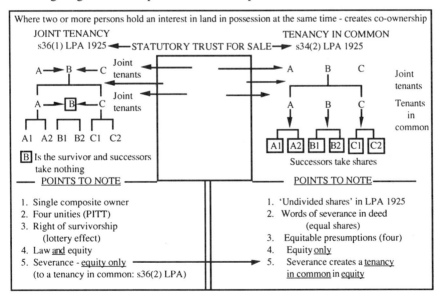

Effect on co-ownership of 1925 property legislation

a)   Land held on trust for sale (s30 LPA 1925)

51

b) Legal estate must be held as joint tenants

c) Equitable interests may be held as either joint tenants or tenants in common

Distinguish several ownership - owner entitled in own right with no other person - and concurrent interest or co-ownership where owner and others have simultaneous interests in the land.

Cheshire: 'Land may the subject of several, that is separate ownership, or co-ownership.'

4.2   Key points

Where two or more persons hold an interest in land in possession at the same time.

a) *Joint tenancy* - where land is conveyed to two or more persons without WORDS OF SEVERANCE indicating distinct shares.

   i) Characteristics of joint tenancy

     • Survivorship - jus accrescendi - lottery effect

     • The four unities:

       - Unity of possession - all joint tenants

       - Unity of interest - same in quality

       - Unity of title - same document

       - Unity of time - vests at the same time.

   ii) Joint tenancy after 1925 - s34(2) LPA 1925.

     No severance of legal joint tenancy to create a tenancy in common at law is possible - s36(2) and s1(6) LPA 1925

b) *Tenancy in common* - no longer exists at law - s1(6) LPA 1925

   i) Undivided shares

   ii) Difference between tenancy in common and joint tenancy

     • Not subject to four unities - only unity of possession required

     • No jus accrescendi - undivided shares pass to personal representatives for person entitled on will or intestacy on statutory trusts - s35 LPA 1925.

     • Not necessarily in equal shares

   iii) Determination of tenancy in common

     • Partition - each becomes sole owner of part

     • Sale - purchaser takes free of interests of co-owners - those interests continue in the purchase money.

     • Acquisition by one tenant of the shares of his co-tenants

iv) Presumptions in favour of tenancy in common

- Purchase money in unequal shares: *Bull* v *Bull* [1955] 1 QB 234 - origin of trust for sale - s36(4) SLA 1925.

- Loan by co-mortgagees in equal or unequal shares

- Partnership property: *Barton* v *Morris* [1985] 2 All ER 1032

- Where grantees hold premises for their several individual business purposes: *Malayan Credit Ltd* v *Jack Chia-MPH Ltd* [1986] 1 All ER 711

c) *Severance of joint tenancy* - equity only - s36(2) LPA 1925 - severance means conversion in equity from a joint tenancy to a tenancy in common.

Four methods

i) Inter vivos alienation

ii) Later acquisition of another interest in the land

iii) Agreement to hold as tenants in common - memorandum of severance on the original conveyance.

iv) Notice in writing: s36(2) LPA 1925 *Burgess* v *Rawnsley* [1975] Ch 429 - unilateral oral declaration may lead to severance. Look for 'a course of dealing'.

d) *Party walls*

i) The problem - alternatives were available as follows:-

- Tenants in common

- Ownership to mid point of width of wall

- Ownership to mid point plus cross-easements of support

- Owned entirely by one neighbour subject to an easement in favour of other

ii) The statutory solution is contained in s38 LPA 1925: *Bradburn* v *Lindsay* [1983] 2 All ER 408

This was needed because the definition of 'land' in the LPA would include party walls - leading to the creation of a trust for sale of the party wall. Now deemed to have been severed vertically but with cross rights of support and user as would be enjoyed by a tenant in common.

4.3　Recent cases and statutes

Harman v *Glencross* [1986] 1 All ER 545

Malayan Credit Ltd v *Jack Chia-MPH Ltd* [1986] 1 All ER 711

Goodman v *Gallant* [1986] 1 All ER 311

Grant v *Edwards* [1986] 2 All ER 426

Martin v *Martin* (1987) 54 P & CR 238; cf *Joyce* v *Barker Bros (Builders) Ltd* (1980) 40 P & CR 512 - the phrase in a conveyance reads 'as beneficial joint tenants in common in equal shares'. Two solutions - in *Joyce* v *Barker Bros (Builders) Ltd* (1980) take the first sensible words in the deed hence - beneficial joint tenants. But in *Martin* v *Martin* (1987) the court read the earlier words as words of severance which override the apparent joint tenancy to create a tenancy in common. This was done by considering two notional deeds, the first created the joint tenancy and the second severed it.

AG Securities Ltd v *Vaughan*; *Antoniades* v *Villiers* [1988] 3 All ER 1058

Perry v *Phoenix Assurance plc* [1988] 3 All ER 60

Lloyds Bank plc v *Rosset* [1990] 2 WLR 867

Springette v *Defoe* (1992) The Independent 24 March

4.4   Analysis of questions

The links with other subjects are apparent in this area of Land Law. The links with trusts for sale were mentioned in chapter 3 - the modern question may also contain a registered land element and a knowledge of the decision in *Williams & Glyn's Bank Ltd* v *Boland* [1980] 3 WLR 138 is always a useful base. In addition this is an area of change where for many years three presumptions of an equitable tenancy in common were recognised but suddenly these became four in *Malayan Credit Ltd* v *Jack Chia-MPH Ltd* [1986] 1 All ER 711 with the suggestion from the Privy Council that there may be others.

Generally the questions are popular and many of the answers are very good.

4.5   Questions

Question 1

In 1985 James conveyed The Meadows to his sons Kenneth, Lionel, Mike and Ned as joint tenants. Ned, the youngest brother, was aged 17. In 1987 Kenneth died, leaving all his property to Oswald. In 1988 Mike sold his interest to Paul, and in 1989 Paul died, leaving all his realty to Quentin, and all his personalty to Robert and Simon in equal shares. Lionel now wishes to sell The Meadows, but Ned objects. Advise Lionel.

If The Meadows is sold, how should the proceeds of sale be divided?

University of London LLB Examination
(for External Students) Land Law June 1977 Q4

General comment

To illustrate many of the facets of co-ownership. Note the infant element.

Skeleton solution

THE MEADOWS

EVENT 1: Conveyance 'as joint tenants'	K L M	Joint tenants
[N - s19(2) LPA 1925] 'Statutory trusts' s35 LPA 1925	K L M N	Joint tenants
EVENT 2: Death of K	L - M	Joint tenants [Oswald gets nothing]
Jus accrescendi praefertur ultimae voluntatii	L M N	Joint tenants
EVENT 3: M sells to P	L - M	Joint tenants
Severance of joint tenancy in equity only	L N - P	L N joint tenants 2/3 : P tenant in common 1/3
s36(2) LPA - no severance at law	2/3	1/3 undivided share
EVENT 4: Death of P	L - M	Joint tenants [Quentin - realty - gets
Conversion - *Re Kempthorne* [1930] 1 Ch 268	L N R & S	nothing]
	2/3	1/3 in equal shares - personalty
	Joint tenants	Tenants in common

EVENT 5: Sale now - s25 - power to postpone sale - all must agree - *Re Mayo* (1943)

s30 - any person interested - apply to court - such order as it thinks fit.

Court considers - purpose of the trust - *Re Buchanan-Wollaston's Conveyance* (1939)

Re Evers's Trust (1980)

EVENT 6: Division of proceeds of sale: L & N - $2/3$ [effectively $1/3$ each]
R & S - $1/6$ each Undivided shares

Suggested solution

The original conveyance of The Meadows in 1985 would vest the property in Kenneth, Lionel, Mike and Ned as joint tenants. As Ned was, then, only 17 the effect of the conveyance will be controlled by s19(2) of the Law of Property Act 1925 which states:

'(2) A conveyance of a legal estate in land to an infant, jointly with one or more other persons of full age, shall operate to vest the legal estate in the other person or persons on the statutory trusts, but not so as to sever any joint tenancy in the net proceeds of sale or in the rents and profits until sale...'

The effect will be that Kenneth, Lionel and Mike will hold the legal estate on the statutory trusts for the benefit of the four sons. The phrase 'statutory trusts' is defined in s35 of the LPA 1925 as being land held:

'... upon trust to sell the same and to stand possessed of the net proceeds of sale, after payment of costs, and of the net rents and profits until sale after payment of rates, taxes, costs of insurance, repairs, and other out-goings, upon such trusts, and subject to such powers and provisions, as may be requisite for giving effect to the rights of the persons ... interested in the land ...'

The jus accrescendi will operate on the death of Kenneth and his interest in The Meadows will pass to Lionel, Mike and Ned by the right of survivorship. This right of survivorship takes precedence over any disposition made by Kenneth of his will and as a result no interest in The Meadows will pass to Oswald.

When Mike sells his interest to Paul in 1988 this effects a severance of the joint tenancy in equity and Paul will take a one third interest as a tenant in common whilst Lionel and Ned continue as joint tenants of the remaining interests in The Meadows. By s36(2) of the LPA 1925 there can be no severance of the joint tenancy of the legal estate because this would create a tenancy in common in the legal estate and no tenancy in common can exist at law after 1925: s1(6) LPA 1925. The effect is that Mike would continue to be a statutory trustee for sale as a joint tenant of the legal estate, but in view of his transaction with Paul he could relinquish his trusteeship leaving Lionel and Ned as the trustees.

When Paul died in 1989 he left all his realty to Quentin and all his personalty to Robert and Simon in equal shares. The effect of the equitable doctrine of conversion upon the statutory trust for sale is that a notional conversion takes place even before sale and Paul's one third interest in The Meadows is converted into an interest in the proceeds of sale when The Meadows is, eventually, sold. The result is that Paul's interest is an interest in personalty and Paul has left all his personalty to Robert and Simon in equal shares. The effect is that the use of the words 'in equal shares' makes Robert and Simon tenants in common of Paul's share in the proceeds of sale of The Meadows. If Robert or Simon were to die the jus accrescendi would not operate.

In the case of the statutory trust for sale the overriding obligation is to sell but there is a power to postpone the sale. Section 25 of the LPA 1925 implies in a trust for sale the power to postpone sale unless there is a contrary intention. The power to postpone must be exercised unanimously and, if there is any disagreement, s30 of the LPA 1925 gives the court a discretion to direct that the sale be carried out. Section 30(1) of the LPA 1925 states:

'If the trustees for sale refuse to sell ... any person interested may apply to the court for a vesting or other order for giving effect to the proposed transaction or for an order directing the trustees for sale to give effect thereto, and the court may make such order as it thinks fit.'

For Ned to succeed in his objections to the sale he must have the unanimous support of all the trustees for sale: if he is unable to command such support the duty to sell will prevail.

The exercise of the discretion given to the court has been considered in a number of cases including *Jones* v *Challenger* (1961) in which Donovan J, sitting in the Court of Appeal, said:

'The language of s30 could hardly be more apt to confer a complete discretion on the court which considers an application under the section. The court is, inter alia, to make "such order as it thinks fit". The discretion must, of course, be exercised judicially, and the principles which govern its exercise are those set forth in this court in *Re Buchanan-Wollaston's Conveyance* [1939] Ch 738.'

Lord Greene there said (at page 747): 'It seems to me that the Court of Equity, when asked to enforce the trust for sale, whether one created by a settlement or a will or one created by the statute, must look into all the circumstances of the case and consider whether or not, at the particular moment and in the particular circumstances when the application is made to it, it is right and proper that such an order shall be made.'

If Ned continues to object it is open to Lionel to apply to the court under s30 of the LPA 1925 for an order for sale.

If Ned withdraws his objection, or the court orders a sale, the proceeds of sale of The Meadows will be divided as to two-thirds to Lionel and Ned as the surviving joint tenants. The remaining one-third share will go on the basis of the severance of the equitable interest by Mike to Robert and Simon in equal shares under the disposition of his personalty set out in Paul's will. On this basis Robert and Simon will each get one-sixth of the proceeds of sale of The Meadows.

Tutorial comments

a) Treatment of chronological questions on co-ownership.

b) Effect of conversion.

c) Use of s30 LPA 1925 and the discretion of the court.

Question 2

The Gables was conveyed in 1986 to Ada and Bertha, who were sisters, as joint tenants. Ada and Bertha lived in The Gables on friendly terms until earlier this year, when Ada decided that she would prefer to live on her own, and she told Bertha that she wanted to end the joint tenancy. They therefore discussed the possibility of selling The Gables and buying two smaller houses with the proceeds. They advertised the property but received no satisfactory offers. They also discussed the possibility of splitting the house up into two separate flats, but had come to no firm decision about this. They were however still living together in The Gables when Ada died last month. In her will Ada left her share in The Gables to another sister, Clara. Bertha claims that as the sole survivor of joint tenants she is entitled to The Gables.

Discuss.

University of London LLB Examination
(for External Students) Land Law June 1978 Q4

General comment

The question deals with the rights of co-ownership, the manner in which a joint tenancy may be severed to create a tenancy in common and the rights of devolution upon the death of a co-owner.

Skeleton solution

THE GABLES

Ada - Bertha: express joint tenants: law and equity - severance in equity only - consider various activities as potential evidence of severance:-

a)	A decided she would prefer to live on own:	No
b)	A told B she wanted to end joint tenancy:	Yes
c)	They advertised property - received no satisfactory replies:	Yes
d)	Discussed possibility of splitting house into 2 separate flats:	No

Severance: any course of dealing?: s36(2) LPA 1925

'… where a legal estate … is vested in joint tenants beneficially, and any tenant desires to sever the joint tenancy in equity, he shall … do such other acts or things as would… have been effectual to sever the tenancy in equity…'

Re Draper's Conveyance (1969); *Burgess v Rawnsley* (1975) - beneficial joint tenancy severed by Mrs R's oral agreement to sell her share - even though not specifically enforceable did evince an intention that property be held in common and not jointly. Lord Denning:

'It is sufficient if there is a course of dealings in which one party makes clear to the other that he desires that their shares should no longer be held jointly but be held in common.' Apply 1 to 4 above.

a) Not made clear to Bertha.

b) This is clearly a desire no longer to hold jointly.

c) Action which supports 2.

d) Does not evince any intention that shares be held in common.

Clearly Ada and Bertha have entered on a course of dealings which indicates their interests shall be held as tenants in common in equity even though they were still living together when Ada died.

Clara will be entitled to Ada's undivided share in The Gables.

[A share in the proceeds of sale of The Gables - effect of conversion on the trust for sale.]

Suggested solution   Alice

The Gables was conveyed in 1986 to Ada and Bertha as joint tenants. There are two essential attributes of a joint tenancy: the need for the presence of the four unities and the right of survivorship. As we are told the conveyance was expressed to be as joint tenants the presence of the four unities may be presumed. We must, however, consider the effect of the jus accrescendi, the right of survivorship. This is the right of the survivor or survivors under a joint tenancy to succeed to a fellow joint tenant's interest on his or her death which continues until there is only one survivor who holds the land as his or her sole property. If Ada and Bertha continue to be joint tenants of The Gables until the death of Ada then the claim of Bertha to be entitled to The Gables as the sole survivor of the joint tenants will be valid and will prevail against the claim of Clara under the will of Ada.

Prior to the death of Ada has any event taken place which could change this nature of the holding and, if so, what is the effect thereof? We are told that earlier this year Ada decided that she would prefer to live on her own and she told Bertha that she wanted to end the joint tenancy. This was a serious proposal which led to the advertising of The Gables but they received no satisfactory offers. The sisters considered two alternatives - the sale of The Gables or the splitting up of the house into two separate flats. Following this failure to sell the house no firm decision had been reached on the alternative and they were still living together in The Gables when Ada died. The question to consider is whether any of these events amounts to a severance of the joint tenancy which would convert into a tenancy in common the equitable interest of the sisters in the proceeds of sale. After 1925 tenants in common are entitled to land in undivided shares. The effect is that the legal estate would vest in them as joint tenants upon trust for sale and they would hold the net proceeds of sale and the net rents and profits, if any, until sale for themselves as tenants in common in equity.

As a tenancy in common can no longer exist at law after 1925, the severance can only affect the equitable interest in the proceeds of sale and not the legal estate. The result of severance would be to give Ada and Bertha undivided shares in The Gables whereas before each had no more than a potential share under the jus accrescendi.

The methods of severance are first where a joint tenant disposes of her interest in equity and thus takes that share out of the joint tenancy. There was no such inter vivos alienation in this case. Secondly, if either sister had acquired another interest in The Gables and thus destroyed the unity of interest. This had not occurred either. If the sisters had specifically agreed to hold as tenants in common this could be an express agreement or be implied from their conduct, but it is probably true that if they had been asked the nature of their intentions they would have been unable to place them precisely in any specific category. This method of severance has been reinforced by s36(2) of the Law of Property Act 1925 which provides that:

'... where a legal estate (not being settled land) is vested in joint tenants beneficially, and any tenant desires to sever the joint tenancy in equity, he shall give to the other joint tenants a notice in writing of such desire or do such other acts or things as would, in the case of personal estate, have been effectual to sever the tenancy in equity...'

It is the nature of the 'other acts or things' capable of effecting a severance which has exercised the courts in recent years. In *Re Draper's Conveyance* (1969) a matrimonial case, there was evidence of a firm agreement that husband would buy the wife's share in the matrimonial home but the agreement was not in writing. Although it was not specifically enforceable it was held to be sufficient to effect a severance under s36(2) of the LPA 1925. On the other hand, Walton J in *Nielson-Jones* v *Fedden* (1974) had thought no conduct was sufficient to sever a joint tenancy unless it was irrevocable. The decision in *Re Draper's Conveyance* was supported by the Court of Appeal in *Burgess* v *Rawnsley* (1975).

In this case a house had been bought by the defendant, Mrs Rawnsley, and a Mr Honick for £850 each paying half the price. The house was conveyed to them jointly upon trust for sale and to hold the proceeds upon trust for themsleves as joint tenants. At the time Mr Honick contemplated marrying Mrs Rawnsley but had not told her of his intention whereas she had no other intention than merely to live in an upstairs flat in the house. In 1968 Mrs Rawnsley orally agreed to sell her share in the house to Mr Honick for £750 but subsequently refused to sell and she never did live in the house. Mr Honick died in 1971. The action was to determine if his estate was entitled to a half share in the house and it was held by the Court of Appeal that the beneficial joint tenancy had been severed by Mrs Rawnsley's oral agreement to sell her share to Mr Honick even though it was not specifically enforceable. It did evince an intention by both parties that the property should be held in common and not jointly. Lord Denning MR summarised the position today:

'The thing to remember today is that equity leans against joint tenants and favours tenancies in common ... It is sufficient if there is a course of dealing in which one party makes clear to the other that he desires that their shares should no longer be held jointly but be held in common... Similarly it is sufficient if both parties enter on a course of dealing which evinces an intention by both of them that their shares shall henceforth be held in common and not jointly.'

The Court of Appeal was unanimous in finding that even though the oral agreement by the joint tenants was not enforceable for want of evidence under s40 LPA 1925 (see now s2 of the Law of Property (Miscellaneous Provisions) Act 1989) it was a course of dealing which was sufficient to effect a severance. It was an example of 'such other acts or things' which would satisfy the requirements of s36(2) LPA 1925.

In the problem in hand there is clearly no written evidence of severance to satisfy the provisions of s40 LPA 1925 (see now s2 of the 1989 Act, above). On the other hand there is clear evidence of a desire to sever with the two proposals of either selling The Gables, which was carried to the point of placing The Gables on the market, or the discussion of the possibility of splitting the house up into two separate flats. These actions could be used by Clara as evidence of 'other acts or things' necessary to support her claim that the equitable joint tenancy of Ada and Bertha had been severed and that, she, Clara was entitled to the share in The Gables left to her in Ada's will.

To refute this Bertha would have to distinguish *Burgess* v *Rawnsley* (1975) by showing that all the discussions were no more than tentative as evidenced by the fact that they were still living together in The Gables when Ada died. Bertha could maintain that beyond placing the house on the market, with no success, the proposals were no more than alternative ideas at the time she became entitled to the whole interest in The Gables by virtue of the jus accrescendi on the death of Ada.

Tutorial comments

a) Severance of the joint tenancy in equity only.

b) What does *Burgess* v *Rawnsley* [1975] Ch 429 really decide?

c) The extent of the 'course of dealing' to become 'other acts or things' within s36(2) LPA 1925.

Question 3

In 1973 Arthur bought Manor Farm, the title to which is unregistered, for £50,000. Manor Farm consists of a farmhouse, and several acres of farmland. In 1975 Arthur married Bertha, and they have two children, Carol born in 1978 and Donald born 1981. In 1985 Arthur's mother, Ethel, came to live with them. In 1986 Arthur executed a trust deed in which he declared that he held Manor Farm on trust for himself, Bertha, Carol, Donald and Ethel in equal shares.

Arthur has just sold Manor Farm for £250,000 to Fred, a property developer, who intends to build a housing estate on the land. The title disclosed by Arthur consisted only of the conveyance to him in 1973. Fred made a close inspection of the land before buying, but did not bother to look round the farmhouse.

Bertha, Carol, Donald and Ethel wish to remain at Manor Farm.

a) Advise Fred.

b) Would it make any difference if the title to Manor Farm were registered?

University of London LLB Examination
(for External Students) Land Law June 1986 Q4

General comment

A very good question with references to a very contemporary problem relating to the sale of land held on trust for sale where the trust itself is not disclosed to the purchaser. The opportunity to compare the effect in both unregistered and registered land will be welcomed by the candidate. The question offers ample scope for the good candidate to demonstrate his knowledge of recent case law on this topic.

Skeleton solution

a) *Unregistered land*

Nature of trust deed of 1986.

Rules of notice - *Caunce* v *Caunce* (1969); cf Russell LJ in *Hodgson* v *Marks* (1971)

Estoppel - *Midland Bank Ltd* v *Farmpride Hatcheries Ltd* (1981)

Duty to sell, power to postpone - *Re Mayo* (1943)

Single trustee for sale - *Bull* v *Bull* (1955)

Conclusion

b) *Registered land*

Overriding interest under s70(1)(g) LRA 1925

Williams & Glyn's Bank Ltd v *Boland* (1980)

Problems posed by *Paddington Building Society* v *Mendelsohn* (1985)

Conclusion

Suggested solution

a) There is little need to rehearse all the facts. Suffice it to say that following the conveyance of Manor Farm to Arthur in 1973 various events took place which resulted in the execution of a trust deed in 1986 in which Arthur declared he held Manor Farm on trust for himself; Bertha, his wife; Carol and Donald, their children; and Ethel, his mother. It should be noted that the above five people held 'in equal shares'. As these words were in the trust deed itself they will constitute words of severance indicating that the five held their interests as tenants in common in equity. The trust deed, apparently, failed to appoint any trustees and a minimum of two trustees are required to give a valid receipt for purchase money of land held on trust for sale: s14(2) Trustee Act 1925 and s27(2) LPA 1925.

When Arthur purported to sell Manor Farm to Fred he did not disclose the trust deed but only the conveyance of 1973, in which event it is assumed Arthur sold 'as beneficial owner' rather than 'as trustee'. If the latter formula had been used Fred would have been made aware of the need for a second trustee. In the event it will be assumed that Fred believed he was purchasing the Manor Farm from Arthur as the sole beneficial owner. It should be noted that the four other beneficiaries, Bertha, Carol, Donald and Ethel, wish to remain at Manor Farm.

As to advice to Fred on the basis that the title to the land was not registered, there is no question that Fred had no knowledge of the trust deed of 1986 and that he took title on the basis of the 1973 conveyance. In such a case the ordinary rules of notice apply and a bona fide purchaser of the legal estate for value without notice of the trust will take free from any trust. The question to consider is whether the action of Fred was sufficient in all the circumstances. He made a close inspection of the land before buying but did not bother to look around the farmhouse. If he had done so evidence of the occupation by Bertha, Carol, Donald and Ethel would have become apparent. The present rule as to constructive notice is to be found in s199 LPA 1925 which provides:

'1) A purchaser shall not be prejudicially affected by notice of - ... (ii) any other instrument or matter or any fact or thing unless - (a) it is within his own knowledge, or would have come to his knowledge if such inquiries and inspections had been made as ought reasonably to have been made by him ...'

If Fred had made a detailed inspection of the farmhouse would this necessarily have given him knowledge of the 1986 trust deed? It would appear that Fred does not have such constructive notice because, at present, the law would not require him to ask such detailed questions of the occupiers of unregistered land as to reveal their interest under the trust deed. This is the effect of the decision of Stamp J in *Caunce v Caunce* (1969). This was a matrimonial home case in which Stamp J said of the wife who was alleging constructive notice:

'She was there ostensibly because she was the husband's wife and her presence was wholly consistent with the title offered by the husband to the bank.'

It should, however, be noted that this decision is not free from criticism and Russell LJ in *Hodgson* v *Marks* (1971) made the following comment:

'In so far as the judgment might appear to lay down a general proposition that enquiry need not be made of any person on the premises if the proposed vendor himself appears to be in occupation, I would not accept them.'

In the context of registered land, Lord Wilberforce said in *Williams & Glyn's Bank Ltd* v *Boland* (1981):

'But the presence of the vendor, with occupation, does not exclude the possibility of occupation of others.'

Both these comments were applied at first instance in *Kingsnorth Finance Co* v *Tizard* (1986). The position in unregistered land is clearly unsatisfactory and whilst Fred may well not be visited with constructive notice in these circumstances, there is always the possibility of litigation between the beneficiaries as to the division of the proceeds of sale. The rules of overreaching would clearly apply here to relieve Fred of any anxiety as to his title to the land and farm.

The rules of estoppel may also apply to these circumstances if the title of Fred is challenged. By his suppression of the 1986 trust deed, Arthur has presented himself as beneficial owner. He would not be allowed to set up the trust deed as a subsequent challenge to that title. By failing to disclose the trust deed, Arthur has encouraged Fred to believe he can sell as beneficial owner and Arthur would be estopped from relying upon the doctrine of constructive notice: *Midland Bank Ltd* v *Farmpride Hatcheries Ltd* (1981). Although this would prevail against Arthur there is no clear authority to indicate that the other beneficiaries would be similarly estopped. The answer to the other beneficiaries should be that as the land is held on trust for sale the duty to sell must prevail over the power to postpone: *Re Mayo* (1943). As one of the beneficiaries has sought sale this must prevail. The answer to the other four is that their interest has, throughout, been in the proceeds of sale and Arthur has merely implemented the sale.

A final problem for Fred might arise through the reading of *Bull* v *Bull* (1955). The facts are well known in that mother and son contributed to the purchase of a house in which title was vested in the son alone. There was a presumption of a tenancy in common in equity but the legal title was in only one trustee, the son. Denning LJ commented:

'The son is the legal owner and he holds it on the statutory trusts for sale. He cannot at the present moment sell the house because he cannot give a valid receipt for the proceeds. It needs two trustees to give a receipt. The son could get over this difficulty by appointing another trustee who would agree with him to sell the house.'

Fred has acquired title without such an appointment of another trustee, the overreaching provisions of s27 LPA 1925 will not apply and prima facie Fred is subject to the interest of the beneficiaries. As indicated above, the answer for Fred is the plea of bona fide purchaser for value of the legal estate without notice.

From the various approaches that may be made to the problem, it appears that Fred may well have a good title. This will leave the remaining beneficiaries with personal rights to compel Arthur to account for their respective shares of £50,000 in the proceeds of sale of Manor Farm.

b) If the title to the land is registered a very different set of principles apply. The position of Bertha, Carol, Donald and Ethel appears to be much more secure. Section 70(1)(g) LRA 1925 protects as an overriding interest 'the rights of every person in actual occupation of the land or in receipt of the rents and profits thereof, save where enquiry is made of such person and the rights are not disclosed'.

For our purposes s70(1)(g) has three important aspects. The 'rights' which are protected will be those under the trust deed of 1986 to hold Manor Farm in equal shares. The 'actual occupation' is the key to the protection of these rights and we are told that they wish to remain in Manor Farm and so they are in actual occupation. Fred cannot rely on the saving clause because, although he inspected the fields closely, he 'did not bother to look around the farmhouse'. In fact looking around and seeing the occupants would not be sufficient. He would have had to ask Bertha, Carol, Donald and Ethel respectively as to their rights and they must have refused to disclose such rights. The strength of this protection was recognised by the House of Lords in *Williams and Glyn's Bank Ltd* v *Boland* (1981) and has recently been supported by the decision of the Court of Appeal in *City of London Building Society* v *Flegg* (1987).

The only problem is the date of the trust deed. The farm was conveyed to Arthur in 1973 but the trust deed was only executed in 1986. It appears that if the trust deed is executed later it will be implied that the trust deed is then subject to any intervening rights of third parties, such as a mortgagee, who may then prevail over the apparent 'rights' of the person in actual occupation. An intention is imputed to postpone the interests of the occupier to the mortgagee: see *Paddington Building Society* v *Mendelsohn* (1985).

One commentator on this decision has made the following observation:

'In policy terms, there may be much to be said for the decision in *Mendelsohn*, easing as it does the problems created for the institutional lenders by the *Boland* decision. It is disturbing, however, to see such a policy shift being effected by means of transparently superficial reasoning. Regrettably, it is thought that it has now become necessary for this matter to be ventilated again in the House of Lords. As the law now stands, what was seen as a landmark decision, as it seems clear it was intended to be, has now become something of a damp squib.': M P Thompson (1986) Conv 60-61.

Damp squib or not, the body of law surrounding *Williams & Glyn's Bank* v *Boland* and s70(1)(g) will certainly help the beneficiaries to remain in the property and would be very damaging to Fred. The outcome may be rectification of the register under s82(3) LRA 1925 to give effect to their overriding interest under s70(1)(g) LRA 1925. If so, this would merely leave Fred with an application for indemnity under s83(1) for any 'loss by reason of any rectification of the register'. Fred may even have problems here because his loss may well be due to his own failure to make direct enquiries of Bertha, Carol, Donald and Ethel within the saving provisions of s70(1)(g) LRA 1925. Compare the decision in *Re Chowood's Registered Land* (1933).

Tutorial comments

a) The full effect of the decision in *Williams and Glyn's Bank Ltd* v *Boland* [1980] 3 WLR 138.

b) Is there a further need to consider this decision in the light of later decisons?

c) Analyse the effect of the decision of the House of Lords in *Lloyds Bank plc* v *Rosset* [1990] 2 WLR 867. Consider also Peter Sparkes' article 'The discoverability of occupiers of registered land' *Conveyancer and Property Lawyer*, September/October 1988, p342.

Question 4

In 1984 Tom, Dick and Harry, three wealthy businessmen, clubbed together to purchase a block of offices as an investment. Each contributed one-third of the purchase price and the property was conveyed 'to Tom, Dick and Harry, to hold unto themselves in fee simple'. In April last Tom decided to live in the South of France and wrote to Dick and Harry, 'I shall now be moving all my property out of England, so the office block must be sold unless you buy me out'. Before Dick and Harry could reply, Tom was killed in a car accident; by his will he left all his property to his wife, Alice. Last week Dick died suddenly; by his will he left all his property to his wife, Beatrice.

a) Who is now entitled to (i) the legal estate and (ii) the beneficial interests in the block of offices?

b) If there is a sale, who should be the vendor or vendors?

University of London LLB Examination
(for External Students) Land Law June 1985 Q2

General comment

Students might well have difficulty with this question in that a fundamental decision has to be derived from the first line in order to establish whether the three are joint tenants or tenants in common in equity. Some students may be tempted to answer the question in the alternative but this may be seen as indecision in the eyes of the examiner. In any event this question does illustrate a major problem with co-ownership questions; if you get it wrong on the first line your answer may never recover. The same sentiment may well apply to the questions as well as the answers. Thereafter the question raises a number of interesting points and the candidate should have enjoyed the question once any initial doubts had been dispelled. The answer will then become the traditional chronological questions much favoured in relation to concurrent interests and should be dealt with on that basis by considering events in 1984, 1989 and 1990 and then considering points raised in parts (a) and (b) respectively of the question.

Skeleton solution

1984   Law - joint tenants - s36(1) LPA 1925

   Equity - presumptions - equal shares - one-third each - no presumption

   BUT - commercial undertaking

   Equitable presumption in favour of tenancy in common.

Result   T D H - law - joint tenants

   T D H - equity - one-third each as tenants in common

1989   Tom to South of France - effect of letter? No severance because already tenants in common in equity. Cf *Harris* v *Goddard* (1983).

   Death of Tom - will to wife - Alice

   Right of survivorship at law

   Equitable interest passes under will to Alice

Result   D H - law - joint tenants

   Alice - D - H - equity - one-third each as tenants in common

a) 1990 Death of Dick - will to Wife - Beatrice

   Right of survivorship at law - H surviving joint tenant

   Equitable interest passes under will to Beatrice.

   i) Result H - law - surviving joint tenant

   ii) Alice - Beatrice - H - equity - one-third each as tenants in common

b) Law of Property (Joint Tenants) Act 1964 does NOT apply. H cannot give a valid receipt as a single trustee: s14(2)(a) Trustee Act 1925.

   H must appoint additional trustee(s) before sale: s36(6)(b) Trustee Act 1925.

Suggested solution

The effect of the conveyance in 1984 was to vest the fee simple in Tom, Dick and Harry as joint tenants upon trust for sale. Although the conveyance was to Tom, Dick and Harry, to hold unto themselves in fee simple, the necessary trust for sale will be derived from s36(1) LPA 1925.

'1) Where a legal estate (not being settled land) is beneficially limited to or held in trust for any persons as joint tenants, the same shall be held on trust for sale ...'

The effect in equity may be different. There are three cases where equity will presume a tenancy in common. One of these relates to mortgages and has no relevance here. Of the other two, there is a presumption in favour of an equitable tenancy in common where the purchase price is provided in unequal shares. The purchase price was by way of contribution of one-third each so, again, this presumption will not apply where the contributions are by way of equal shares. The third presumption poses a problem in that it is based on a maxim which, apparently, is wider than the presumption today. The maxim is jus accrescendi inter mercatores locum non habet pro beneficio comercii - the right of survivorship has no place in business. The acquisition of the block of offices was clearly a business venture 'as an investment'. The maxim however has generally been restricted to partnership property and there is clearly a presumption of tenancy in common where land is bought as partnership property. Megarry and Wade say:

'The rule extended to any joint undertaking carried on with a view to profit, even if there is no formal partnership between the parties ... ' quoting, inter alia, *Lake* v *Gibson* (1729). Cheshire is not so forthright but does say: ' ... that persons who make a joint purchase for the purposes of a joint undertaking or partnership, either in trade or in any other dealing, are to be treated in equity as tenants in common.'

If these statements are applied in the context of the question then Tom, Dick and Harry become tenants in common in equity. This conclusion is achieved with some reluctance especially in the light of Cheshire's conclusion that: 'Despite these exceptional cases, the fundamental rule is that wherever land is granted ... to two or more persons singly and without words of severance, the donees become joint tenants holding a single title'. The fact that these are mere presumptions which give way to any express statement to the contrary is clearly illustrated by the recent decision in *Barton* v *Morris* (1985).

The next point to consider is the effect in April 1989 of Tom's decision to live in the South of France and the letter he wrote to Dick and Harry. The move will have no effect on the legal estate which remains in Tom, Dick and Harry as joint tenants on trust for sale. As it has been decided that they hold the beneficial interest as tenants in common there is also no need to consider whether the letter is an act of severance. It is interesting to note that the phrasing of the letter that the property 'must be sold unless you buy me out' indicates some doubt in Tom's mind as to how to achieve whatever result he desires. To that end the following words of Lawton LJ in *Harris* v *Goddard* (1983) at page 246 should be noted: 'I am unable to accept the submission of counsel for the plaintiffs that a notice in writing which shows no more than a desire to bring the existing interest to an end is a good notice.'

In 1989 Tom died in a motor car accident and in his will he left all his property to his wife, Alice. The effect of Tom's death must be considered both at law and in equity. At law the right of survivorship applies and the legal estate is now vested in Dick and Harry. In equity the three held as tenants in common so Dick and Harry continue to hold a one-third share each whilst the one-third share of Tom will pass under his will to his widow, Alice.

The death of Dick in 1990 provides the opportunity to answer the various parts of the question itself.

a)   i)   The legal estate will now be vested in Harry as the surviving joint tenant at law. He will continue to hold the property on trust for sale. It should be noted that the Law of Property (Joint Tenants) Act 1964 does not apply because Harry is not a surviving joint tenant who is solely and beneficially entitled to the land. The equitable interests continue in various persons.

      ii)   Dick died leaving in his will all his property to his wife, Beatrice. As a tenant in common in equity his one-third share in the block of offices will pass to his widow, Beatrice. The effect is that Harry now holds the legal estate, as a sole trustee, on behalf of himself as to a one-third share, a one-third share to Alice, the widow of Tom, and a one-third share to Beatrice, the widow of Dick. All the shares will be held as tenants in common in equity.

b) The block of offices is held on trust for sale and the problem is: if and when a sale is effected who can make title as the vendor? The legal estate is vested in Harry but he is a sole trustee for sale and a sole trustee is unable to give a valid receipt for the purchase money. Section 14(2)(a) Trustee Act 1925 provides:

'2) This section does not, except where the trustee is a trust corporation, enable a sole trustee to give a valid receipt for -

a) the proceeds of sale or other capital money arising under a ... trust for sale of land.'

This problem was recognised by Denning LJ in *Bull* v *Bull* (1955):

'The son is the legal owner and he holds it on the statutory trusts for sale. He cannot at the present moment sell the house because he cannot give a valid receipt for the proceeds.

It needs two trustees to give a receipt. The son could get over this difficulty by appointing another trustee who would agree with him to sell the house.'

Thus Harry must appoint a new trustee under the provisions of s36(6) Trustee Act 1925 which state:

'6) Where a sole trustee, other than a trust corporation, is or has been originally appointed to act in a trust, or where, in the case of any trust, there are not more than three trustees (none of them being a trust corporation) either original or substituted and whether appointed by the court or otherwise, then and in any such case -

a) the person or persons nominated for the purpose of appointing new trustees by the instrument, if any, creating the trust; or

b) if there is no such person, or no such person able and willing to act, then the trustee or trustees for the time being;

may, by writing appoint another person or other persons to be an additional trustee or additional trustees ... '

Assuming that no one else has the power under s36(6)(a) then Harry may appoint an additional trustee, in writing, under the provisions of s36(6)(b) Trustee Act 1925.

Tutorial comments

a) The need for care in this type of chronological question.

b) The equitable presumptions in favour of a tenancy in common.

Question 5

Mike, Pat, Rob and Saul formed a pop group and decided to buy a house together situated near the recording studios. All four of them contributed equally to the purchase price and the house was conveyed into the joint names of Mike, Pat and Rob; Saul was aged 17 at the time of the conveyance. The pop group was not a success and in 1990 Mike sold his interest in the house to Pat. Shortly afterwards Rob wrote to Pat offering to sell him his interest for a certain price. Pat replied that he would be happy to purchase Rob's interest, but that the price was too high. Before any negotiations took place Rob was killed in a motor accident. Saul now wishes the house to be sold whereas Pat wishes to continue living there.

Saul would like to know whether he can force a sale of the house and, if so, how the proceeds would be divided.

Advise Saul.

> University of London LLB Examination
> (for External Students) Land Law June 1992 Q8

General comment

A fairly straightforward question on severance of a joint tenancy and the operation of s30 LPA 1925. The only 'tricky' part lies in the fact that one joint tenant sells to another, so that that other remains a joint tenant of his original share and becomes a tenant-in-common in respect of his 'new share'.

Skeleton solution

- Co-ownership trust for sale - s34-36 LPA 1925.

- Joint tenancy - four unities - contributions.

- Severance - *Williams* v *Hensman* (1861).

- Sale to existing joint tenant - *Re Mayo* (1943).

- Section 30 LPA 1925 application for order for sale - secondary or collateral trusts - *Jones* v *Challenger* (1961).

Suggested solution

Whenever two or more people contribute to the purchase of property which is not conveyed into all of their names, the Law of Property Act (LPA) 1925 brings into play a trust for sale in favour of the co-owners.

Mike, Pat, Rob and Saul contribute equally to the purchase of the house, and they are thus co-owners. As Saul is a minor he cannot hold the legal estate (s1(6) LPA 1925), and so the house is conveyed into the names of Mike, Pat and Rob who hold it on trust for sale for themselves and Saul in equity (ss34-36 LPA 1925). The legal estate is held by the three of them as joint tenants as a tenancy-in-common cannot exist at law.

All four hold the equitable interests as joint tenants for the following reasons. Firstly, the four unities (possession, interest, time and title) appear to be present as all of them are entitled to possess and occupy the house, all of them have the same interest (presumably fee simple), they all acquired that interest at the same time, namely, the date of conveyance, and they all acquired it under the same act or document, viz, the purchase of the house. Secondly, they have contributed equally to the purchase in which case equity presumes a joint tenancy. Thirdly, the house is purchased to be lived in, it is not purchased as a business asset or as business premises (see *Malayan Credit* v *Jack Chia* (1986)), although it will enable them to get to the recording studio easier.

As they are joint tenants none of them can point to a specific share of the property as being theirs - they each own the entirety, although upon sale they will each be entitled to a quarter share of the proceeds. Moreover, as there is a joint tenancy the doctrine of survivorship operates so that, unless a joint tenant has severed his interest during life, his interest passes to the other joint tenants on his death.

The interests of the four could be expressed as follows:

Mike	Pat	Rob		Legal Title (Joint Tenants)
Mike	Pat	Rob	Saul	Equity
JT	JT	JT	JT	
$\frac{1}{4}$	$\frac{1}{4}$	$\frac{1}{4}$	$\frac{1}{4}$	

A joint tenancy can be severed by a joint tenant acting upon his 'share', eg by selling it. In fact the tenancy will have been severed the moment Mike entered into a specifically enforceable contract of sale with Pat. The transaction has no effect on the legal title and Mike remains a trustee for sale. As far as the equitable interests are concerned, Mike drops out of the picture and is no longer a beneficiary behind the trust for sale. Pat will remain a joint tenant in equity of his original interest vis-à-vis Rob and Saul, and will have become a tenant-in-common in respect of the share he has acquired from Mike. He cannot be a joint tenant in respect of this share because unity of title is missing.

The interests of the parties can now be expressed as follows:

Mike	Pat	Rob		Legal Title (Joint Tenants)
Mike	Pat	Rob	Saul	Equity
(TIC)	JT	JT	JT	
$\left(\frac{1}{4}\right)$	$\frac{1}{4}$	$\frac{1}{4}$	$\frac{1}{4}$	

Although a joint tenancy can be severed by way of mutual agreement or mutual conduct (see *Williams* v *Hensman* (1861)), neither could be said to have occurred here, as the price had not been agreed (contrast: *Burgess* v *Rawnsley* (1975)). The letter then has no effect on either the legal or beneficial interests.

Rob's death does not effect a severance of his interest in the house, but survivorship operates and his share passes to the two remaining joint tenants, Pat and Saul. The legal estate is now vested in Mike and Pat as trustees for sale on trust for Saul and Pat as joint tenants of their original shares and the share of Rob which has passed to them by survivorship, and Pat as tenant-in-common in respect of the share he purchased from Mike, viz:

Mike	Pat		Legal Title (Joint Tenants)
Pat	Pat	Saul	Equity
(TIC)	JT	JT	
$\left(\frac{2}{8}\right)$	$\frac{3}{8}$	$\frac{3}{8}$	

By definition, trustees of a trust for sale must sell. That notwithstanding, s25 LPA 1925 gives trustees a power to postpone sale provided that they act unanimously - in the absence of unanimity the duty to sell prevails: *Re Mayo* (1943). Hence, Mike and Pat can agree to postpone sale. It would not avail Saul to rely on s26(3) LPA 1925 as that section only requires the trustees to consult the beneficiaries, and where practicable, give effect to the wishes of the majority. On the facts Pat has the majority interest $\left(\frac{5}{8}\right)$, and anyway the trustees only have to consult not obey.

Saul could make an application to the court under s30 LPA 1925 for an order for sale, as he is clearly an interested party for the purposes of that section. In deciding whether or not to order sale the court will consider whether there was a secondary or collateral purpose to the trust, and whether that purpose still exists. If it does, sale will not be ordered: see *Jones* v *Challenger* (1961); *Re Buchanan Wollaston's Conveyance* (1939). It could be argued that the secondary or collateral purpose lay in the fact that the purchase of the house was connected to the four's membership of the pop group and as the group has since disbanded, the secondary purpose has ceased to exist and sale should be ordered.

If sale is ordered pursuant to s30 LPA 1925 Saul will receive $\frac{3}{8}$ and Pat $\frac{5}{8}$ of the proceeds.

5 LANDLORD AND TENANT

5.1   Introduction

5.2   Key points

5.3   Recent cases and statutes

5.4   Analysis of questions

5.5   Questions

5.1   Introduction

More than any other area of Land Law this is a topic where the exact knowledge of the syllabus and the style of previous papers will help the student. Some examiners load their Land Law paper with questions relating to landlord and tenant, others relegate to merely one question in the recognition of the width of a pure Land Law syllabus. In between the two extremes a typical nine question Land Law paper will probably carry two or three questions directly or indirectly related to landlord and tenant. These could include the following:

a) A three or four part question on general principles of landlord and tenant, including:

  i)   perpetually renewable leases: s145 and 15th Schedule LPA 1922

  ii) s1(1)(b) + s205(1) (xxvii) LPA 1925

  iii) s149(3) or s149(6) LPA 1925

b) Areas relating to security of tenure - assured tenancy - assured shorthold tenancy

  i)   Methods to secure re-possession - compare Rent Act 1977 (Schedule 15) and Housing Act 1988

  ii) Licence as a method of avoiding Rent Act (1987-1988 cases)

     Brooker Settled Estates v *Ayers* (1987) 1 EGLR 50; *Hadjiloucas* v *Crean* [1987] 3 All ER 1008

     Ashburn Anstalt v *Arnold* [1988] 2 All ER 147; *AG Securities* v *Vaughan*; *Antoniades* v *Villiers* [1988] 3 All ER 1058, House of Lords

     Mikeover Ltd v *Brady* [1989] 3 All ER 618

     Aslan v *Murphy (No 1)* [1990] 1 WLR 766

  iii) Other methods of avoidance

c) Covenants: remedies for breach, relief against forfeiture, running of covenant

    i) Covenant to pay rent

    ii) Covenant to repair and the repair/renewal debate

       Post Office v *Aquarius Properties Ltd* [1987] 1 All ER 1055; *Stent* v *Monmouth Borough Council* (1987) 282 EG 705: *Irvine* v *Moran* (1992) 24 HLR 1

    iii) Covenant not to assign or underlet

       s19(1) Landlord and Tenant Act 1927 and ss1, 2 Landlord and Tenant Act 1988

       International Drilling Fluids Ltd v *Louisville Investments (Uxbridge) Ltd* [1986] 2 WLR 581

    iv) Different rules as to relief against forfeiture - forfeiture clause

    v) Running of the benefit and burden of covenants

       City & Metropolitan Properties Ltd v *Greycroft Ltd* (1987) 283 EG 199

       Rhone v *Stephens* (1993) The Times 21 January

5.2 Key points

Meaning of 'term of years absolute': LPA 1925 s205(1)(xxvii). It is 'absolute' even though it may be determined by notice to quit, operation of law, re-entry or a provision for cesser on redemption. 'Year' includes a term for less than a year.

Note concurrent legal estates possible: LPA s1(5).

a) *Unusual leases*

    i) Lease 'in perpetuity' is void

    ii) Perpetually renewable leases allowed pre-1926, but converted by LPA 1922 s145 and 15th Schedule into 2000 year term. May be created inadvertently.

    iii) LPA s149(6) - abolished leases for lives by providing that a lease at a rent for life or lives for a term of years determinable on life or lives becomes a 90 year term, determinable after the event by one month's notice expiring on a quarter day.

    iv) Reversionary leases - s149(3) LPA 1925. Void if takes effect more than 21 years from the instrument creating it.

b) *Terminology*

Privity of contract - binds original parties by a direct contractual relationship. Privity of estate - binds whoever is presently in the position of landlord and tenant.

Lease/tenancy/term of years

Lessee is possessed of a term which he may assign

Lessor leases, or demises, the term and retains a reversion which he may convey (if fee simple) or assign (if a superior lease)

The lessee may sub-demise (underlease) to sub-lessee (underlessee).

Always distinguish the assignment of the whole interest from the sub-lease where a reversion remains.

c) *Nature of terms of years*

Lessor may confer upon lessee the right to exclusive possession of land for a period which must be either definite or capable of definition. Consider three essentials of a lease:

   i) Exclusive possession

   See the words of Lord Templeman in *Street* v *Mountford* [1985] 2 WLR 877: 'Where the only circumstances were that residential accommodation was offered and accepted with exclusive possession for a term at a rent - the result was a tenancy.'

   Necessary but not sufficient. Compare 'licence' - see chapter 6. The general control by owner negatives lease, eg, service occupant.

   But no need for rent - *Ashburn Anstalt* v *Arnold* [1988] 2 All ER 147 - Fox LJ.

   ii) Definite period - certainty of duration

   Beginning and end must be capable of being ascertained: LPA s149(3) provides:

   • leasehold term at rent to take effect 21 + years from the instrument creating it is void; and

   • a contract to create 'such a term' is also void.

   End of term must be capable of being fixed before the lease takes effect:

   Lace v *Chantler* [1944] 1 All ER 305. But premature termination is permitted, eg, a term for 21 years or death whichever is the sooner is valid.

   Prudential Assurance Co Ltd v *London Residuary Body* [1992] 3 WLR 279.

   iii) Form

   Deed: s52 and s54(2) LPA 1925 - term not exceeding 3 years - oral or written - in possession, at best rent. Section 54(2) is not affected by the Law of Property (Miscellaneous Provisions) Act 1989: see s2(5) of the 1989 Act.

d) *Methods of creation*

Compare 'lease' with an 'agreement for a lease' - the latter forms a contract by an intending landlord to grant a lease and by the tenant to take a lease once it has been granted by deed (if required).

ii) Formalities for legal lease

- Originally a mere contract - even oral would suffice.

- 1677-1845: Statute of Frauds 1677 required writing, signed by the party or agent authorised in writing, exception for certain leases not exceeding 3 years.

- 1845-1925: replaced writing by need for deed - retaining 3 year exception - Real Property Act 1845.

- Now LPA 1925 ss52 and 54 [ss52(2)(d) and 54(2)] - s2 of the Law of Property (Miscellaneous Provisions) Act 1989 does not apply to s54(2): s2(5)(a) of the 1989 Act.

  Lease void at law unless by deed. But no deed or writing required for lease taking effect in possession for not more than 3 years at best rent without a fine.

  Deed always required for assignment of a legal lease, even if created orally.

  The doctrine of frustration may apply to leases, but see *National Carriers Ltd* v *Panalpina (Northern) Ltd* [1981] AC 675.

iii) Formalities for agreement for a lease

- Final agreement in writing is required. Note that agreement 'subject to contract' is no contract.

  Chillingworth v *Esche* [1924] 1 Ch 97 - 'subject to a proper contract to be prepared by the vendor's solicitors'.

  Branca v *Cabarro* [1947] KB 854 - a 'provisional agreement until a fully legalised agreement drawn up by a solicitor and embodying all the conditions herewith stated is signed'.

  See also *Tiverton Estates Ltd* v *Wearwell Ltd* [1974] 1 All ER 209.

- LPA 1925 s40(1) is repealed and replaced by s2(1) Law of Property (Miscellaneous Provisions) Act 1989 from the 27 September 1989. Section 2(1) provides: 'A contract for the sale or other disposition of an interest in land can only be made in writing and only by incorporating all the terms which the parties have expressly agreed in one document or, where contracts are exchanged, in each.' By s2(3) the contract must be signed by or on behalf of each party to the contract.

- LPA 1925 s40(2) is also repealed by s2(8) of the 1989 Act. The effect of this repeal is that the rules of part performance for alleged contracts relating to land may not survive s2(1) of the 1989 Act in respect of contracts made after the 27 September 1989. Consideration should now be given to the application of the rules of estoppel to replace the doctrine of part performance in this area of Land Law.

iv) Effect of informal leases

Equity treated an imperfect lease as a contract then ordered specific performance of it. After the Judicature Act 1873 equitable rules prevail: *Walsh* v *Lonsdale* (1882) 21 Ch D 9. An enforceable agreement for a lease is almost as good as a lease, BUT;

- dependent upon specific performance - a discretionary remedy
- void against third parties unless registered as an estate contract - land charge Class C(iv), s4(6) LCA 1972
- not a 'conveyance' within LPA 1925 s62 and thus does not pass easements and rights
- burden of covenant does not run.

LAW - LEGAL ESTATE	EQUITY - EQUITABLE INTEREST
Grants A lease	Agrees to grant a lease

Deed - s52(1) LPA 1925 or oral/writingfor term not exceeding three years. S54(2) LPA 1925 [in possession: at best rent]
 	
Requirements of a valid lease:
1) Correct form [ss52/54 LPA 1925]
2) Certainty of duration
   Lace v *Chantler* [1944] 1 All ER 305
3) Exclusive possession
   Street v *Mountford* [1985] 2 WLR 877
[Answer by landlord must reserve a rightof re-entry by way of a forfeiture clause]
 	
'Term of years absolute'. A legalestate within s1(1)(b) LPA 1925
	Agreement - must now satisfy s2(1) of the Law of Property (Miscellaneous Provisions) Act 1989 - contract for disposition of an interest in land can only be made in writing and (by s2(3)) must be signed by each party to the contract. Rules of part performance may no longer apply BUT estoppel may become the alternative answer.

Consequence of *Walsh* v *Lonsdale* (1882) 21 Ch D 9 - if a conflict between a specifically enforceable agreement for a lease (equity) and a legal periodic tenancy arising from a payment of rent (law) - equity will prevail. But an agreement for a lease is not as good as a lease - because:
1) Discretionary remedies
2) s62 LPA 1925 only applies to a 'conveyance'
3) 3rd party rights
   a) unregistered land charge Class C(iv) - ss2(4), 4(6) LCA 1972
   b) registered: minor interest - notice - s48 LRA 1925 or
      overriding interest: s70(1)(g) LRA 1925 but not s70(1)(k) LRA 1925
      City Permanent Building Society v *Miller* [1952] Ch 840
4) No privity of estate between landlord and assignee of equitable lease
5) 'Usual covenants' only implied in an agreement for a lease.

v) Summary

- Lease UNDER SEAL for any period creates legal estate: LPA s52

- Oral or written lease for 3 years or less may create a legal estate: LPA s54

- Lease or agreement MADE IN WRITING for period exceeding 3 years may confer equitable term: LP(MP)A 1989 s2.

e) *Tenancies*

Distinguish between specific tenancies and periodic tenancies.

i) Specific tenancy: a term of certain duration limited to expire at end of term for which granted.

ii) Periodic tenancy: granted for definite period, but which continues thereafter until determined. Note: length of notice to quit required: s5 Protection from Eviction Act 1977. Residential property not less than 4 weeks' notice. Any notice to quit must be given to expire at end of period for which it has been granted.

Note also:

iii) Tenancy at will: equitable interest for no certain duration to continue during the joint will of both parties. Converted to a tenancy from year to year by payment and acceptance of a yearly rent. Occurs where negotiations for a lease are proceeding - must be consent of landlord.

iv) Tenancy at sufferance: tenant remaining in possession after lease expires but without the consent of the landlord.

v) Statutory tenancies - see paragraph j.

vi) Licences - see chapter 6.

f) *Form and assignment of lease*

i) A lease by deed must be written or printed and be signed, sealed and delivered.

ii) Legal lease, however created, transferable inter vivos only by deed: LPA s52. An informal assignment may be effective under *Walsh* v *Lonsdale* (1882) 21 ChD 9 principle.

Note: distinguish assignment from sub-lease.

iii) LPA 1925 s62 'general words' clause. A lease of land or land + house passes to the lessee - in the absence of stipulation to the contrary - all fixtures, easements and other things: *Wright* v *Macadam* [1949] 2 KB 744 - renewed lease - existing use of coal shed passed on renewal.

g) *Determination of a lease may be effected as follows:*

   i)   Expiry by effluxion of time - specific tenancy ceases when term for which granted comes to an end.

   ii)   Exercise of express power by break clause in lease of commercial premises - often found in association with a rent review clause.

   iii)   Forfeiture - every lease should contain a forfeiture clause which allows the landlord to renter on breach of covenant.

     Relief against forfeiture:

     The rules for relief vary - distinguish the rules relating to:

- non-payment of rent - from
- breach of other covenants: s146 LPA 1925 - repair - Leasehold Property (Repairs) Act 1938

   iv)   Notice to quit - see s5 Protection from Eviction Act 1977

   v)   Surrender - to the landlord - the tenant voluntarily yields up the term to the landlord

   vi)   Merger - to the tenant or a third party. The tenant retains the lease and acquires the reversion or both vest in a third party.

   vii)   Satisfied term, eg, a portions term under the SLA 1925.

   viii)   Enlargement - s153 LPA 1925 - lease for over 300 years, no rent and still over 200 years to run.

   ix)   Disclaimer - s315 Insolvency Act 1986.

   x)   Enfranchisement: Leasehold Reform Act 1967 - must be a house, rateable value limited but a long lease, at a low rent of less than two-thirds rateable value. Tenant in occupation for last 3 years (or 3 of last 10 years). Tenant may acquire reversion or extend term for 50 years. *Tandon* v *Trustees of Spurgeon's Homes* [1982] AC 755.

h) *Rights and duties of landlord and tenant*

   i)   Implied obligations of landlord

- Covenant for quiet enjoyment
- Fitness for habitation: Landlord and Tenant Act 1985 s8 - *Quick* v *Taff-Ely Borough Council* [1985] 3 All ER 321
- No derogation from grant - landlord must do nothing to make the property substantially less fit for the purpose for which let.

   ii)   Implied obligations and rights of tenant

- Obligation to repair and also not to commit waste

- Obligation to pay rent derived from words such as 'yielding and paying'
- Obligation to pay rates and taxes - because the tenant is in occupation
- Right to remove fixtures: trade - remove during term; ornamental or domestic - may remove without injury to the property; agricultural - up to two months after term ends.

iii) 'Usual covenants' - agreement for a lease only. *Chester* v *Buckingham Travel Ltd* [1981] 1 All ER 386

iv) Express obligations of tenant

- Covenant to pay rent
- Covenant to repair
    - Extent of obligation. As to the distinction between repair or renewal, the following points should be noted:

        Repair is to replace subsidiary parts of premises no longer repairable, not rebuild entire premises. *Post Office* v *Aquarius Properties Ltd* [1987] 1 All ER 1055.

        Repair and inherent defects. The basic decisions are:

        Ravenseft Properties Ltd v *Davstone (Holdings) Ltd* [1979] 1 All ER 929

        Insertion of expansion joints into cladding of a building - did not change character of building - within repair covenant - tenant liable to repair.

        Elmcroft Developments Ltd v *Tankersley Sawyer* (1984) 270 EG 140

        Landlords required to insert damp-proof course within repairing covenant - not a new or wholly different building than when demised - landlord liable to repair.

        Quick v *Taff-Ely Borough Council* [1985] 3 All ER 321

        Only damage was outside covenant to repair - condensation due to faulty design and building not in need of structural repair - landlord not liable.

        Post Office v *Aquarius Properties Ltd* [1987] 1 All ER 1055

        Defect in structure of basement - not worse but allowed water into basement - not within repair covenant to remedy original construction defect - tenant not liable.

        Stent v *Monmouth Borough Council* (1987) 282 EG 705

        Defective door - let in water - damage to carpets - landlord must remedy defective door - damage established breach of reparing obligation - landlord liable to repair.

        See also: *Irvine* v *Moran* (1992) 24 HLR 1

79

Principles derived from above cases:

If an inherent defect remedial work not within repair covenant unless defect has caused some damage to the buildings: *Quick* v *Taff-Ely Borough Council.*

If inherent defect causes deterioration to the building it does not justify work beyond terms of the repairing covenant: *Elmcroft Developments Ltd* v *Tankersley Sawyer.*

If that remedial work is necessary within the terms of the covenant to repair then this may extend to the remedy of the There is no disrepair within the covenant to repair if there is no proof of physical deterioration to the building: *Quick* v *Taff-Ely Borough Council* and *Post Office* v *Aquarius Properties Ltd.*

Note meaning of 'fair wear and tear excepted'.

Regis Property Co Ltd v *Dudley* [1959] AC 370 relieves tenant from liability for any disrepair which he can show has resulted from the reasonable use of the premises - but there is liability for consequential damage.

- Normal standard of repair:

Such repair as having regard to the age, character and locality of the premises would make them reasonably fit for occupation of a reasonably minded tenant of the class that would be likely to take them: *Proudfoot* v *Hart* (1890) 25 QBD 42.

- Covenant construed as at start of lease:

Anstruther-Gough-Calthorpe v *McOscar* [1924] 1 KB 716

- Varying obligations - depends on the above standard of repair at the beginning of the lease.

to 'put' into repair. Imposes obligation to reinstate.

to 'keep' in repair. As in (a) + keep at all times and implied that premises be left in repair: NB - 'to repair' means to keep in repair.

to 'leave' in repair. Must be in repair at end of lease.

- Absolute liability

Repairing covenant imposes an absolute liability

- Remedies for non-repair

At common law - action for damages

NOTE: Measure of damages and Landlord and Tenant Act 1927 s18(1) - the amount by which the value of the reversion is reduced by the breach. Action usually at the end of the lease. *Jones* v *Herxheimer* [1950] 2 KB 106

If power in lease then lessor may enter and do the repair and charge the lessee.

Probably right of re-entry and forfeiture for breach of covenant reserved in lease, but note:

By statute

LPA 1925 s146(1):

Notice to be served on lessee: specifying the particular breach complained of, requiring remedy if possible and requiring money compensation: *Scala House & District Property Co Ltd* v *Forbes* [1973] 3 All ER 308

If breach of covenant against assignment/underletting this is incapable of remedy - any notice need not require the breach to be remedied in such a case.

See also:

Rugby School (Governors) v *Tannahill* [1935] 1 KB 87

Glass v *Kencakes Ltd* [1966] 1 QB 611

Expert Clothing Service & Sales Ltd v *Hillgate House Ltd* [1985] 3 WLR 359

British Petroleum Pension Trust Ltd v *Behrendt* (1985) 276 EG 199

Billson v *Residential Apartments Ltd* [1992] 1 AC 494

Reasonable time allowed for compliance and lessee must be told of right to serve a counter-notice (below).

Landlord and Tenant Act 1927 s18(2):

Right of forfeiture not enforceable unless lessor proves above notice known to lessee or occupier and sufficient time elapsed to enable repairs to be carried out.

Leasehold Property (Repairs) Act 1938:

If lease for 7 years or more and at least 3 years to run, lessee may serve a counter-notice and then lessor cannot proceed further without permission of court. Note s1(5) as to the grounds for giving permission:

Immediate remedy to prevent substantial diminution in the value of the reversion.

To give effect to some bye-law.

In the interests of the occupier.

Small expense now compared with greater expense later.

It is just and equitable to give such permission.

SEDAC Investments Ltd v *Tanner* [1982] 1 WLR 1342

Hamilton v *Martell Securities Ltd* [1984] 1 All ER 665

LPA 1925 s147:

May relieve from liability for internal decorative repair.

LPA 1925 s146(4) - relief for sub-tenants.

- Covenants to insure against fire: Fires Prevention (Metropolis) Act 1774 - use of insurance money to restore the premises.

- Covenants against assignment, underletting or parting with possession. Distinguish:

  - Absolute prohibition

  - Qualified prohibition: s19(1) Landlord and Tenant Act 1927 - such consent is not to be unreasonably withheld. *International Drilling Fluids Ltd* v *Louisville Investments (Uxbridge) Ltd* [1986] 2 WLR 581 Balcombe LJ Landlord and Tenant Act 1988 ss1 and 2 now places the burden of proof on the landlord. The onus is on the landlord to reply to any request within a reasonable time and provide adequate reasons for any refusal. The interpretation of 'unreasonably withheld' for the purposes of s19(1) of the 1927 Act is unaltered.

i) *Enforcement of covenants*

Distinguish the rules relating to rent from other covenants.

  i) Covenants to pay rent

  - By proceeding for re-entry through forfeiture:

    High Court - see ss210-212 Common Law Procedure Act 1852.

    County court - *Di Palma* v *Victoria Square Property Co Ltd* [1985] 3 WLR 207

    s138 County Courts Act 1984 and s55 Administration of Justice Act 1985

  - Action on the covenant for arrears

  - Distress:

    - Essentials

    - What may be distrained

    - How distress levied

    - When distress may be levied

- How much rent can be recovered

- Tenants' remedies for wrongful distress

NOTE: Waiver of breach: *Central Estates (Belgravia) Ltd* v *Woolgar (No 2)* [1972] 1 WLR 1048 where the landlord shows the tenancy to be continuing, eg, demands and accepts rent either himself or through an agent.

   ii)   Enforcement for other covenants

- Action for damages

- Injunction

- Forfeiture under s146 LPA 1925

Relief of sub-tenants under s146(4) LPA 1925

Abbey National Building Society v *Maybeech Ltd* [1984] 3 All ER 262 and *Smith* v *Metropolitan City Properties Ltd* (1986) 277 EG 753 - these two cases give conflicting views on whether there is an inherent equitable jurisdiction to grant relief.

   iii)   Problem of enforcing covenants. Can A sue B for breach of covenant, assuming that the lease contains a right of re-entry for breach of the covenant? See diagram overleaf.

j) *Security of tenure*

   i)   Agricultural tenancies

Agricultural Holdings Act 1986

   ii)   Business tenancies

Part II Landlord and Tenant Act 1954

   iii)   Residential tenancies: has been described as a 'status of irremovability'

Rent Act 1977 - *Hampstead Way Investments Ltd* v *Lewis-Weare* [1985] 1 WLR 164

Housing Act 1980

Rent (Amendment) Act 1985

Landlord and Tenant Act 1985

Housing Act 1985

Housing Act 1988 (from 15 January 1989)

The effect of the 1988 Act may be reviewed as follows:

- Existing lettings continue to have Rent Act protection. Only new lettings are subject to these provisions.

- Reduction of transmissions to one is the only significant alteration to existing lettings (s39).

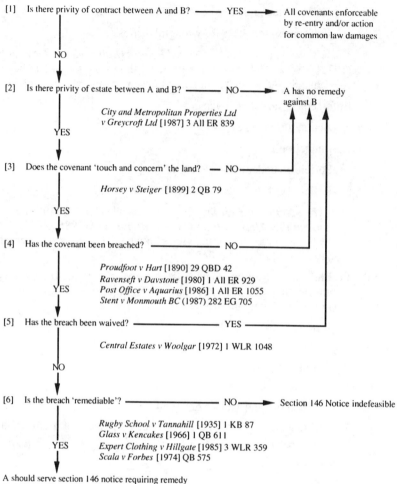

[1] Is there privity of contract between A and B? —— YES —→ All covenants enforceable by re-entry and/or action for common law damages

NO

[2] Is there privity of estate between A and B? —— NO —→ A has no remedy against B

City and Metropolitan Properties Ltd v Greycroft Ltd [1987] 3 All ER 839

YES

[3] Does the covenant 'touch and concern' the land? — NO

Horsey v Steiger [1899] 2 QB 79

YES

[4] Has the covenant been breached? —— NO

Proudfoot v Hart [1890] 29 QBD 42
Ravenseft v Davstone [1980] 1 All ER 929
Post Office v Aquarius [1986] 1 All ER 1055
Stent v Monmouth BC (1987) 282 EG 705

YES

[5] Has the breach been waived? —— YES

Central Estates v Woolgar [1972] 1 WLR 1048

NO

[6] Is the breach 'remediable'? —— NO —→ Section 146 Notice indefeasible

Rugby School v Tannahill [1935] 1 KB 87
Glass v Kencakes [1966] 1 QB 611
Expert Clothing v Hillgate [1985] 3 WLR 359
Scala v Forbes [1974] QB 575

YES

A should serve section 146 notice requiring remedy
(unless breach consists of failure to pay rent)

- New protected tenancies become assured tenancies (the Housing Act 1980 tenancies become 'new' assured tenancies: s1(3) HA 1988). No assured tenancies under the Housing Act 1980 will be created after 15 January 1989.

- Schedule 2 HA 1988 contains (Grounds 1-8) mandatory grounds for possession, such as:

    Ground 6 - wish to develop the site, or

    Ground 8 - three months' rent in arrears

and (Grounds 9-16) discretionary grounds for possession. In the latter case the court must be satisfied that it is reasonable to make an order.

- From 15 January 1989 any new letting becomes an assured tenancy with similar security of tenure but no control on amount of rent. (No 'fair' rent.)

- Landlord can increase rent by giving notice (minimum one month). This notice can be referred to Rent Assessment Committee to fix open market rent for premises. Note: no control on original rent charged.

- End of protected shortholds, but existing ones continue (s34).

- New: assured shorthold tenancies (AST) (s20) - short, fixed term lettings with landlord guaranteed possession at end of term - minimum six months (formerly twelve). Notice procedure simplified (compare s21 1988 Act and case 19 Schedule 15 Rent Act 1977). Must serve notice on tenant, before tenancy commences, that it is an assured shorthold tenancy.

- Some rent control on the AST because the tenant may refer this rent to the Rent Assessment Committee at any time on the ground of excessive rent, and the committee can fix a lower rent on comparison with similar houses let on assured tenancies (s22(3)). A peson cannot contract out of these shorthold provisions (s22(4)(b)).

iv) The effect of security of tenure on the various types of tenancy may be summarised as follows:

- Agricultural tenancies: Agricultural Holdings Act 1986

  Statutory notice to quit at least 12 months. If tenant issues a counter-notice then agricultural lands tribunal must consent to possession.

- Business tenancies: Part II Landlord and Tenant Act 1954

  Lease continues automatically. Landlord's notice between 12 and 6 months from end of tenancy. Parties may negotiate new tenancy.

  Note: Landlord's grounds for opposing a new tenancy: s30(1).

- Long residential tenancies [+ 21 years at low rent]

  - Part I Landlord and Tenant Act 1954 - tenant continues in occupation

  - Leasehold Reform Act 1967 - enfranchisement

- Other residential tenancies - Rent Act 1977 - Protection from Eviction Act 1977 and Housing Act 1980 - Housing Act 1988 (from 15.1.89) - new contracts create assured tenancies.

  Protected tenancy into statutory tenancy.

Note:

- Grounds for possession: s98 and Schedule 15 1977 Act
- Restricted contract lettings: s19(1) 1977 Act
- Shorthold lettings (ss52-55 Housing Act 1980) now
- Assured shorthold tenancies (AST): s20 Housing Act 1988

• Lease/licence debate - *Street* v *Mountford* [1985] 2 WLR 877

- Application to commercial property
- Meaning of exclusive possession in this context.
- The non-exclusive agreement. Joint tenants? No! See House of Lords in *AG Securities* v *Vaughan*; *Antoniades* v *Villiers* [1988] 3 WLR 1205
- Continuing exceptions. No intention to create legal relations. Rent Act 1977 itself:

  Holiday lettings: s9

  Student lettings: s8

  Substantial board and attendance: s7

  Mixed business and residential: s24(3)

5.3   Recent cases and statutes

AG Securities v *Vaughan* and *Antoniadies* v *Villiers* [1988] 3 All ER 1058

Street v *Mountford* [1985] 2 WLR 877

Royal Philanthropic Society v *County* (1985) 276 EG 1068

London and Associated Investment Trust plc v *Calow* (1986) 280 EG 1252

Brooker Settled Estates Ltd v *Ayers* (1987) 1 EGLR 50

Bass Holdings Ltd v *Lewis* (1986) 280 EG 771

James v *UK* (1986) 8 EHRR 123

Ponderosa International v *Pengap Securities (Bristol) Ltd* (1986) 277 EG 1252

Manorlike Ltd v *Le Vitas Travel Agency* [1986] 1 All ER 573

Field v *Barkworth* [1986] 1 All ER 362

Smith v *Metropolitan City Properties Ltd* (1986) 277 EG 753

Post Office v *Aquarius Properties Ltd* [1987] 1 All ER 1055

City and Metropolitan Properties Ltd v *Greycroft Ltd* (1987) 283 EG 199

Celsteel Ltd v *Alton House Holdings Ltd (No 2)* [1987] 1 WLR 291

Stent v *Monmouth BC* (1987) 282 EG 705

Mikeover Ltd v *Brady* [1989] 3 All ER 618

Aslan v *Murphy* [1989] 3 All ER 130

Landlord and Tenant Act 1988

Housing Act 1988

5.4 Analysis of questions

The questions are wide ranging and cover general principles, the creation of the lease and the agreement for a lease, the covenants which are commonly found in leases and the rules relating to security of tenure.

5.5 Questions

Question 1

What formalities are required, in unregistered and registered conveyancing, for the creation of a lease, and what is the effect, at common law, and in equity, of the absence of such formalities?

University of London LLB Examination
(for External Students) Land Law June 1983 Q2

General comment

This question appeared in a Land Law paper where three of the nine questions were devoted to landlord and tenant matters. This is a warning to question spotters who should never be tempted to 'drop' landlord and tenant from their revision programme. On the other hand this is an interesting question and the introduction of registered land adds an extra dimension which should be well within the ability of the candidate who has correctly 'programmed' his revision. The candidate must keep in mind all the facets of this question and not be deterred by the word 'conveyancing'.

Skeleton solution

UNREGISTERED LAND

a) *Lease*

  i) Must be by deed: s52(1) LPA 1925

  ii) If not exceeding 3 years may be oral/writing: s54(2) LPA 1925

b) *Absence of formalities*

  i) Equity

   • Agreement for a lease formerly had to satisfy s40 LPA 1925 but must now be made in writing and signed by both parties within s2 Law of Property (Miscellaneous Provisions) Act 1989.

   • Formerly there may have been an act of part performance: *Steadman* v *Steadman* [1974]. See now the effect of the repeal of s40(2) LPA 1925 by s2 LP(MP)A 1989. Part performance no longer applies in Land Law but the rules of estoppel may apply.

- Conflict: consider effect of *Walsh v Lonsdale* (1882) - equity prevails. 'He holds under the same terms in equity as if a lease had been granted': Jessel MR.

- Any such agreement for a lease must be protected as a land charge Class C(iv) - estate contract: void against a purchaser if not so registered: s4(6) LCA 1972.

ii) Common law

If possession and payment of rent - will create a legal periodic tenancy.

REGISTERED LAND

a) *Lease*

i) To create a valid legal lease - must use a deed within s52(1) LPA 1925

ii) If term for more than 21 years then lease must be registered within two months of completion: s123 LRA 1925, as amended by s2 LRA 1986.

iii) Any legal lease granted for a term of 21 years or less is an overriding interest within s70(1)(k) LRA 1925 as amended by s4 LRA 1986. [No longer need for rent.]

b) *Absence of formalities*

i) Equity

- Any agreement for a lease probably still does not come within s70(1)(k) LRA (*City Permanent Building Society v Miller* (1952)) but may be a 'right' within s70(1)(g) LRA 1925 which will become an overriding interest when protected by 'actual occupation' and no enquiries made of tenant in person.

- Such an agreement is a minor interest - protected by entry of a notice on the register: s52(1) LRA 1925.

ii) Common law

Any other legal lease - periodic and not granted - will probably come within s70(1)(g) LRA 1925 as a 'right' protected by possession ('actual occupation').

Suggested solution

The system of registration of title does not, in itself, create any new land law. It is merely a system for the transfer of title which uses the existing divisions of legal estate and legal and equitable interests identified in s1 of the Law of Property Act 1925. On the other hand because of some rather curious drafting of the Land Registration Act 1925 it is necessary to give particular attention to leases of three varying lengths: those up to 21 years, those between 21 and 40 years and those over 40 years.

The formalities for a lease are, today, covered by ss52 and 54 of the Law of Property Act 1925. The fundamental provision is contained in s52(1) which provides:

'(1) All conveyances of land or of any interest therein are void for the purpose of conveying or creating a legal estate unless made by deed.'

This means that all leases must be a deed accompanied by the requirement of being 'signed, sealed and delivered'. Section 52 goes on to identify an exception:

'(2) This section does not apply to:

(d) leases or tenancies or other assurances not required by law to be made in writing:'

The answer as to which are such 'leases or tenancies' is given in s54(2) Law of Property Act 1925 (to which s2 Law of Property (Miscellaneous Provisions) Act 1989 does not apply: s2(5)(a)):

'(2) Nothing in the foregoing provisions of this Part of this Act shall affect the creation by parol of leases taking effect in possession for a term not exceeding three years (whether or not the lessee is given power to extend the term) at the best rent which can be reasonably obtained without taking a fine.'

The position is well summarised by Cheshire:

'Moreover the above represents the legal position at the present day if we confine our attention to the common law. A conveyance of land, and this includes a lease, is void under the Law of Property Act 1925, for the purpose of creating a legal estate unless made by deed (except of course in the case of a lease not exceeding three years), but nevertheless, if the tenant enters into possession and pays a yearly rent, he will become a yearly tenant. Again, by the same Act a term exceeding three years which is not put in writing is to have the force and effect of an interest at will only, but, given the same two facts of possession and payment of rent, it also will be converted into a legal yearly tenancy.'

This quotation recognises, clearly, the major common law exception to the statutory rules that where a tenant enters into possession and pays a rent a tenancy is recognised for a period relative to that rental period.

In addition equity looked at the circumstances where the statutory rules were not fulfilled and supplied an alternative solution. Equity considered that the lease must be examined with care - if it were not possible to construe a valid statutory lease then, provided the evidence was satisfied, it might be construed as a contract for a lease. The statutory evidence must be in writing, see s2 of the 1989 Act, above. If the evidence is satisfactory then specific performance was available as an equitable remedy. This divergence of the rules of common law and equity was fully considered in *Walsh* v *Lonsdale* (1882) ; and the oft-quoted words of Sir George Jessel MR should be considered as a conclusion to this aspect of the answer:

'There is an agreement for a lease under which possession has been given. Now since the Judicature Act the possession is held under the agreement. There are not two estates as there were formerly - one estate at common law by reason of the payment of the rent from year to year, and an estate in equity under the agreement. There is only one court, and the equity rules prevail in it. The tenant holds under an agreement for a lease. He holds, therefore, under the same terms in equity as if a lease had been granted... he is protected in the same way as if a lease had been granted ...'

This rule in *Walsh* v *Lonsdale* now covers all leases which do not come within ss52 and 54 of the Law of Property Act 1925, and if the tenant can satisfy these equitable rules he can call for specific performance of his rights.

In the case of registered land the lease must still satisfy ss52 and 54 of the Law of Property Act 1925, or if these are not fulfilled, the rules of equity may be called into play. Thus a written agreement for a lease for seven years will be recognised under *Walsh* v *Lonsdale*: then the problem arises as to where it fits in the registration system introduced by the Land Registration Act 1925. This system must be briefly summarised by reference to the terms of the lease.

Leases granted for a term not exceeding 21 years cannot be registered but may be protected as overriding interests under s70(1)(k) Land Registration Act 1925 as amended by s4 LRA 1986. If the lease is not granted but is an equitable lease and the tenant has gone into actual occupation, there will be a possible overriding interest within s70(1)(g) LRA 1925. A new lease for a period exceeding 21 years granted out of land which is already registered may be registered under a separate title with the appropriate type of leasehold title.

If the new lease is for a period of more than 21 years it must be registered under a separate title where the land is in a compulsory area of registration of title: s123 LRA 1925 as amended by s2 LRA 1986.

Thus a written agreement for a lease for, say, seven years may be an overriding interest under s70(1)(g) LRA 1925 where the tenant has gone into occupation and, probably, regardless of whether rent is paid or not. The agreement for the lease could be the 'right' protected under s70(1)(g). It is, however, clear that such an agreement for a lease is not within s70(1)(k) LRA 1925 because it is not granted as a legal lease: *City Permanent Building Society* v *Miller* (1952). This remains the law in spite of s3(x) LRA 1925 which says '"lease" includes an under-lease and any tenancy or agreement for a lease, under-lease or tenancy.'

What is clear is that a formal lease granted for seven years will come within s70(1)(k) LRA 1925, where the title to the land is registered.

Apart from these complications arising from s70(1)(k) LRA 1925 it is broadly true to say that the question of formalities in the creation of leases has the same effect whether the title to the land is registered or unregistered.

Tutorial comments

a) Consider ss52-54 LPA 1925.

b) If no formalities, requirement of an agreement for a lease had to satisfy s40 LPA 1925 but see now s2 of the Law of Property (Miscellaneous Provisions) Act 1989. In particular consider the effect on part performance of the provisions of the 1989 Act.

c) Registered land - registered interest (s123 LRA 1925) or overriding interest (s70(1)(k) LRA 1925).

d) The amendment by the LRA 1986.

e) The continuing effect of *City Permanent Building Society* v *Miller* [1952] Ch 840.

Question 2

a) Professor Jones owns a house in Cardiff and is the tenant of a flat in London. He occupies the flat three days a week while he teaches in London. The flat is in a quiet area near to where he works. He has just received a letter from his landlord saying that the landlord requires the flat and offering him a smaller flat on a main road at a lower rent but which is further away from Professor Jones' work.

Advise the Professor.

b) William, who lives in London, has just bought a bungalow at a seaside resort. He wishes to have the bungalow as an investment, but may decide to live there when he retires. He is presently 61 and now works for his firm only on weekday mornings. It is too late to let the bungalow for the summer but he tells you that he plans to let it for seven months from October to April and then to let it on short lets for seaside holidays. He asks you whether there is likely to be any difficulty in getting possession of the bungalow next April or at any time in the future if he decides to live there eventually.

What steps should he take to protect his position?

University of London LLB Examination
(for External Students) Land Law June 1987 Q4

General comment

This question is welcomed to give specific emphasis to the terms of any syllabus which clearly includes 'security of tenure under Rent Acts'. Probably only a limited number of candidates attempted the question, but it should have been popular and provides an interesting application of the practical problems associated with modern Land Law. Some candidates may feel that both parts of the question require something more than the land law form of 'outline' of the Rent Acts to do full justice to the points raised. The writer is of the opinion that this is a perfectly fair question and should have been within the knowledge of the candidates. The question was set before January 1989, but today reference should be made to the effect of the Housing Act 1988 on new tenancies entered into after 15 January 1989.

Skeleton solution

a)   i)   Protected tenancy under s1 Rent Act 1977

      Effect of two homes

        Langford Property Co Ltd v *Tureman* (1949)

        Hampstead Way Investments v *Lewis-Weare* (1985)

      Effect - the Professor has a protected tenancy.

Possession: s98 Rent Act 1977.

Schedule 15 Part (iv) - suitable alternative accommodation.

Three points -

- new flat smaller;

- on a main road;

- further away from the work.

Cases - mainly use:

Hill v *Rochard* (1983)

Redspring Ltd v *Francis* (1973)

Proposed flat is not suitable. Professor remain where he is as a protected tenant. DO NOT LEAVE VOLUNTARILY.

ii)   After January 1989 under the Housing Act 1988 - discretionary Case 9

b)   i)   Holiday letting exempt from Rent Act: s9 RA 1977

Meaning of 'holiday' - *Buchmann* v *May* (1978)

Proposal to let from October-April - off season letting.

Schedule 15 Case 13 RA 1977.

But only applies if previously let for 'holiday' purposes.

Advise William to take a summer holiday in the bungalow; or use the retirement home provisions of Schedule 15, Case 12, RA 1977.

Must serve notice on tenant beforehand and genuinely retire from regular employment.

ii)   After January 1989 under the Housing Act 1988 - mandatory Case 3.

Suggested solution

a)   i)   Under the Rent Act 1977

Section 1 of the Rent Act 1977 provides that '... a tenancy under which a dwelling-house (which may be a house or part of a house) is let as a separate dwelling is a protected tenancy for the purposes of this Act.' In advising the Professor we must first establish whether he is a protected tenant within the Rent Act 1977.

The flat must be within the meaning of s1 as a dwelling-house. As part of a house may be a dwelling there is little doubt that the premises do come within s1. On the basis that the flat is let as a single dwelling, does the Professor qualify as a protected tenant because he also owns a house in Cardiff?

In *Langford Property Co Ltd* v *Tureman* (1949), the defendant owned a cottage in the country and took a tenancy of a flat in London in order to have somewhere to stay during business visits. He slept in the flat, on average, two nights a week, but rarely had a meal there. The Court of Appeal held the defendant to be a protected tenant. He was in personal occupation of the flat and there was nothing in the Rent Act to prevent a person having more than one home. This is especially true where his profession required it. The dividing line is very narrow as was seen in the decision of the House of Lords in *Hampstead Way Investments* v *Lewis-Weare* (1985). A tenant of a flat married and went to live with his wife and stepchild in a nearby house. He retained his flat and slept there five nights a week so as not to disturb his family; his adult step-son also lived there. The tenant paid all the outgoings but never ate at the flat. The House of Lords confirmed that it was possible for a person to occupy two dwellings as his residence: it was a question of fact and degree. Here the tenant made only limited use of the flat, and then only for part of his daily living because he did not eat there. On the facts the tenant was not protected.

In our problem the Professor occupies the flat for three days and on the basis that he sleeps there for three nights and has his meals in the flat he appears to have a tenancy protected by the Rent Act 1977. In the *Hampstead Way Investments Ltd* v *Lewis-Weare* case Lord Brandon gave this very important warning when seeking to apply decisions on the Rent Act 1977 to a given set of circumstances:

'It is, in my view, essential to bear in mind that all these Rent Act cases turn on their particular facts, and it is seldom helpful to decide one case with one set of facts by reference to another case with a different set of facts.'

In spite of these cautionary and helpful words we must advise Professor Jones that he has a protected tenancy. We must now consider the effect this has on his own particular circumstances.

The first point to make is that the Professor has a protected tenancy so long as he remains in occupation of the flat. He should not leave the flat of his own accord. It is up to the landlord to discover and prove the appropriate grounds for obtaining possession. This is the effect of s98(1) Rent Act 1977 which provides:

'(1)... a court shall not make an order for possession of a dwelling-house which is for the time being let on a protected tenancy or subject to a statutory tenancy unless the court considers it reasonable to make such an order and either -

a) the court is satisfied that suitable alternative accommodation is available for the tenant or will be available for him when the order in question takes effect, or

b) the circumstances are as specified in any of the Cases in Part 1 of Schedule 15 to this Act.'

Schedule 15 sets out the discretionary and mandatory grounds for possession of dwelling houses which are subject to protected tenancies. These do not concern Professor Jones but Part IV of Schedule 15 does relate to suitable alternative accommodation. Paragraph 5 considers the nature of this alternative accommodation and states that it must be 'reasonably suitable to the needs of the tenant and his family as regards proximity to place of work, and either -

a) similar as regards rental and extent to the accommodation afforded by dwelling-houses provided in the neighbourhood by any local housing authority for persons whose needs as regards extent are, in the opinion of the court, similar to those of the tenant and of his family, or

b) reasonably suitable to the means of the tenant and to the needs of the tenant and his family as regards extent and character ...'

The flat which is being offered by the landlord appears to have three major drawbacks:

- it is smaller;
- it is on a main road - whereas the existing flat is in a quiet area;
- it is further away from the Professor's work because the existing flat is said to be 'near where he works'.

If the Professor wishes to object to the proposed flat, as it is assumed he will, he must demonstrate the disadvantages. If the flat is smaller it may well not accommodate all his books or furniture and this was held to be unsuitable in *McDonnell* v *Daly* (1969) and *McIntyre* v *Hardcastle* (1948).

The proposed accommodation appears to offer an inferior environment to the Professor. The court will compare the present environment of the tenant and that offered in the alternative accommodation on an objective basis: *Hill* v *Rochard* (1983).

It has been held that accommodation was not suitable where it was situated in a busy road with a nearby hospital and fish and chip shop in place of the tenant's quiet residential flat: *Redspring Ltd* v *Francis* (1973).

The advice to the Professor must, therefore, be to refuse the landlord's offer of the smaller flat and remain where he is on the basis that he has a protected tenancy of his existing London flat. Under no circumstances must he voluntarily surrender his flat to the landlord.

ii) Under the Housing Act 1988

The offer of suitable alternative accommodation is now discretionary Case 9 of Schedule 2 for a court order for possession under the Housing Act 1988. This will be used if Professor Jones had been granted an assured tenancy. The existing law above on Schedule 15 would, at this stage, still apply as to the suitability of the alternative accommodation which has been offered.

b) i) Under the Rent Act 1977

William has recently bought a bungalow at a seaside resort but has never lived in the premises. He regards it as an investment but may retire to the bungalow in due course. In the meantime can he let the premises but be able to obtain possession again as and when he wishes?

Section 9 Rent Act 1977 provides:

'A tenancy is not a protected tenancy if the purpose of the tenancy is to confer on the tenant the right to occupy the dwelling-house for a holiday.'

The Act does not define 'holiday' but the courts are aware of the risk of abuse in this area. In *Buchmann* v *May* (1978), Sir John Pennycuick took the definition of 'holiday' from the Shorter Oxford English Dictionary as 'a period of cessation from work or a period of recreation'. He then went on to describe the attitude of the court in this context. 'The court would be astute to detect a sham when it appeared in the context of the Rent Acts, but the burden is on the tenant to prove it, not on the landlord to show that the agreement was correct.' In this case a tenancy agreement for a term of three months stated: 'It is mutually agreed and declared that the letting hereby made is solely for the purpose of the tenant's holiday in the London area.' The Court of Appeal held that this was a holiday letting and so outside the Rent Acts. Where parties to an instrument express their purpose in entering into the transaction or the purposes for which the demised property is to be used then this expression is, at least, prima facie evidence of their true purpose and can only be displaced by evidence that the express purpose does not represent the true purpose. The burden of such proof, as indicated above, is on the tenant.

The advice to William is that s9 Rent Act 1977 will exempt a genuine holiday letting from the protection of the Rent Act 1977. William, however, proposes a letting for seven months from October to April. Such out of season lettings may create problems within the above definition of 'holiday'. A proposed period of seven months takes us to Schedule 15, Case 13 of the Rent Act 1977. This provides a mandatory ground for possession:

'Where the dwelling-house is let under a tenancy for a term of years certain not exceeding eight months and -

a) not later than the relevant date the landlord gave notice in writing to the tenant that possession might be recovered under this Case; and

b) that dwelling house was, at some time within the period of twelve months ending on the relevant date, occupied under a right to occupy it for a holiday.'

Paragraph (b) above contains a cautionary phrase. We are told it is too late to let the bungalow for the summer but if William is to let the bungalow between October and April he must show that within the twelve months to next April it has been 'occupied under a right to occupy it for a holiday.' The advice to William must be that he looks jaded and deserves a holiday. He should spend more time in the bungalow in August and September on a genuine holiday, then he can use the out of season letting provisions of

Case 13. He can then follow a cycle of summer holiday lets and longer-term out of season lettings until he decides to retire. This sequence would ensure no occupier could claim to hold a protected tenancy and would satisfy the terms of reference in the question as to 'any difficulty in getting possession of the bungalow next April or at any time in the future if he decides to live there eventually.'

If he merely regards the bungalow as a long term retirement home prospect with no short-term holiday factor then William should also consider the alternative prescribed by the mandatory Case 12 of Schedule 15. In this case the court must grant William possession if he shows he intends to occupy the bungalow as his residence when he retires from his regular employment on weekday mornings. He must be able to show he had let the bungalow on a regulated tenancy before he retired and:

- before the tenancy commenced he gave the tenant written notice that possession might be recovered on this ground; and

- the bungalow has not since 1974 been let by him on a protected tenancy without the notice being served; and

- the court is satisfied that William has retired from regular employment and needs the bungalow as his residence.

On the basis that the weekday mornings do come within the meaning of 'regular employment' William could adopt this procedure and let the bungalow as his ultimate retirement home when he finally retires.

ii) Under the Housing Act 1988

Holiday lettings are excluded from the definition of an 'assured tenancy': Schedule 1 Housing Act 1988. But Case 3 of Schedule 2 under the Housing Act 1988 does allow a 'holiday landlord' to recover possession from an assured tenant who is not on holiday. This is one of the mandatory grounds.

Tutorial comments

a) Protection under the Rent Act 1977

i) The two-home tenant - *Hampstead Way Investments Ltd* v *Lewis-Weare* [1985] 1 WLR 164

ii) The provision of suitable alternative accommodation - *Hill* v *Rochard* [1983] 2 All ER 21

iii) Holiday lettings - Case 13, Schedule 15, Rent Act 1977.

b) Protection under the Housing Act 1988 - assured tenancies

i) Discretionary Case 9 is the provision for obtaining possession of an assured tenancy.

ii) Mandatory Case 3. But holiday lettings are excluded from assured tenancy.

Question 3

In 1964, Lionel, by deed, granted to Thomas a lease of Blackacre (a house with a tennis court), for 30 years. In the lease Thomas covenanted (inter alia) to pay the rent, to keep the house in repair, not to do anything that might be a nuisance or annoyance to neighbours, and to allow Lionel to use the tennis court on one day each week; the lease also reserved to the lessor a right of re-entry on breach of covenant. In December 1988 Thomas by deed sublet Blackacre to Victor for the residue of the term less three days, and shortly afterwards (in 1989) assigned his lease to William. Lionel consults you, saying that the house is in disrepair, that Victor has been convicted of possessing cannabis found on Blackacre and that he (Lionel) has not been allowed to play tennis this year.

Advise Lionel.

University of London LLB Examination
(for External Students) Land Law June 1985 Q5

General comment

Questions on covenants in leases are always welcome and the majority of candidates should have a good look at this question and realise that this would be well within their capabilities.

In all landlord and tenant questions a useful introduction is to draw the relationship of the parties in some diagrammatic form. This serves two functions in that it sets the events of the question clearly in the mind of the candidate and as he proceeds through the question it may prevent any subsequent confusion as to the relationship of the parties inter se.

Skeleton solution

(See diagram in suggested solution.)

Covenants - rent;

repair;

not to do anything which might be a nuisance or annoyance to neigbours;

allow Lionel to use the tennis court.

Events - disrepair;

conviction of Victor for possession of cannabis found on Blackacre;

Lionel has not been allowed to play tennis.

Repair - notice s146(1) LPA 1925;

Leasehold Property (Repairs) Act 1938, s1;

standard of repair - *Proudfoot* v *Hart* (1890);

measure of damages - s18(1) Landlord and Tenant Act 1927.

Nuisance/ annoyance -	s146(1) notice - capable of being remedied;
	Rugby School (Governors) v *Tannahill* (1935);
	Sublease - *Glass* v *Kencakes* (1966).
Tennis -	does not touch and concern land;
	Thomas liable on privity of contract;
	Horsey Estates Ltd v *Steiger* (1899).

Suggested solution

In diagramatic form we have:

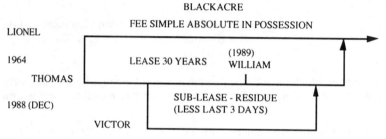

The lease of 1964 contained a number of covenants including:

> to pay rent;
>
> to repair;
>
> not to do anything which might be a nuisance or annoyance to neighbours ;
>
> to allow Lionel to use the tennis court.

The events which are significant are:

> the sublease to Victor;
>
> the assignment of the residue of the term to William.

There has to be considered:

> disrepair;
>
> the conviction of Victor for possessing cannabis found on Blackacre;
>
> the fact that Lionel has not been allowed to play tennis.

Blackacre is now in disrepair and Lionel must be advised as to responsibility and the steps which can be taken to remedy the disrepair.

A covenant to repair does touch and concern the land so the liability will pass from Thomas to William upon the assignment of the residue of the lease to William. The problem, of course, is that the sub-lease means that Victor is in occupation and, presumably, he is responsible for the disrepair. The lease contains a right of re-entry for breach of covenant so the remedy for Lionel is to serve a notice on William under s146(1) LPA 1925. This notice will specify the breach (the want of repair in this case), require the breach to be remedied, if this is possible, and require William to make compensation in money for the breach if Lionel requires compensation. Lionel is unable to serve any such notice on Victor but the effect of the notice on William is that if the repairs are not carried out and relief is not sought by William the lease could be forfeited which would in turn bring the sub-lease to an end.

If William does not receive a notice Lionel must be advised of the effects of s1 of the Leasehold Property (Repairs) Act 1938. These provisions apply to leases of not less than seven years of which at least three years remain unexpired. William may within 28 days of receiving the notice serve a counter-notice on Lionel claiming the benefit of the Act. This means that no proceedings may then be taken by Lionel to enforce the right of re-entry unless he obtains the leave of the court.

In advising Lionel information must be obtained as to the exact nature of the disrepair and reference should be made to the standard of repair expressed in *Proudfoot* v *Hart* (1890) that, after making due allowance for the locality, character and age of the premises at the time of the lease, the tenant must keep the premises in the condition in which they would be kept by a reasonably minded owner. This standard of repair is set at the commencement of the lease: *Anstruther-Gough-Calthorpe* v *McOscar* (1924). If Lionel seeks damages for the lack of repair the measure of damages is set out in s18(1) of the Landlord and Tenant Act 1927 as follows:

'Damages ... shall in no case exceed the amount (if any) by which the value of the reversion (whether immediate or not) in the premises is diminished ...'

This diminution in the value of the reversion may not be easy to assess and must represent the cost of making Blackacre reasonably fit for the type of tenant likely to take it. If the calculation poses a problem it has been held, as a last resort, that the cost of the repairs represents the diminution in the value of the reversion - see *Jones* v *Herxheimer* (1950).

Thus Lionel may proceed for forfeiture on the grounds of disrepair and look for compensation for the loss incurred due to the disrepair.

A second route to forfeiture may be through the covenant not to do anything which might be a nuisance or annoyance to neighbours. The question to resolve is whether the conviction of Victor for possessing cannabis found on Blackacre is a breach of such a covenant. It is surprising that this particular point is not so well covered by judicial precedent whereas certain forms of moral stigma to the property have been the subject of a number of cases. The main points at issue are two-fold: is the conviction a breach of the covenant and, if so, is the breach capable of being remedied? The words 'nuisance' and 'annoyance' pose problems but on the assumption that the events surrounding the arrest and subsequent conviction have 'annoyed' neighbours, what remedy is given to Lionel?

Lionel can serve a notice under s146(1) LPA 1925 but in view of the stigma now attached to Blackacre he need not require the breach to be remedied because it has been held that in some circumstances breaches are not capable of remedy - see *Rugby School (Governors)* v *Tannahill* (1935), which was recently reviewed in *Expert Clothing Services and Sales Ltd* v *Hillgate House Ltd* (1986).

On the other hand the conviction is not of William but of Victor. If Lionel serves a s146(1) notice on William it is then up to William to serve a similar notice on Victor. If, as is usual, the sub-lease of December 1988 contains similar covenants to those in the 1964 lease then William will be able to allege Victor is in breach of covenant. If William then succeeds in obtaining possession from Victor, for breach of covenant, the breach has been remedied and Lionel will not be able to proceed on his notice because the breach has now been remedied. This is a direct result of the decision in *Glass* v *Kencakes Ltd* (1966).

The covenant to allow Lionel to use the tennis court on one day a week is a personal covenant between Lionel and Thomas. It does not touch and concern the land and the burden will not run from Thomas to William. This view is not entirely without doubt and Cheshire expresses the doubt in clear terms:

'On principle a right of re-entry for breach of covenant should be exercisable against any assignee of the lease ... whether or not the covenant touches and concerns the land: for a right of re-entry is a proprietary interest in its own right (quoting s1(2)(e) LPA 1925) ... But the only direct decision holds that the burden of a condition of re-entry will run with the lease at law only if the condition touches and concerns the land (quoting *Horsey Estates Ltd* v *Steiger* [1899] 2 QB 79 at pp88 and 89). If this is right, the condition will be exercisable against an assignee only if the covenant itself runs with the land.'

This is a persuasive point of view and will leave Lionel with an action against Thomas only on the contract which exists between them for the whole thirty year duration of the lease.

Tutorial comments

a) Consider the effect of the most common covenants such as repair.

b) Consider the effect of sub-leasing on the running of covenants.

Question 4

In 1980 Peter granted a lease of a house to Thomas for a term of 30 years subject to covenants to pay rent, to keep the house in a good state of repair and not to use the house for business purposes. Performance of the tenant's covenants was guaranteed by a surety, Simon. In 1989 Thomas granted a sublease of the house to Richard for a term of ten years and in 1990 Thomas assigned his lease to Stephen. In 1991 Peter assigned his reversion to Arthur.

Arthur has received no rent this year, the house is in urgent need of repair and Richard is proposing to start a business in the house.

What remedies does Arthur have, and against whom?

University of London LLB Examination
(for External Students) Land Law June 1991 Q2

General comment

A fairly standard question on the enforceability of leasehold covenants which covered privity of estate and contract and remedies available to the landlord. The well-prepared student should have had no real difficulty in coping with any of the points raised.

Skeleton solution

Has benefit or covenants passed to A? - LPA 1925 s141, privity of estate - No privity between A & R? - Has burden passed to S? - Enforcement procedures against S: for failure to pay rent and other covenants - Is there a forfeiture clause? If not, breach of condition? - s146 procedure - Can A proceed against T? - Does benefit of S's covenant run with freehold?

Suggested solution

There is privity of estate and contract between the original landlord and tenant, both of whom remain liable to each other on the covenants in the lease throughout the term. Thomas, as original tenant, remains liable on the covenants in the lease even after he has assigned the lease to Stephen. Arthur is not the original landlord but the assignee of the reversion and in order to enforce the covenants he must show first that the benefit of the covenants has passed to him. By s141 LPA 1925 the benefit of all covenants 'having reference to the subject-matter' of the lease pass with the reversion to the assignee. Such a covenant is said to touch and concern the land or affect the landlord in his normal capacity as landlord or the tenant in his normal capacity as tenant. The covenants in this question are to pay the rent, to keep the property in good repair and not to use the property for business purposes. All these covenants are classic examples of covenants which touch and concern the land and thus the benefit of the three covenants has passed to Arthur.

Arthur may not bring proceedings for breach of covenant against Richard as although the benefit of the covenant has passed to Arthur there is no privity of estate or contract between him and Richard. Richard is only the sub-tenant. As the user covenant is a negative one, it might be directly enforceable against Richard under the law of restrictive covenants, but insufficient information is given to enable this possibility to be considered further. Whether Richard is in breach of his sub-lease, depends on its terms.

In order to enforce the covenants against Stephen, Arthur must show that the burden of the covenants has passed to Stephen and that there is privity of estate or contract between them. At common law the burden of covenants in the lease which touch and concern the land pass with an assignment of the lease (*Spencer's Case* (1583)). All three covenants touch and concern the land. There is no privity of contract between Stephen and Arthur as they are not the original parties to the lease but there will be privity of estate provided that the lease and the assignment were both legal and not merely equitable. Thus Arthur may enforce the covenants against Stephen.

Arthur may enforce payment of the rent directly by an action for the money or by seizing Stephen's goods through the procedure of distress. He may also be entitled to bring proceedings for forfeiture. The lease is only subject to forfeiture if the covenants are framed as conditions or there is a forfeiture clause in the lease. It is standard for a lease to contain an express forfeiture clause. If there is a forfeiture clause in the lease, Arthur must first make a formal demand for the rent, unless the lease exempts him from so doing. Stephen may obtain relief from forfeiture if he pays the rent due and any costs incurred by Arthur, provided that it is just and equitable to grant relief. The application for relief must be made within six months of the landlord obtaining judgment. If there is at least six months rent in arrears, Stephen has a statutory right to have the proceedings stayed if he pays the arrears of rent and costs before trial. Forfeiture of the lease will automatically determine the sublease to Richard, although Richard has a right to apply for relief independently.

Arthur may sue for damages for breach of the repairing covenant and for an injunction in respect of the user covenant (although this will be of little benefit as Stephen has not himself committed the breach), but he may be entitled to bring forfeiture proceedings if there is a forfeiture clause in the lease. He must first serve notice under s146 LPA 1925 and the notice must specify the breach, require it to be remedied if possible, and require the tenant to pay compensation, if the landlord requires compensation. Arthur must allow Stephen a reasonable time for compliance and three months would probably be sufficient. Certain breaches are considered incapable of remedy but both these breaches are capable of remedy. Stephen may apply for relief on such terms as the court thinks fit and relief is normally granted if the breaches have been remedied. By taking forfeiture proceedings Arthur may indirectly enforce the user covenant against Richard as if the lease to Stephen is forfeited, the sublease will determine. Richard has his own right to ask for discretionary relief.

The performance of the tenant's covenants was guaranteed by Simon as surety. In *P & A Swift Investments* v *Combined English Stores Group* (1988), the House of Lords held that the benefit of a surety covenant could run with the reversion if the surety guaranteed performance of tenants' covenants which themselves touched and concerned the land. Provided that the surety given here was not expressed to be personal (whether given to Peter alone, or in respect of Thomas' personal obligations only) the benefit will pass to Arthur. The remedy against Simon will be in damages only.

Question 5

Last year Michael inherited a flat in London with 65 years of the lease unexpired. As Michael already had a house of his own in London, he decided to have the flat sold and he left the flat empty pending sale. Subsequently the landlords, Limetree Properties Ltd, sent a section 146 notice to the flat stating that the tenant was in breach of a) the covenant to keep the windows clean, b) the covenant to repaint the front door and the window frames before 1 January 1992 and c) the covenant not to place a window box on the window sill. Michael never saw the notice and two weeks later the landlords peaceably re-entered the flat and changed the locks.

Advise Michael.

University of London LLB Examination
(for External Students) Land Law June 1992 Q2

General comment

A question which requires some thought and a particular knowledge of the mechanics of s146 notices. Candidates would be expected to deal with the contents of a s146 notice and its service, particularly where one of the covenants requires some repairs. The issue of relief from forfeiture has to be addressed in the light of *Billson* v *Residential Properties*.

Skeleton solution

- Running of leasehold covenants - *Spencer's Case* (1583).

- Contents of s146 LPA 1925 notices.

- Leasehold Property (Repairs) Act 1938.

- Service of s146 notices.

- Relief from forfeiture - *Billson* v *Residential Apartments Ltd* (1992).

Suggested solution

By virtue of his inheritance Michael has obtained a term of years for a period of 65 years, and, as successor in title to the original tenant, he will take the benefit and the burden of all the covenants which touch and concern the land: see *Spencer's Case* (1583). Consequently the three covenants, being more than personal covenants, are binding on Michael.

The landlord has served a s146 notice alleging breach of the covenants. It is necessary to see whether that notice is valid. In order for the landlord to forfeit the lease in this manner there must be a forfeiture clause in the lease. I assume that this is the case. According to s146, the notice must include a statement of the breaches, require them to be remedied and compensation. However, the cases have relaxed these requirements in appropriate circumstances.

As required by the section, the notice does specify the breaches complained of. It should have required those breaches to be remedied, but, and as far as the cases go, the notice need only require breaches of positive covenants to be remedied - in this case covenants (a) and (b): see *Scala House and District Properties* v *Forbes* (1974). As regards covenant (c), this is negative in nature, and the view expressed in *Governors of Rugby School* v *Tannahill* (1935), was that negative covenants were irremediable and, therefore it was not necessary for the s146 notice to require them to be remedied. In the later case of *Expert Clothing Service and Sales Ltd* v *Hillgate House Ltd* (1986), the Court of Appeal suggested that a negative covenant was capable of remedy. If this is correct then the landlord should have required covenant (c) to be remedied - which, after all, would be a comparatively simple task, namely, removing the window box.

If the landlord required compensation in respect of the breaches then he must have specified this in the notice. An additional element must be included in the s146 notice as the Leasehold Property (Repairs) Act 1938 applies, viz, there is a repairing covenant (covenant (b)) in a lease which was originally for a term in excess of seven years and three years remain unexpired. Under the 1938 Act, the s146 notice should have drawn Michael's attention to his rights under the Act.

Assuming that the s146 notice contains the right elements, it is also necessary to look at whether it has been served correctly. Section 146 notices are served by sending them to the lessee or person interested, or by sending them to the demised premises by registered or recorded delivery, or by attaching it to the demised premises. In this case the letter was sent to the flat so, prima facie, that would be good service on Michael. However, as the notice concerns breach of a repairing covenant s18 Landlord and Tenant Act 1927 should have been complied with. Section 18 requires that service of the notice must be *known* to the lessee, under-lessee or the person who last paid rent. In our case Michael (the new lessee) did not know of the notice and therefore it is invalid.

Insofar as the landlord purported to re-enter pursuant to the notice several points have to be made. Firstly, s18 Landlord and Tenant Act 1927 states that reasonable interval must have elapsed between the date on which service was known to the appropriate person and the actual re-entry. Whether two weeks would be reasonable is a moot point even if it could be shown that Michael knew of the notice. Secondly, and more importantly, it is now settled as a result of the House of Lords' judgment in *Billson* v *Residential Apartments Ltd* (1992), that a tenant can apply for relief from forfeiture under s146(2) whenever a landlord *has* re-entered pursuant to a s146 notice but without a court order - as is the case here. Therefore, following *Billson* it would be open to Michael to apply for relief against forfeiture.

In deciding whether to grant relief, the court will look at the gravity of the breach and all the circumstances of the case in order to see whether it is just and equitable to do so. On the facts breaches of covenants (a) and (c) are of a trivial nature, and whereas covenant (b) is not so trivial, it is not in the nature of breach of a user or assignment covenant. In the circumstances it is quite possible that the court will grant relief, and in doing so it can attach conditions, eg that Michael pay all, or part, of the landlord's expenses.

6   LICENCES

6.1   Introduction

This is an area of Land Law which is in a state of flux. The subject has two distinct areas of study.

a) The licence as a substitute for the lease. This has occupied the courts for some time with two important decisions of the House of Lords, in 1985 (*Street* v *Mountford* [1985] 2 WLR 877) and 1988 (*AG Securities* v *Vaughan*; *Antoniades* v *Villiers* [1988] 3 All ER 1058). The importance of this may diminish with the Housing Act 1988 allowing landlords to create asssured tenancies at a full rent without the problem of security of tenure under the Rent Act 1977. The effect of *Street* v *Mountford* can be demonstrated by the flow chart in section 6.2 below.

b) The licence also operates as a right on its own, a new right in alieno solo is the suggested description. This is the extreme effect but there are graduations of licence beneath that from the bare licence which, in its simplest form is a mere permission to enter the land' to the licence by estoppel which deserves the description of a 'new right in alieno solo'.

6.2   Key points

Licences must be considered in two parts:

A. Lease substitute - often identified by questions incorporating a document headed: 'This licence'.

B. A permission to use the land of another - which emerges in some cases as an equitable right through the rules of proprietory estoppel.

a) *Lease substitute*

Residential occupation - begin with words of Lord Templeman in *Street* v *Mountford* '... relevant ... intention demonstrated by the agreement to grant exclusive possession for a term at a rent'. The test is whether the residential occupier is a 'lodger or a tenant' unless there are exceptional circumstances, as applied in *Royal Philanthropic Society* v *County* (1985) 276 EG 1068 and *AG Securities* v *Vaughan* (1988) (see below). Problems in application:

i) Does it apply to occupiers of commercial premises?

Yes - *London & Associated Investment Trust plc* v *Calow* (1986) 280 EG 1252.

No - *Dresden Estates Ltd* v *Collinson* (1987) 281 EG 1321.

May become restricted to residential occupation.

ii) Is rent necessary for a tenancy?

Section 205(1)(xxvii) LPA 1925 and Fox LJ in *Ashburn Anstalt* v *Arnold* [1988] 2 All ER 147.

iii) What is exclusive possession? The non-exclusive agreement.

If occupier is not a lodger (no attendance/services) it does not necessarily mean there is exclusive possession and a tenancy. Middle ground: *Brooker Settled Estates* v *Ayers* (1987) 1 EGLR 50. Lodging is just one way of not granting exclusive possession but not the only way: *Hadjiloucas* v *Crean* [1987] 3 All ER 1008. The Court of Appeal gave several conclusions:

- Lord Templeman may be too wide in non-exclusive licences;

- may not be relevant to multiple occupations;

- then consider any agreement against factual background (factual matrix) -

  - each occupier is a licensee if cannot exclude others; or

  - parallel leases - if right to exclude; but

  - a joint agreement will not produce a joint tenancy

iv) This joint tenancy approach had been accepted by the Court of Appeal but was rejected by the House of Lords in *AG Securities* v *Vaughan*; *Antoniades* v *Villiers* [1988] 3 WLR 1205. Lord Bridge: 'I do not understand by what legal alchemy they could ever become joint.'

v) Other continuing exceptions: no intention to create legal relations and statute itself: ss 7-9 Rent Act 1977.

v) In addition to *Street* v *Mountford* [1985] 2 WLR 877, see *AG Securities* v *Vaughan*; *Antoniades* v *Villiers*: see also *Mikeover Ltd* v *Brady* [1989] 3 All ER 618 in which *Antoniades* was distinguished.

AG Securities v Vaughan

Facts

The appellants owned a block of flats, one of which contained six living rooms in addition to a kitchen and bathroom. They furnished four living rooms as bedrooms, a fifth as a lounge and the sixth as a sitting room and entered into short-term agreements with four individuals referred to in the relevant agreement as 'licensee'.

The agreements were made at different times and on different terms and were normally for six months' duration. Each agreement provided that the licensee had 'the right to use [the flat] in common with others who have or may from time to time be granted the like right ... but without the right to exclusive possession of any part of the ... flat'. When a licensee left, a new occupant was mutually agreed by the appellants and the remaining licensees.

Held

The occupants were licensees.

Antoniades v Villiers

Facts

The attic of the respondent's house was converted into furnished residential accommodation. Wishing to live together there, the appellants signed identical agreements called 'licences' which were executed at the same time and stressed that they were not to have exclusive possession. In particular, the agreements provided that 'the licensor shall be entitled at any time to use the rooms together with the licensee and permit other persons to use all of the rooms together with the licensee.' No attempt was made by the respondent to use the rooms or to have them used by others. Stressing, too, that the real intention of the parties was to create a licence not coming under the Rent Acts, the agreements provided for a monthly payment of £87 and that they were determinable by one month's notice by either party.

Held

The agreements created a joint tenancy.

Lord Templeman:

'My Lords, in *Street v Mountford* this House stipulated with reiterated emphasis that an express statement of intention is not decisive and that the court must pay attention to the facts and surrounding circumstances and to what people do as well as to what people say...

... My Lords, in the second appeal now under consideration, there was, in my opinion, the grant of a joint tenancy for the following reasons. (1) The applicants for the flat applied to rent the flat jointly and to enjoy exclusive occupation. (2) The landlord allowed the applicants jointly to enjoy exclusive occupation and accepted rent. A tenancy was created. (3) The power reserved to the landlord to deprive the applicants of exclusive occupation was inconsistent with the provisions of the Rent Acts. (4) Moreover, in all the circumstances the power which the landlord insisted on to deprive the applicants of exclusive occupation was a pretence only intended to deprive the applicants of the protection of the Rent Acts.'

Flow chart to demonstrate the effect of *Street* v *Mountford* [1985] 2 WLR 877

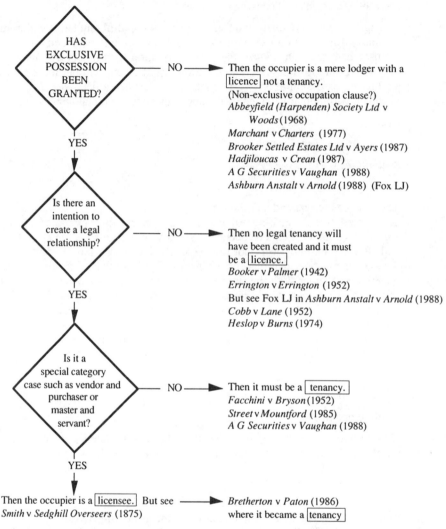

HAS EXCLUSIVE POSSESSION BEEN GRANTED? — NO ⟶ Then the occupier is a mere lodger with a licence not a tenancy.
(Non-exclusive occupation clause?)
Abbeyfield (Harpenden) Society Ltd v *Woods* (1968)
Marchant v *Charters* (1977)
Brooker Settled Estates Ltd v *Ayers* (1987)
Hadjiloucas v *Crean* (1987)
A G Securities v *Vaughan* (1988)
Ashburn Anstalt v *Arnold* (1988) (Fox LJ)

YES

Is there an intention to create a legal relationship? — NO ⟶ Then no legal tenancy will have been created and it must be a licence.
Booker v *Palmer* (1942)
Errington v *Errington* (1952)
But see Fox LJ in *Ashburn Anstalt* v *Arnold* (1988)
Cobb v *Lane* (1952)
Heslop v *Burns* (1974)

YES

Is it a special category case such as vendor and purchaser or master and servant? — NO ⟶ Then it must be a tenancy.
Facchini v *Bryson* (1952)
Street v *Mountford* (1985)
A G Securities v *Vaughan* (1988)

YES

Then the occupier is a licensee. But see ⟶ *Bretherton* v *Paton* (1986)
Smith v *Sedghill Overseers* (1875) where it became a tenancy

Source: Conveyancer and Property Lawyer Sep/Oct 1985 p330

b) *Licence as a right in alieno solo*

Definition: a permission given by the occupier of land which allows the licensee to do some act thereon which otherwise would be a trespass.

i) Types of licence

- Bare licence

  A gratuitous permission which saves the action of the licensee from being a trespass. Revocable at will.

- Licence coupled with an interest or grant

  Licensee given some interest in the land or in something on the land and licence necessary to exploit that interest.

- Contractual licence

  An ordinary contract subject to the usual rules of contract.

- Licence by estoppel

  If an owner permits another person to spend money or alter his position to his detriment in the expectation that he will enjoy some privilege or interest in the land, the owner will be prevented from acting inconsistently with that expectation.

ii) Enforceability of licence between licensor and licensee

- Bare licence - revoke at any time

- Licence coupled with an interst or grant - not revocable

- Contractual licence: *Hounslow London Borough Council* v *Twickenham Garden Developments Ltd* [1970] 3 All ER 326 - depends on the terms of the contract

- Licence by estoppel - not revocable during period for which created - but depends on facts - *Dillwyn* v *Llewellyn* (1862) 4 De GF & J 517 (fee simple): *Pascoe* v *Turner* [1979] 2 All ER 945 (fee simple): *Inwards* v *Baker* [1965] 2 QB 29 (life)

iii) Enforceability of licence against third parties - does the burden run?

- Bare licence - not binding on third parties

- Licence coupled with an interest or grant - probably is binding on third parties

- Contractual licence - cases - *Ashburn Anstalt* v *Arnold* [1988] 2 All ER 147 - not binding on third parties - *Clore* v *Theatrical Properties Ltd* [1936] 3 All ER 483

- Licence by estoppel - the law on this point is still in the process of development, but it seems that a new right in alieno solo is emerging (Cheshire). This is increasingly binding on third parties. Rules of notice apply. *Ives (E R) Investments Ltd* v *High* [1967] 2 QB 379

iv) Assignability of benefit of licence by licensee - does the benefit run?

- Bare licence - no, personal to licensee

- Licence coupled with interest or grant - yes, with the grant

- Contractual licence - yes, unless excluded by contract

- Licence by estoppel - undecided - *Inwards* v *Baker* [1965] 2 QB 29. But see Cumming-Bruce LJ in *Pascoe* v *Turner* [1979] 2 All ER 945 - can be relied upon as a sword not merely as a shield.

These answers to paragraphs ii), iii) and iv) may be illustrated in the following diagrammatic form.

PARAGRAPH	BARE LICENCE	LICENCE COUPLED WITH AN INTEREST	CONTRACTUAL LICENCE	LICENCE BY ESTOPPEL
ii) REVOCABLE	YES Any time. Reasonable notice	NO Must not derogate from grant	DEPENDS ON TERMS May be express/ implied term against revocation. Injunction *Hounslow LBC* v *Twickenham Garden Developments* [1970] 3 All ER 326	HOW TO SATISFY The conveyance of legal estate *Pascoe* v *Turner* [1979] 2 All ER 945 As long as licensee wishes/life *Inwards* v *Baker* [1965] 2 QB 29
iii) BURDEN RUNS?	NO	YES If the interest/ grant is an interest in land	NO Not binding on third parties. *King* v *David Allen* [1916] 2 AC 54 *Ashburn Anstalt* v *Arnold* [1988] 2 All ER 147 Problem case *Binions* v *Evans* [1972] Ch 359	YES Will depend on the rules of notice *Ives (ER) Investments* v *High* [1967] 2 QB 379 'A new right in alieno solo is emerging' Cheshire
iv) BENEFIT RUNS?	NO Personal to licensee	YES May pass with sale of the interest	YES As with benefit of any other contract	DOUBTS - DEPENDS ON FACTS NO - *Inwards* v *Baker* [1965] 2 QB 29 YES - *Ives* v *High* [1967] 2 QB 379 Both a sword and a shield *Pascoe* v *Turner* [1979] 2 All ER 945 Cumming-Bruce LJ

v) Deserted spouse's rights to the matrimonial home:

Matrimonial Homes Act 1983 s2(8) - not an overriding interest for the purposes of s70(1)(g) LRA because s2(8)(b) says so and requires a notice to be entered on the register instead.

CONCLUSION: the lease or licence relationship

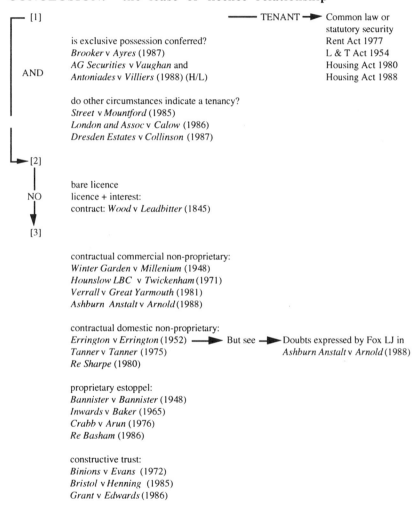

[1]

is exclusive possession conferred?
Brooker v *Ayres* (1987)
AG Securities v *Vaughan* and
Antoniades v *Villiers* (1988) (H/L)

AND

do other circumstances indicate a tenancy?
Street v *Mountford* (1985)
London and Assoc v *Calow* (1986)
Dresden Estates v *Collinson* (1987)

[2]

NO

bare licence
licence + interest:
contract: *Wood* v *Leadbitter* (1845)

[3]

TENANT → Common law or
statutory security
Rent Act 1977
L & T Act 1954
Housing Act 1980
Housing Act 1988

contractual commercial non-proprietary:
Winter Garden v *Millenium* (1948)
Hounslow LBC v *Twickenham* (1971)
Verrall v *Great Yarmouth* (1981)
Ashburn Anstalt v *Arnold* (1988)

contractual domestic non-proprietary:
Errington v *Errington* (1952) → But see → Doubts expressed by Fox LJ in
Tanner v *Tanner* (1975)   *Ashburn Anstalt* v *Arnold* (1988)
Re Sharpe (1980)

proprietary estoppel:
Bannister v *Bannister* (1948)
Inwards v *Baker* (1965)
Crabb v *Arun* (1976)
Re Basham (1986)

constructive trust:
Binions v *Evans* (1972)
Bristol v *Henning* (1985)
Grant v *Edwards* (1986)

6.3 Recent cases and statutes

Bristol and West Building Society v *Henning* [1985] 1 WLR 778

Layton v *Martin* (1985) *The Times* 11 December

Re Basham (deceased) [1986] 1 WLR 1498

J Willis and Son v *Willis* (1985) 277 EG 1133

Hadjiloucas v *Crean* [1987] 3 All ER 1008

Ashburn Anstalt v *Arnold* [1988] 2 All ER 147

AG Securities Ltd v *Vaughan* and *Antoniades* v *Villiers* [1988] 3 All ER 1058

Mikeover Ltd v *Brady* [1989] 3 All ER 618

Aslan v *Murphy* [1989] 3 All ER 130

6.4   Analysis of questions

The questions follow the division mentioned in key points and will alternate between the licence being used as substitute for a lease. The importance of this may decline with the coming into force of the Housing Act 1988. The second aspect relates to the 'pure' licence and the extent to which it may now be recognised as a right in alieno solo.

6.5   Questions

Question 1

a) Charles has been offered a job abroad, initially for six months, but with the possibility of extending this to a maximum of two years. Charles wishes to let his house in London while he is away, but wants to ensure that he can get his house back when he returns.

Advise Charles.

b) Tom is a student at Redbrick University. He lives in a bedsit near the University. He has an agreement with Lionel, described as a licence, whereby Lionel gives Tom the right to occupy the bedsit for one year. Lionel reserves the right to enter the bedsit at any time, and retains a key. Lionel visits the bedsit one day and sees Tom's CND posters on the wall. He immediately gives Tom notice to vacate the bedsit, saying 'I won't have troublemakers living on my property'.

Advise Tom.

University of London LLB Examination
(for External Students) Land Law June 1986 Q7

General comment

Probably the question which most candidates had been hoping to see in the 1986 paper. It would be interesting to know how many, in fact, attempted the question because of the problems they may have had with part (a) of it. In some respects a disappointing question when a more elaborate problem could have given the candidates a much greater opportunity to provide the examiner with a detailed analysis of the present law on licences as lease substitutes.

Skeleton solution

a) Licence - *Addiscombe Garden Estates* v *Crabbe* (1958)

    Street v *Mountford* (1985)

    AG Securities v *Vaughan* (1988)

    Protected shorthold tenancy: s52(1)(a) Housing Act 1980

    After 15 January 1989 - use assured shorthold tenancies - s20 Housing Act 1988

    Lease and rely upon -

    Rent Act 1977, Schedule 15, Part II, Case 11

    Pocock v *Steel* [1985] 1 WLR 229

    Rent (Amendment) Act 1985

    or assured tenancy under Housing Act 1988

b) Section 3(1) Protection from Eviction Act 1977

    Lease or licence - words alone are not enough

    cf *Somma* v *Hazlehurst* (1978) and *Street* v *Mountford* (1985)

    Crancour Ltd v *da Silvaesa* (1986)

    Unlawful eviction - s1(2) Protection from Eviction Act 1977

    Crime and civil remedy - breach of covenant for quiet enjoyment

Suggested solution

a) Charles wishes to let his house confident that he will be able to resume possession when he returns from his job abroad. The major problem for Charles is some uncertainty as to the length of his stay abroad. He knows it will be for at least six months but may be for as long as two years. In 1988 he had three possible solutions: he could grant a licence, he could grant a shorthold tenancy or he could let the house on a regulated tenancy and rely on Case 11 of Schedule 15 to the Rent Act 1977 in order to resume possession when he returns. After 15 January 1989 he could grant an assured shorthold tenancy under the Housing Act 1988 which has replaced the shorthold tenancy.

Charles may seek to use a bare licence which will be revocable at any time. This would be an initial licence for six months with an option to renew the licence for a further single period of eighteen months if both parties agree. The real problem with such a licence is that care must be taken not to create a lease which would give the tenant full protection under the Rent Act 1977. The use of the word 'licence' alone would not be enough if the court construed the whole document as a lease. This problem was illustrated by *Addiscombe Garden Estates* v *Crabbe* (1958). Here the Court of Appeal had to consider an agreement relating to a tennis club carried on in the grounds of a hotel. The agreement was, in the words of Jenkins LJ, 'described by the parties as a licence ... the draftsman had studiously and successfully avoided the use either of the word "landlord" or the word "tenant" throughout the document'. The court concluded, however, that the agreement conferred exclusive possession and thus created a tenancy. Jenkins LJ said:

'The whole of the document must be looked at; and if, after it has been examined, the right conclusion appears to be that, whatever label may have been attached to it, it in fact conferred and imposed on the grantee in substance the rights and obligations of a tenant, and on the grantor in substance the rights and obligations of a landlord, then it must be given the appropriate effect, that is to say, it must be treated as a tenancy agreement as distinct from a mere licence.'

This statement was approved by the House of Lords in *Street* v *Mountford* (1985). Lord Templeman confirmed that the distinction between a lease and a licence was that the lease created a grant for a term at a rent with exclusive possession. He stated that an occupier of residential accommodation at a rent for a term is either a lodger or a tenant and the occupier is a lodger if the landlord provides attendance or services which require the landlord to exercise unrestricted access to and use of the premises. He added:

'If on the other hand residential accommodation is granted for a term at a rent with exclusive possession, the landlord providing neither attendance nor services, the grant is a tenancy: any express reservation to the landlord of limited rights to enter and view the state of the premises and to repair and maintain the premises only serves to emphasise the fact that the grantee is entitled to exclusive possession and is a tenant.'

He then propounded the following test to establish the distinction between a lease and a licence: 'Henceforth, the courts which deal with these problems will, save in exceptional circumstances, only be concerned to enquire whether as a result of an agreement relating to residential accommodation the occupier is a lodger or a tenant.'

The need for a rent in these circumstances was doubted by Fox LJ in *Ashburn Anstalt* v *Arnold* (1988). The general effect of *Street* v *Mountford* was otherwise adopted by the House of Lords in *AG Securities* v *Vaughan* (1988).

In this problem Charles must take care. He is unlikely to be able to make the necessary attendances or services to create a lodging arrangement and any attempt at a licence may well end up as a lease.

In order to avoid these potential problems, before January 1989 Charles might have wished to create a protected shorthold tenancy. As a shorthold tenancy must have been for a term of not less than one year, nor more than five years, Charles would have been advised to create a shorthold tenancy for a term of two years. The problem, of course, is that he may only remain away for six months leaving him to find alternative accommodation in London for himself for the balance of the two years. Under s52(1)(a) of the Housing Act 1980 Charles will not be able to bring the term to a premature end 'except in pursuance of a provision for re-entry or forfeiture for non-payment of rent or breach of any other obligation of the tenancy'.

Under s53(1) of the 1980 Act any tenant would be able to bring the term to an end by three months' notice. At the end of the two years Charles would have grounds for a mandatory order for possession under Rent Act 1977, Schedule 15, Part II, Case 19 which was added by the Housing Act 1980.

This has now been replaced by the assured shorthold tenancy created under s20 of the Housing Act 1988. This will now last for a minimum of 6 months and before the tenancy commences the tenant must receive a notice that it is an assured shorthold tenancy.

If Charles does not wish to risk the problems which may be created by an early end to his appointment abroad then he may create a lease and rely on the provisions of the Rent Act 1977, Schedule 15, Part II, Case 11 to obtain possession when he returns to London. If Charles was not resident in the house before his departure abroad then *Pocock* v *Steel* (1985) discovered a flaw in these provisions by holding that a landlord could not resume possession under Case 11 when he was not in actual occupation immediately prior to the current letting. The relevant words of Case 11 were:

'Where a person who occupied the dwellinghouse as his residence - let it on a regulated tenancy...'

The effect of this decision was altered by the Rent (Amendment) Act 1985 which changed the opening lines of Case 11 to read:

'Where a person (in this Case referred to as "the owner-occupier") who let the dwellinghouse on a regulated tenancy had, at any time before the letting, occupied it as his residence ...'

This reverses the decision in *Pocock v Steel* above and for any new lettings Case 11 will apply if Charles was in occupation at any time in the past.

This final method of using a lease and relying upon Case 11 to obtain possession may well be the most suitable method available for Charles. If the tenancy begins after 15 January 1989 an assured tenancy could be created and then mandatory Ground 1 in the 2nd Schedule to the Housing Act 1988 contains an enlarged version of Case 11 in order to obtain possession.

b) There is no indication of when Tom's licence began but it will be assumed that it was during the currency of the first year that Lionel purported to give Tom notice to vacate the bedsit. If this document did create a licence then the agreement will create a contractual licence for occupation for one year and the notice to quit itself would not be effective.

In any event Tom may rely upon the provisions of s3(1) and (2) of the Protection from Eviction Act 1977, as amended, which provides:

'(1) Where any premises have been let as a dwelling under a tenancy which is neither a statutorily protected tenancy nor an excluded tenancy and -

a) the tenancy (in this section referred to as the former tenancy) has come to an end, but

b) the occupier continues to reside on the premises or part of them,

it shall not be lawful for the owner to enforce against the occupier, otherwise than by proceedings in the court, his right to recover possession of the premises.

(2) In this section "the occupier", in relation to any premises, means any person lawfully residing in the premises or part of them at the termination of the former tenancy.'

A further s3(2A) was added by s69(1) of the Housing Act 1980 to extend the above provisions to a restricted contract under the Rent Act 1977 which creates a licence.

It does appear that s3 of the Protection from Eviction Act 1977 would protect Tom if his arrangement was a contractual licence.

It may be, however, that Tom has even more protection in that he has been granted exclusive possession of the bedsit and, thereby, has a lease and not merely a licence. The words of Lord Denning MR in *Facchini v Bryson* (1952) still apply:

'Their relationship is determined by the law and not by the label which they choose to put on it.'

The question to be determined is whether Tom has exclusive possession even though Lionel has reserved the right to enter the bedsit at any time, and retained a key. The courts are now anxious to establish whether such an agreement is a sham especially after the comment of Lord Templeman in *Street v Mountford* (1985) that the decision in *Somma v Hazlehurst* (1978) was wrongly decided. On the other hand too much must not be read into *Street v Mountford* and where exclusive possession is not granted a licence may still be created. This is seen in the decision of the Court of Appeal in *Crancour Ltd v da Silvaesa* (1986). It is interesting to note that in this case the licensor was to retain keys 'in order to obtain access at all times for the purpose of exercising management and control, carrying out repairs and providing attendance, and in order to remove or replace such items of furniture as the licensor saw fit'. In considering this clause along with a number of others the Court of Appeal took no exception to such a provision in deciding that the arrangement was not necessarily a sham. The word 'pretence' was preferred to 'sham' when the House of Lords further considered this question of exclusive possession in *AG Securities v Vaughan; Antoniades v Villiers* (1988).

As a consequence, Tom may be a lodger but he most certainly should not leave on that account. Lionel will have to seek possession through the courts when Tom may then use two separate forms of defence. First, that the agreement creates a lease and not a licence. Second, that in any event he has an agreement for one year and does not appear to have broken any term of that agreement by the display of posters on the wall. There is certainly no implied term that CND posters should not be displayed on the wall. Finally Tom should not leave his bedsit in response to the notice he has received from Lionel.

Tom should be reminded that s1(2) of the Protection from Eviction Act 1977 does make it an offence for any person unlawfully to deprive a residential occupier of any premises of his occupation of the premises or any part of them. It is also an offence to attempt any such deprivation. The term 'residential occupier' is defined by s1(1) as a person occupying the premises as a residence, whether under a contract, statute or rule of law. The protection will be afforded to tenants, licencees and lodgers.

In addition to a crime, it is provided by s1(5) PEA 1977 that civil remedies remain available to a residential occupier who is unlawfully evicted. As a consequence, Tom could pursue an action in trespass for breach of the implied (probably) covenant for quiet enjoyment in the agreement: *McCall v Abelesz* (1976).

Tutorial comments

a)   i)   Consider three choices in 1988

- Licence

- Protected shorthold tenancy

- Lease and Rent Act 1977, Schedule 15, Case 11

ii) Consider three choices in 1989

- Licence

- Assured shorthold tenancy under Housing Act 1988

- Assured tenancy under the Housing Act 1988 and Schedule 2, Ground 1

b) Protection from Eviction Act 1977 s3(1)

Lease/licence debate

Unlawful eviction under s1 Protection from Eviction Act 1977.

Question 2

'A disposition or licence properly passeth no interest nor alters or transfers property in anything ...'

(Vaughan CJ)

'The doctrine of the licence ... is no more than a mechanism by which the law sanctions the informal creation of proprietary rights in land.' (Moriarty)

Does either of these statements accurately reflect the current status of licences in property law?

University of London LLB Examination
(for External Students) Land Law June 1987 Q6

General comment

Another question to be welcomed in an area which any Land Law student should be able to consider at length. The form of the question may well give the examiner the opportunity to study the examination techniques of the candidates. There are many ways of attempting such an answer and it could well be that technique alone will raise the marks awarded to those candidates who are able to assemble their answers in a logical and progressive form outside the stricter discipline of a problem-style question.

Skeleton solution

Briefly outline four types of licence: (use numbers below)

1) Bare licence

2) Licence coupled with an interest

3) Contractual licence - *Hounslow LBC* v *Twickenham Garden Developments Ltd* (1970)

4) Licence by estoppel - Lord Kingsdown - *Ramsden* v *Dyson* (1866); *Inwards* v *Baker* (1965)

Quote 1: 'A disposition or licence properly passeth no interest nor alters or transfers property in anything.'

1) TRUE

2) NOT TRUE

3) TRUE - *Clore* v *Theatrical Properties Ltd* (1936) - confirmed by *Ashburn Anstalt* v *Arnold* (1988)

BUT NOTE EXCEPTION: *Binions* v *Evans* (1972)

4) A state of change from TRUE TO NOT TRUE: *Ives (E R) Investments Ltd* v *High* (1967)

Quote 2: 'The doctrine of the licence... is no more than a mechanism by which the law sanctions the informal creation of proprietary rights in land.'

1) Mainly TRUE

2) Mainly TRUE

3) TRUE - *BUT* see the exceptions above. Quote: Megarry and Wade

4) More to the licence by estoppel than this: *Pascoe* v *Turner* (1979)

Cheshire: '... a new right in alieno solo has emerged ...'

Conclusion: Can the word 'licence' continue to describe such diverse interests?

Suggested solution

There are four main types of licence:

1) BARE LICENCE

2) LICENCE COUPLED WITH AN INTEREST

3) CONTRACTUAL LICENCE

4) LICENCE BY ESTOPPEL OR PROPRIETARY ESTOPPEL

In relating the current status of licences in property law to the given statements of Vaughan CJ and Moriarty it is necessary to briefly analyse each of these four types of licence and then to apply the respective quotations to each in turn. In this way we should establish whether either statement does accurately reflect the current status of the various forms of licence in property law.

1) Bare licence. This is a gratuitous permission which protects the licensed activity from becoming a trespass. The licence is revocable at any time and is not enforceable against subsequent holders of the land.

2) Licence coupled with an interest. The licensee receives some proprietary interest in the land and the licence is necessary to enter in order to exploit that interest. The licence and the interest tend to become inter-connected and each survives with the other.

3) Contractual licence. This is basically an ordinary contract which creates a licence supported by consideration. It creates a contractual right to do things on land which would otherwise be a trespass. The contract itself, however, is construed as any ordinary contract: *Winter Garden Theatre (London) Ltd* v *Millenium Productions Ltd* (1948).

The courts will not recognise any wrongful repudiation of the contract: *Hurst* v *Picture Theatres Ltd* (1915). The law relating to contractual licences is summarised by Megarry J in *Hounslow London Borough Council v Twickenham Garden Developments Ltd* (1971): 'I find it difficult to see how a contractual licensee can be treated as a trespasser so long as his contract entitled him to be on the land... I do not think that the licence can be detached from the contract and separately revoked.'

This is emphasised by Megarry and Wade:

'The judicial consensus is now to the effect that a licensor has no right to eject a licensee in breach of contract, even where equity will not assist the licensee, and that if he does so forcibly the licensee can sue for assault.'

4) Licence by estoppel. Now recognised as a separate form of licence following earlier links with both contractual licences and the constructive trust. If an owner permits another person to spend money or alter his position in any way to his detriment in the expectation that he will enjoy some interest in the land that owner will be prevented from acting inconsistently with the expectations raised. The licence emerges from the words of Lord Kingsdown in a dissenting speech in *Ramsden v Dyson* (1866):

'If a man, under a verbal agreement, with a landlord for a certain interest in land, or, what amounts to the same thing under an expectation, created or encouraged by the landlord, that he shall have a certain interest, takes possession of such land with the consent of the landlord and upon the faith of such promise or expectation, with the knowledge of the landlord, and without objection by him, lays out money upon the land, a Court of Equity will compel the landlord to give effect to such promise or expectation.'

119

The proprietary estoppel will be enforced as an equitable proprietary interest. It is this area of licences which has seen most expansion over recent years. The estoppel is created by either expenditure on the land or encouragement or acquiescence by the land owner. The essence of the licence was described by Lord Denning MR in *Inwards v Baker* (1965):

'If the owner of land requests another, or indeed allows another, to expend money on the land under an expectation created or encouraged by the owner of the land that he will be able to remain there, that raises an equity in the licensee such as to entitle him to stay.'

The Master of the Rolls went on to say:

'All that is necessary is that the licensee should, at the request or with the encouragement of the owner of the land, have spent money in the expectation of being allowed to stay there. If so, the court will not allow that expectation to be defeated where it would be inequitable so to do.'

The licence by estoppel is protected in equity but in the case of unregistered land it is not capable of being registered as a land charge for the purposes of the Land Charges Act 1972. As a consequence it relies for protection against third parties on the equitable doctrine of notice: *Ives (E R) Investments Ltd v High* (1967).

Most of the discussion today on the exact nature of the licence is related to this expansion in the licence by estoppel.

Each quotation will now be considered in relation to these four forms of licence.

'A disposition or licence properly passeth no interest nor alters or transfers property in anything.' (Vaughan CJ)

1) Bare licence. True, it creates no interest in the land and is not enforceable against subsequent holders of the land.

2) Licence coupled with an interest. If the subject matter of the grant is an interest in land and the legal interest has passed the licence does become a 'property' which will be binding on third parties.

3) Contractual licence. Generally does not create any interest which would be enforceable against third parties: *Clore* v *Theatrical Properties Ltd* (1936). This view was confirmed by the Court of Appeal in *Ashburn Anstalt* v *Arnold* (1988) where Fox LJ confirmed that *Errington* v *Errington* (1952) was wrongly decided.

However there is one case which goes against this statement and which prevents a clear cut answer on this point.

In *Binions* v *Evans* (1972), the widow who occupied a cottage after the death of her husband was held to be protected against purchasers of the cottage who knew of her occupation and even paid a reduced price because of it. The problem with this decision is that, although the Court of Appeal were unanimous in protecting the widow, their unanimity did not extend to the reasons. The majority decided that Mrs Evans was a tenant for life under the SLA 1925, whereas Lord Denning held that she was a contractual licensee and that the licence created a constructive trust which bound the plaintiffs to permit Mrs Evans to live in the cottage during her life or for as long as she wished. Whatever the reason Mrs Evans could remain, the problems created by these conflicting views are still with us.

4) Licence by estoppel. There is an increasing willingness to recognise an interest which is enforceable against third parties. This is seen in *Ives (E R) Investments Ltd* v *High* (1967), where the Court of Appeal held that High had a right of estoppel which was not capable of registration as a land charge, but it was binding on the plaintiffs who had purchased the legal estate with actual notice.

'The doctrine of the licence ... is no more than a mechanism by which the law sanctions the informal creation of proprietary rights in land.' (Moriarty)

1) Bare licence. Mainly true, it is worthy of an over-statement where the bare licence is concerned because there is no attempt to create any proprietary right in the land, merely a provision to use the land for a limited time.

2) Licence coupled with an interest. Again there is more to this licence and a formal right may exist to which the licence is ancillary.

3) Contractual licence. The exceptional case of *Binions* v *Evans* (1972) mentioned above does create problems in relation to this statement. The statement is probably true in certain very exceptional circumstances as indicated by Megarry and Wade:

'The law for so long set its face firmly against the notion that a contractual licence could be binding on the licensor's successor in title, on the principle that licences were personal transactions which created no proprietary interests in land. A purchaser of the licensor's land therefore had no concern with any mere licence, even when he bought with express notice of it.'

Megarry and Wade conclude:

'All the indications now are that contractual licences are capable of binding successors in title as equitable interests ... In this development the useful mechanism of the constructive trust is clearly destined to play a part ... The courts appear to be well on their way to creating a new and highly versatile interest in land which will rescue many informal and unbusinesslike transactions, particularly within families, from the penalties of disregarding legal forms. Old restraints are giving way to the demands of justice.'

But this must now be read in the light of the words of Fox LJ in *Ashburn Anstalt* v *Arnold* (1988) where the two exceptional cases were reduced to only *Binions* v *Evans* (1972). The future may well be with the constructive trust: *Grant* v *Edwards* (1986).

4) Licence by estoppel. It is here where the development of new interests is most clear. The estoppel interests do bind third parties and the debate is now as to the extent, if any, of this as a proprietary right in land. The general view is that it is an interest in land. Gray and Symes in 'Real property and real people' said:

'This result adds to the category of unregisterable, non-overreachable equitable interests in land, with consequent insecurity and uncertainty for both the licensee and the purchaser.'

The extent of this licence by estoppel is best seen in *Pascoe v Turner* (1979) where the right enabled a successful claim for the conveyance of the fee simple to be made. The second quotation is, therefore, probably most apt in describing the licence by estoppel. The licence has, however, gone further by the recognition which has been given to those 'proprietary rights in land'. Cheshire probably provides the most apposite conclusion:

'The law on this point is still in the process of development but it seems that a new right *in alieno solo* has emerged in this century as did one in the previous century under the doctrine of *Tulk* v *Moxhay*.'

The time is now here when the word 'licence' is too broad to cover the various rights which now shelter beneath its umbrella. The above analysis shows that generalised phrases which may refer to the bare licence are quite inappropriate when the more sophisticated relationships arising out of the licence by estoppel have to be considered and construed.

Tutorial comments

a) Outline the four types of licence.

b) Quotation 1 - consider the effect on the contractual licence of the decision of the Court of Appeal in *Ashburn Anstalt* v *Arnold* [1988] 2 All ER 147.

c) Quotation 2 - consider the four licences again, and conclude with Cheshire's comment on the emergence of a new right in alieno solo.

Question 3

As Ann and Liza were close friends and were doing the same post-graduate course, they decided to share a flat. After looking for a month they found a two-room flat belonging to Lionel which suited them. Lionel insisted on each of them entering into separate but identical 'licence' agreements. Each agreement provided that the licence was to run for nine months from 1 September 1990 and that the licensee agreed to pay £200 per month as licence fee as well as 50% of the outgoings on the flat. The agreement further stated that the licensor should retain a key to the flat and that he reserved the right to occupy the flat whenever he wished. The agreement denied that the licensee was to have exclusive possession of the flat or any part of the flat. Ann and Liza each signed their agreements and entered into possession of the flat on 1 September 1990. Nine months later Lionel told them to leave and, when they refused, he began making abusive telephone calls to them in the middle of the night.

Advise Ann and Liza.

University of London LLB Examination
(for External Students) Land Law June 1991 Q3

General comment

This was a predictable question on the lease/licence distinction with particular reference to sharing arrangements. Students who had actually read the relevant cases would have had a definite advantage in answering the question.

Skeleton solution

Is it a lease or licence? - Importance of distinction re security of tenure - Any remedy for harassment under Protection from Eviction Act 1977? - Is there exclusive possession? - Main cases on sharing agreements: joint tenancy or licence? - Is the term reserving to Lionel the right to occupy a sham? - Are separate obligations to pay fatal to a joint tenancy? - Conclusion: suggest on balance points more towards a lease but emphasise this area of law changing all the time.

Suggested solution

The real issue in this case is whether Ann and Liza are tenants or licensees. If they are tenants they may be entitled to security of tenure under the Rent Acts, whereas if they are licensees, their rights depend on the terms of the licence and they will have no security of tenure as the Rent Acts will not apply. Whether they are licensees or tenants they may have a remedy against Lionel's abusive telephone calls under the Protection from Eviction Act 1977. This Act makes it an offence to harass a residential occupier with the intention of causing him to give up his occupation.

Therefore Ann and Liza may be able to prosecute Lionel under this Act, but this will not help them remain in occupation although it may give them some personal satisfaction.

A lessee must have exclusive possession and if there is no grant of exclusive possession there is no lease, although it is possible to have exclusive possession but still a licence. In *Street* v *Mountford* (1985) Lord Templemann said 'Where the only circumstances are that residential accommodation is offered and accepted with exclusive possession for a term at a rent, the result is a tenancy.' The court will construe the agreement made by the parties and if, in substance, the agreement is a lease, it is a lease, no matter that the parties have called it a licence. In *Street* v *Mountford* the agreement was held to create a lease even though it clearly stated that it was only a licence. In this case the crucial question is whether Ann and Liza have been granted exclusive possession and the fact that the agreement calls itself a licence is not decisive.

There have been several recent cases on the difficult issues raised by multiple occupation and sharing agreements. Where there are several occupiers there may be a grant of exclusive possession to them all as joint tenants, or there may be no grant of exclusive possession so that all the occupiers are merely licensees. A third possibility, which does not seem to have been argued in the cases, would be that each occupier has a grant of exclusive possession of his own room with a shared right to use the common parts. In *AG Securities* v *Vaughan* (1988) there was a six-roomed flat occupied by four persons. Each occupier signed an individual 'licence' agreement and the amount he paid depended on which room he occupied. There was a fairly high turnover of occupants and when one left, either the remaining occupiers found a replacement or the owners advertised for a replacement. A new occupier had to be acceptable to the owners. It was held by the House of Lords that this arrangement created a series of licences not a lease. It was not possible to say that there had been a grant of exclusive possession to the occupiers together. The occupiers had no right to exclude a new occupier introduced by the owners when one occupier left and this term to allow the introduction of new occupiers was clearly not a sham. The four unities essential for joint tenancy were not present. Different occupiers arrived at different times, paid different amounts and stayed for different periods. The argument that when one occupier left, his agreement was terminated and there was an implied surrender by the others followed by a new grant, was considered 'unreal' by the House of Lords.

This case is different to that of *AG Securities* in many respects. There is a term that Lionel may occupy the flat whenever he wishes, but that may well be a sham here. The flat has only two rooms and it is unlikely that it was ever intended by anyone that Lionel would actually move in. In *Antoniades* v *Villiers* (1988) the owner granted a 'licence' to an unmarried couple to occupy a two-roomed flat and purported to reserve the right to go into occupation with the couple or introduce another occupier, but the House of Lords said that there had been a grant of exclusive occupation as this term was never intended to be acted upon and was a sham. It seems that in this case both Ann and Liza would have signed or neither. It does not seem to be material that they are two ladies rather than an unmarried couple. In *Hadjiloucas* v *Crean* (1987) two ladies agreed to take a two-roomed flat with kitchen and bathroom. Each signed a separate agreement to pay and to use the flat with one other person and if one agreement was terminated the owner could require another person to move in. A retrial was ordered by the Court of Appeal but Lord Templemann in *AG Securities* clearly thought that this arrangement had created a lease with exclusive possession.

One problem does arise as each has a separate obligation to pay. Joint tenancy requires unity of obligation. In *Antoniades* v *Villiers* there were separate obligations to pay but Lord Templemann still held that there was a joint grant of exclusive possession. He said 'A tenancy remains a tenancy even though the landlord may choose to require each of two joint tenants to agree expressly to pay one-half of the rent.' However in the later case of *Mikeover* v *Brady* (1989) the fact that there were separate obligations to pay was regarded as a fatal objection to any finding of joint tenancy. In that case there were two 'licence' agreements which imposed separate obligations to pay, although the agreements did not contain any express power to introduce new occupiers and the occupiers did not have the right to leave early on notice. Although the agreements appeared to grant joint exclusive occupation, the Court of Appeal held that there was no joint tenancy because of the separate obligations to pay.

Again in *Stribling* v *Wickham* (1989) there were three separate agreements to use premises on a shared basis. It was held that the court must consider all the circumstances and construe the agreement in the light of the circumstances. Here each occupier was responsible for his own payment only and could terminate his own agreement on 28 days notice without affecting the rights of the others. Occupiers changed from time to time and the agreements were not leases but true licences as there was no grant of exclusive occupation. By contrast in *Nicolaou* v *Pitt* (1989) there was held to be a grant of exclusive possession and hence a lease in a sharing agreement. In that case the court considered that there had been no real contemplation of introducing another occupier.

Thus some factors in this case seem to point towards a lease and some towards a licence. Ann and Liza appear to have exclusive possession despite Lionel's retention of a key and the term that allows Lionel to occupy the flat with them seems to be a sham as one cannot imagine that the parties ever intended it should be acted upon. However the existence of two separate obligations to pay points away from a joint tenancy and thus towards a licence. If the court is prepared to construe the two agreements together as in *Antoniades* v *Villiers* it is likely that a lease exists. On balance this situation seems closer to *Antoniades* v *Villiers* than *AG Securities* v *Vaughan* or *Stribling* v *Wickham*. Both the latter cases were situations of a fluctuating number of occupiers when each occupier clearly was independent of each other. Here the two agreements appear to be dependent on each other, there is no provision for one of the occupiers to leave early, and the term allowing Lionel to occupy looks like a sham. Therefore it is suggested that Ann and Liza may well have a tenancy and thus protection under the Rent Acts and security of tenure. This area is one where the law is still changing and subsequent cases may point more firmly towards a lease or towards a licence. Lionel would have been better advised to use the new provisions of the Housing Act 1988 to grant a short-hold tenancy with guaranteed recovery of possession at the end of the term. Whether they have a lease or licence, Ann and Liza probably have some remedy against Lionel under the Protection from Eviction Act 1977 in respect of his abusive telephone calls.

Question 4

Distinguish a lease from a licence. To what extent is the distinction important today?

University of London LLB Examination
(for External Students) Land Law June 1992 Q1

General comment

A slight variation on the typical lease/licence question as it is neither solely about *Street* v *Mountford* nor licences as interests in land. The good candidate will cover both these issues in order to answer the question.

Skeleton solution

- Define lease and licence.
- Security of tenure.
- Exclusive possession.
- *Street* v *Mountford* (1985).
- Protection against third party purchasers.
- Licence coupled with interest.
- Licences and constructive trusts.
- Estoppel licences.

Suggested solution

A lease is a document which creates a term of years in land, in other words it creates an interest in land - a proprietary right. Leases can be legal, ie made by deed in accordance with s52 Law of Property Act (LPA) 1925, or by parol, if they take effect in possession for a term not exceeding three years at the best rent reasonably obtainable (s54 LPA 1925). Licences on the other hand are, generally, merely personal rights giving no interest in land.

The distinction is of fundamental importance in relation to occupancy of residential premises because of the differing degrees of protection afforded to lessees and licensees. In short, lessees are afforded security of tenure whereas licensees are not. If a lease is found to exist the tenant will have the protection of the Protection from Eviction Act 1977, the Rent Act 1977 and the Housing Act 1988. The former governs the periods of notice to quit and the latter two give the tenant valuable rights in terms of security of tenure and the devolution of tenancies. For instance, under both the Rent Act and the Housing Act (with the exception of the assured shorthold tenancy under the latter) a tenant can only be removed from the premises if the landlord can show a mandatory or discretionary ground for possession. Until that time the tenant remains in possession. Similarly, a tenancy can be succeeded to twice under the Rent Act (in favour of a spouse and then members of the tenant's family) and once under the Housing Act. The Rent Act tenant also has valuable rights in relation to rent assessment, whereby rents are subject to review by an adjudication officer.

Licensees on the other hand have no security of tenure, or rent control. They can be removed from the premises following a valid notice to quit, and there is no statutory control of rents. Not surprisingly in the light of the above there has been a continuous battle between landlords, who have constantly tried to create licences out of leases, and tenants who claim the latter. As a result of *Street* v *Mountford* (1985), a standard test became applicable in deciding whether an agreement was a lease or not - if the agreement gave the occupant exclusive possession, for a term and at a rent, it was a lease despite any label to the contrary. Subsequent cases have refined that approach and it is now relevant to look not just to the agreement itself but the parties intentions at the time of its making, and how they operated the agreement in practice: *Antoniades* v *Villiers* (1988). As a result of these cases certain propositions have emerged. Firstly, in cases of multiple occupancy licences can still exist if there is an absence of the four unities: *AG Securities* v *Vaughan* (1988).

Secondly, in exceptional circumstances licences will exist despite the occupant's exclusive possession, eg where the occupant is in possession pursuant to a contract of employment or pending conveyance of the property to him, or pursuant to a local authority's statutory duties. On balance, however, the practice has been to favour the tenant by finding a lease with all its concomitant rights.

The distinction is also important in relation to protection against third parties. A lease is a legal estate in land and if over 21 years and legal, in an area subject to the Land Registration Act 1925, it will be registered as title. If it is legal and under 21 years it will take effect as an overriding interest under s70(1)(k), and is not capable of being overreached. If it is not made by deed and is an equitable lease of any duration, then it can be protected by the entry on the register as a minor interest or, failing that, as an overriding interest under s70(1)(g), although this can be overreached: *City of London Building Society* v *Flegg* (1988). By contrast, a licence cannot be protected as title or a minor interest and cannot fall within s70(1)(g) as it is not an interest in land. In the case of land within the ambit of the Land Charges Act 1925, the legal lease will bind 'in rem' and the equitable one can be registered as a C(iv) land charge (estate contract). The licence, on the other hand, has no measure of protection and is not capable of binding third parties.

However, it must not be thought that the licence has no value whatsoever. It has always been recognised that a licence, coupled with an interest or profit, is capable of binding third parties if properly registered. Similarly, some cases of recent origin, eg *Binions* v *Evans* (1972), have held that in appropriate cases a purchaser who has knowledge of a contractual licence will be bound by a constructive trust. Others have taken the view that contractual licences have the status of an equity in land (see *Errington* v *Errington* (1952), although this was rejected obiter in *Ashburn Anstalt* v *Arnold* (1987), where the court preferred the traditional view that contractual licences are personal only: see *King* v *David Allen & Sons Billposting Ltd* (1916).

More importantly, however, estoppel licences have been recognised as giving rise to an interest in land capable of binding third parties. These come about on normal estoppel principles, viz, representation and reliance, and are commonly shown by expenditure on the land of another (*Inwards* v *Baker* (1965)), mutual benefit and burden (*Ives* v *High* (1967)) and acquiescence (*Plimmer* v *Mayor of Wellington* (1884)). In any event once the estoppel has arisen the task for the court is how best to satisfy it. Two of the options open to the court are to grant the licensee a life interest (*Inwards*) or to convey the fee simple to him (*Pascoe* v *Turner* (1979)). Like all estoppels, it will bind everyone except the purchaser for value without notice.

Clearly, in terms of residential occupation in the rented sector, the distinction between a lease and a licence is of fundamental importance. Whereas it might be said that the courts favoured the occupant following *Street* v *Mountford*, the Housing Act 1988 has redressed the balance somewhat by the introduction of the assured short-hold tenancy. That said, the licence in other areas is afforded some value, not least through the concept of estoppel.

7   COVENANTS RELATING
       TO LAND

7.1	Introduction
7.2	Key points
7.3	Recent cases and statutes
7.4	Analysis of questions
7.5	Questions

7.1   Introduction

This chapter covers two distinct areas. The first relates to the running of the benefit and burden of covenants in leases. This is, in effect, a continuation of part of chapter 6. The second area is the predominant part of the chapter and relates to covenants affecting land held in fee simple. In this area two important preliminary points must be established. The first is to establish the nature of the covenant, whether it is positive or negative. Then, secondly, to consider the different rules which apply to the running of the benefit and burden of those covenants.

As an aid to revision this may be expressed in the form shown on the page opposite.

FIRST: Consider nature of covenant: whether positive or negative.

THEN: Apply following rules as to running of the benefit and burden following the sequence of arrows from (1) to (4).

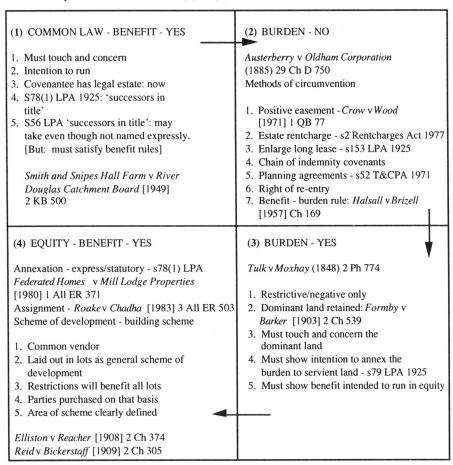

(1) COMMON LAW - BENEFIT - YES	(2) BURDEN - NO
1. Must touch and concern 2. Intention to run 3. Covenantee has legal estate: now 4. S78(1) LPA 1925: 'successors in title' 5. S56 LPA 'successors in title': may take even though not named expressly. [But: must satisfy benefit rules] *Smith and Snipes Hall Farm* v *River Douglas Catchment Board* [1949] 2 KB 500	*Austerberry* v *Oldham Corporation* (1885) 29 Ch D 750 Methods of circumvention 1. Positive easement - *Crow* v *Wood* [1971] 1 QB 77 2. Estate rentcharge - s2 Rentcharges Act 1977 3. Enlarge long lease - s153 LPA 1925 4. Chain of indemnity covenants 5. Planning agreements - s52 T&CPA 1971 6. Right of re-entry 7. Benefit - burden rule: *Halsall* v *Brizell* [1957] Ch 169
(4) EQUITY - BENEFIT - YES	(3) BURDEN - YES
Annexation - express/statutory - s78(1) LPA *Federated Homes* v *Mill Lodge Properties* [1980] 1 All ER 371 Assignment - *Roake* v *Chadha* [1983] 3 All ER 503 Scheme of development - building scheme 1. Common vendor 2. Laid out in lots as general scheme of development 3. Restrictions will benefit all lots 4. Parties purchased on that basis 5. Area of scheme clearly defined *Elliston* v *Reacher* [1908] 2 Ch 374 *Reid* v *Bickerstaff* [1909] 2 Ch 305	*Tulk* v *Moxhay* (1848) 2 Ph 774 1. Restrictive/negative only 2. Dominant land retained: *Formby* v *Barker* [1903] 2 Ch 539 3. Must touch and concern the dominant land 4. Must show intention to annex the burden to servient land - s79 LPA 1925 5. Must show benefit intended to run in equity

Covenants created before 1926   -   Protected by doctrine of notice

Covenants created after 1925   -   Land charge Class D(ii) s2 LCA 1972

7.2   Key points

a) *Covenants in LEASES*

   i) Privity of contract + indemnity provisions - s77 and 2nd Schedule Pt IX LPA 1925 - may be an alternative claim in quasi-contract provided the liability is the same - *Moule* v *Garrett* (1872) LR 7 Ex 101.

ii) Privity of estate

- Where the tenant has assigned his interest: ss78 (benefit) and 79 (burden) LPA 1925

- Where the landlord has assigned his reversion: ss141 (benefit) and 142 (burden) LPA 1925

b) *Covenants affecting FEE SIMPLE*

Note s56 LPA 1925: 'A person may take an immediate or other interest in land or other property, or the benefit of any ... covenant ... although he may not be named as a party ...' Section 56 is NOT concerned with the rules for passing the benefit BUT the giving of the benefit to other persons not named in the deed: *Smith and Snipes Hall Farm* v *River Douglas Catchment Board* [1949] 2 KB 500.

i) Do benefit and burden of covenants affecting fee simple bind successive owners?

- Original parties

- 3rd parties or successors: see s56 LPA 1925

ii) Running of covenants at common law

- Benefit - note conditions: must touch and concern land of covenantee and covenantee has legal estate.

- Burden, not at common law - *Austerberry* v *Oldham Corporation* (1885) 29 Ch D 750. See also *Rhone* v *Stephens* (1993) The Times 21 January

- Consider methods of circumvention.

  These are alternative methods for the running of the burden of positive covenants.

  - Positive easement - *Crow* v *Wood* [1971] 1 QB 77

  - Estate rentcharge - s2 Rentcharges Act 1977

  - Chain of indemnity covenants

  - Planning agreements under s52 Town and County Planning Act 1971

  - Long lease which is then enlarged into the fee simple under s153 LPA 1925.

  - The benefit/burden rule in *Halsall* v *Brizell* [1957] Ch 169 by which anyone who enjoys the benefit of an obligation must also pay the corresponding burdens.

iii) Intervention of equity

- Burden of a restrictive covenant runs with the land in equity:

  Tulk v *Moxhay* (1848) 2 Ph 774 - originally based on NOTICE.

- Characteristics and enforceability of restrictive covenants

  - Must be negative in nature - substance NOT form

  - Must be dominant land retained by the covenantee: *Formby* v *Barker* [1903] 2 Ch 539

  - Successor to dominant land must prove benefit has passed to him

  Methods of acquiring benefit:

  - Annexation express or by statute - s78 LPA 1925 - *Federated Homes Ltd* v *Mill Lodge Properties Ltd* [1980] 1 All ER 371

  - Express assignment - *Roake* v *Chadha* [1983] 3 All ER 503

  - Scheme of development - building scheme - *Elliston* v *Reacher* [1908] 2 Ch 374

  The five requirements of a building scheme to create the 'local law' are:

  - Common vendor

  - Estate laid out in lots consistent with a scheme of development

  - Restrictions benefit all the lots

  - The parties purchased on that basis

  - The area must be clearly defined: *Reid* v *Bickerstaff* [1909] 2 Ch 305

iv) Enforceability

  Persons against whom restrictive covenant enforceable:

  - Before 1926 - doctrine of notice applies

  - After 1925 - unregistered land - land charge Class D(ii), ss2 and 4 LCA 1972. Registered land - minor interst - protect by NOTICE on the charges register - s50 LRA 1925

v) Discharge of restrictive covenants

  - In equity: *Chatsworth Estates Co* v *Fewell* [1931] 1 Ch 224. Covenants may be lost by showing that because of change in character of neighbourhood no value left in covenant or that this change has arisen by acts or omissions of covenantee which give rise to belief that covenants would no longer be enforced.

  - By statute:

    - LPA s84(1), (1A), (1B), (1C) - *Gilbert* v *Spoor* [1983] Ch 27 and *Re Martin's Application* (1989) 57 P & CR 119

    Lands Tribunal on four grounds:

    1) Obsolete

2) Obstructs reasonable use and no substantial benefit or contrary to public interest

3) Parties agree

4) No injury

Appeal from the Land Tribunal is to the Court of Appeal.

- LPA s84(2) - declaration by court whether or not land is affected by a covenant and its nature and extent - *J Sainsbury plc* v *Enfield London BC* [1989] 2 All ER 817

- Housing Act 1985 s610. County court may allow conversion to two or more tenements within one house.

- Town and Country Planning Act 1971 s127. Local planning authority only may carry out development contrary to an easement or restrictive covenant with compensation.

• Unity of seisin: - where a person becomes entitled to BOTH the dominant and servient land to which the covenant relates.

Re Tiltwood, Sussex, Barrett v *Bond* [1978] Ch 269

Texaco Antilles Ltd v *Kernochan* [1973] AC 609 - but not if in a building scheme.

• Insure against the risk of enforcement

vi) Relationship between restrictive covenants and the law of town and country planning - BOTH private and public codes must be satisfied - but planning permission may show that the covenant is no longer in the public interest for the purposes of an application to the Lands Tribunal under s84(1) LPA 1925: cf *Gilbert* v *Spoor* [1983] Ch 27. Otherwise the law of restrictive covenants is quite distinct from the law of town and country of planning - a person wishing to develop land must be able to do so under BOTH private and public branches of the law - a grant of planning permission does *not* itself entitle a person to breach a restrictive covenant. *Re Martin's Application* (1989) 57 P & CR 119.

7.3   Recent cases and statutes

Abbey Homesteads (Developments) Ltd v *Northamptonshire County Council* (1986) 278 EG 1249

City and Metropolitan Properties Ltd v *Greycroft* (1987) 283 EG 199

J Sainsbury plc v *Enfield London BC* [1989] 2 All ER 817

Re Martin's Application (1989) 57 P & CR 119

Rhone v *Stephens* (1993) The Times 21 January

The controversy over the decision in *Federated Homes Ltd* v *Mill Lodge Properties* [1980] 1 All ER 371 continues. It may be useful to appreciate the facts and decision in the following form:

FEDERATED HOMES LTD v *MILL LODGE PROPERTIES LTD* [1980] 1 All ER
371

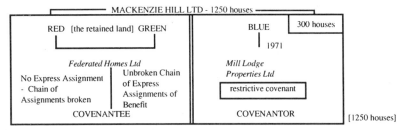

1970 - M Ltd - outline planning permission to develop whole site - set maximum
number

1971 - conveyance of blue land contained |restrictive covenant| 'not to build at a
greater density than a total of 300 dwellings' [so as not to reduce the number
of units which the vendor (M Ltd) might eventually build on the retained land
[red and green].

1977 - planning permission to F to develop red and green land. Defendants had also
obtained planning permission to develop blue land at higher density than
covenant. Action by F to restrain defendants from breaking the restrictive
covenant.

Question: Had benefit passed to F in respect of red land?

Court of Appeal held: If restrictive covenant touched and concerned
covenantee's land then s78(1) LPA 1925 annexed the benefit of the covenant
to that land. The restrictive covenant was for the benefit of the retained land
and that was sufficiently described in the 1971 conveyance for the purposes of
annexation.

Section 78(1) annexed the benefit to the retained land for the benefit of M Ltd
and their successors in title and persons deriving title under them. Thus
s78(1) caused the benefit to run with every part of the retained land including
the red land. F could enforce for both red and green land.

But will not apply if contrary intention is shown - by stipulation that benefit will only
pass by express assignment: *Roake v Chadha* [1983] 3 All ER 503.

7.4 Analysis of questions

The questions on restrictive covenants have changed in recent years. Formerly the
questions would be either on the creation or the discharge of restrictive covenants.
Now the law has changed since the decision of the Court of Appeal in *Federated Homes*
v *Mill Lodge Properties* [1980] 1 All ER 371 to the extent that it is not always easy
to set a question merely on restrictive covenants. As a consequence examiners have
been linking subjects and a typical question may now cover BOTH

restrictive covenants and easements. If a question does relate to covenants always establish the substance of the covenant as to whether it is positive or negative.

7.5 Questions

Question 1

Vincent was the registered proprietor of Blackacre, a house in extensive grounds, and of Whiteacre, an adjoining plot of land. In 1984 Vincent sold and transferred Whiteacre to Peter. Peter covenanted 'with Vincent' (i) to build and maintain a wall between the two properties, and (ii) not to build more than one house on Whiteacre. Vincent also granted to Peter an easement over a private road which ran across Blackacre, and Peter covenanted to pay one third of the cost of maintaining the road.

In 1986 Peter sold and transferred Whiteacre to Quentin.

In 1987 Vincent sold and transferred Blackacre to Walter.

Consider how far these covenants are now enforceable.

University of London LLB Examination
(for External Students) Land Law June 1985 Q6

General comment

An excellent and enjoyable question which gives the candidate every opportunity to marshal his material and present the answer in a logical manner. The element of registered land is a particularly interesting feature and could enable the better student to earn an additional mark or two. On the other hand no answer should contain references to land charges Class D(ii).

Skeleton solution

(See diagram in suggested solution.)

Covenant 1984 'with Vincent'

a) To build and maintain a wall between the two properties - positive benefit - yes common law - *The Prior's Case* (1368)

   Burden - no common law - *Austerberry* v *Oldham Corporation* (1885)

   ? Indemnity covenant

   Easement - *Crow* v *Wood* (1971)

b) Not to build more than one house on Whiteacre - negative

   Benefit - yes common law

   Burden - yes equity - *Tulk* v *Moxhay* (1848)

   Note: title registered

   Reconsider benefit in light of *Federated Homes Ltd* v *Mill Lodge Properties Ltd* (1980) and s78 LPA 1925

c) Easement over private road and covenant to pay one-third cost of maintaining the road

Benefit - yes common law

Burden - no BUT see benefit/burden rule in *Halsall v Brizell* (1957)

Suggested solution

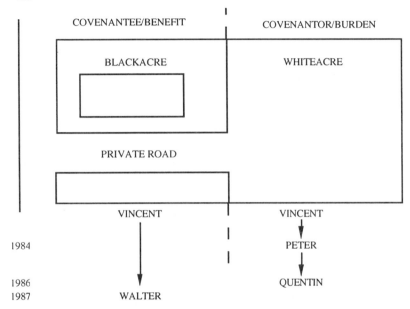

On the basis that Vincent was the registered proprietor of the freehold estate in Blackacre and that the covenants contained in the transfer of Whiteacre in 1984 to Peter would be entered in the register and be shown on the land certificate issued to Peter, there are at least two methods of answering the question, either by using the covenants as the base point and considering the effect on each of the respective events or dealing with the respective events as the base point showing how each covenant was affected by that transaction. Using the first method we shall look at the events as they affect each covenant in turn.

a) *To build and maintain a wall between the two properties*

This is a positive obligation and the benefit would pass to Walter in 1987 upon the sale of Blackacre. See *The Prior's Case* (1369), above.

The burden of a positive obligation does not run with the fee simple at common law:

Austerberry v Oldham Corporation (1885).

Thus the liability to build and maintain the wall would remain in Peter as a matter of contract following the sale of Whiteacre to Quentin in 1986. The onus would be

135

on Peter to avoid this liability and he should have inserted an indemnity in the transfer to Quentin by which Quentin would agree to indemnify Peter in the event of any breach. As this was a two-part covenant Quentin would only give the indemnity if Peter, in fact, had built the wall and had thereafter maintained the wall up until the date of the transfer in 1986. Another method of avoidance of the problem would have been to create an estate rentcharge as defined in s2 Rentcharges Act 1977 in order to pay for the upkeep of the wall once it had been built.

On the information available it would appear that Peter remains liable as the original covenantor. If it is not possible to recover from Peter the cost of maintaining the wall and Quentin denies liability as indicated above a further step open to Walter would be to examine the precise terminology of the covenant in the 1984 transfer to see if it could be construed as an easement rather than a covenant per se. If this were possible then Walter could rely upon the decision in *Crow v Wood* (1971), and, in particular, the words of Lord Denning MR when considering a question of the right to have a wall or fence maintained by an adjoining owner:

'It is not an easement strictly so called because it involves the servient owner in the expenditure of money. It was described by Gale as a "spurious kind of easement". But it has been treated in practice by the courts as being an easement ...

It seems to me that it is now sufficiently established - or at any rate, if not established hitherto, we should now declare - that a right to have your neighbour keep up the fences is a right in the nature of an easement which is capable of being granted by law so as to run with the land and to be binding on successors. It is a right which lies in grant.'

Thus the benefit will be in Walter but the burden (liability) will be in Peter unless one of the above 'methods of circumvention' can be used in order for the liability to fall upon the present owner of Whiteacre, Quentin.

b) *Not to build more than one house on Whiteacre*

The benefit of the covenant will, again, pass at common law provided the same essentials operate, ie:

   i)   the covenant touches and concerns the land;

  ii)   there is an intention that the benefit should run with Blackacre expressed at the date of the covenant. (In this transfer the covenant was 'with Vincent' so this condition may not be fulfilled. See later);

 iii)   Vincent, as the original covenantee, had the legal estate in Blackacre as the land to be benefited;

 iv)   Walter, as the assignee who now seeks to enforce the covenant must, at common law, have the same legal estate in the land as Vincent the original covenantee.

This final rule (iv) has been modified by s78(1) LPA 1925 which provides that:

'A covenant relating to any land of the covenantee shall be deemed to be made with the covenantee and his successors in title and the persons deriving title under him or them, and shall have effect as if such successors and other persons were expressed ...'

Thus Walter could enforce the covenant as a 'successor in title' to Vincent. The burden of a covenant does not run at common law but the burden of a negative or restrictive covenant may run in equity. This is the outcome of the decision in *Tulk* v *Moxhay* (1848). The rule emerges from the words of Lord Cottenham: 'It is said that, the covenant being one which does not run with the land, this court cannot enforce it: but the question is, not whether the covenant runs with the land, but whether a party shall be permitted to use the land in a manner inconsistent with the contract entered into by his vendor, and with notice of which he purchased.'

From this decision and these words of Lord Cottenham the following rules have emerged:

i) The covenant must be negative in nature. This is already the case as it is both expressed negatively and restricts the building to only one house.

ii) The covenantee must have at the time of the creation of the covenant and afterwards owned land for the protection of which the covenant is made. At the time of the transfer in 1984 Vincent owned the adjoining land, Blackacre, and it would be clearly advantageous to Blackacre if only one house were built on Whiteacre.

iii) The covenant must touch and concern the dominant land. This covenant will benefit Blackacre and fulfils the test suggested by Farwell J in *Rogers* v *Hosegood* (1900): '... the covenant must either affect the land as regards mode of occupation, or it must be such as per se, and not merely for collateral circumstances, affects the value of the land.'

This is a question of fact, but as indicated above, Blackacre must benefit from this restriction to one house on the adjoining land.

iv) It must be the common intention of the parties that the burden of the covenant shall run with the land of the covenantor. These covenants were made in 1984 and by s79 LPA 1925 are deemed to be made by Peter on behalf of himself, his successors in title and the persons deriving title under him or them, unless a contrary intention is expressed.

Before we can answer the question in full two further points must be considered. When Lord Cotterham expressed the original rule he based it, in part, on the question of notice. As Blackacre and Whiteacre are registered land the question of notice will play no part. On the other hand, the covenants must be shown as a liability in the charges register relating to Whiteacre: see s50(1) LRA 1925. It may also be that they will be shown as a benefit in the property register relating to Blackacre.

If the burden is to be seen to run then a corresponding rule requires that the benefit has passed with Blackacre. There are, essentially, three methods by which Walter can show he has the benefit. As the original covenant by Peter was 'with Vincent' only one of the three can concern this question but the three methods are:

- by assignment of the benefit;

- by creation of a scheme of development incorporating both properties.

Neither of these would apply here which leaves the third method that:

- the benefit of the covenant has been effectively annexed to the dominant land and that Walter has acquired the land seen to be benefited.

Formerly this rule was expressed in more precise terms and on the interpretation of earlier cases Walter would not have the benefit because he would be unable to show that the benefit was annexed to Blackacre in whole or in part, because it was merely stated to be 'with Vincent'. Any problems have, for the moment, been relieved by the decision of the Court of Appeal in *Federated Homes Ltd* v *Mill Lodge Properties Ltd* (1980).

In this case the Court of Appeal used s78 LPA 1925 to pass the benefit and Brightman LJ said:

'If the condition precedent of s78 is satisfied - that is to say, there exists a covenant which touches and concerns the land of the covenantee - that covenant runs with the land for the benefit of his successors in title, persons deriving title under him or them and other owners and occupiers.'

Cheshire makes the comment: 'This decision simplifies the rules as to the passing of the benefit of a restrictive covenant ... ' and Walter would appear to be a clear beneficiary of this decision. As a consequence, Walter will be able to prevent Quentin exceeding the limit of one house being built on Whiteacre.

c) *Easement over private road running across Blackacre with a covenant to pay one third of the cost of maintaining the road*

This is the method by which all easements should be created - as an express easement. In relation to the covenant to pay the one third of the cost of maintaining the road the same rules as to the passing of the benefit to Walter apply as in the previous parts (a) and (b).

This is a positive covenant to pay money so the burden will not run at common law or in equity under the rule in *Tulk* v *Moxhay* (1848). There is, however, a further rule which may be expressed as the benefit - burden rule by which any person who takes a benefit must pay any corresponding burden. This rule was confirmed in the decision of *Halsall* v *Brizell* (1957). Upjohn J expressed the rule in these words:

'The defendants here cannot if they desire to use this house, as they do, take advantage of the trusts concerning the user of the roads contained in the deed and the other benefits created by it without undertaking the obligations thereunder. Upon that principle, it seems to me that they are bound by this deed, if they desire to take its benefits.'

On this basis if Quentin uses the easement, as presumably he will, then he will have to pay the corresponding burden. This rule in *Halsall* v *Brizell* above has none of the earlier problems relating to the running of benefits and burdens. The simple question is: Do you use the facility? If the answer is 'yes', then the corresponding obligation to pay one third of the cost of maintaining the road must be met.

Tutorial comments

a) Consider the rules of both covenants and easements in preparation for questions of this nature.

b) Note the full consequences of *Federated Homes Ltd v Mill Lodge Properties Ltd* [1980] 1 All ER 371

c) Consider the place of restrictive covenants in registered land and compare the effect of ss2 and 4 LCA 1972 with s50(1) LRA 1925.

Question 2

Why do different principles govern the running of positive and restrictive covenants affecting freehold land? Are the differences justified?

University of London LLB Examination
(for External Students) Land Law June 1987 Q2

General comment

The candidate is given the opportunity to think in the terms of a Law Commissioner considering how to introduce a working paper or a report on the potential for reform in the law of covenants affecting freehold land. Those students who have taken the opportunity to read the Law Commission Report No 127 on the Transfer of Land: The Law of Positive and Restrictive Covenants will be at an advantage in attempting this question.

Skeleton solution

a) *WHY?* - Question of history.

Need to construe with care any obligation to spend money.

Equity introduced reforms but nature of equity jurisdiction ensured these reforms must be limited.

Consequence - different principles for the running of positive and restrictive covenants.

Briefly consider the respective rules:

i) positive - and methods of circumvention;

ii) restrictive - *Tulk* v *Moxhay* (1848).

b) *JUSTIFICATION?* - None.

Problems: they create eg Megarry and Wade

Solutions: land obligations to cover both forms of covenant.

Report of Law Commission No 127, Transfer of Land: The Law of Positive and Restrictive Covenants.

c) *CONCLUSION* - recommendations of Law Commission - in brief. See Part V for full details of the Land Obligation. The report also contains a draft Bill to implement the recommendations.

Suggested solution

The fact that different principles do apply for the running of positive and restrictive covenants affecting freehold land is a question of history. In the case of covenants generally, both positive and negative, the benefit of a covenant will run. Cheshire states: 'The rule at law for several centuries has been that the BENEFIT of covenants, whether positive or negative, which are made with a covenantee, having an interest in the land to which they relate, passes to his successors in title: *The Prior's Case* (1368) YB 42 Ed 3 Hil, pl 14.'

This benefit will pass on four conditions being satisfied:

a) the covenant touches and concerns the land of the covenantee;

b) there is an intention that the benefit should run with the land then owned by the covenantee;

c) the covenantee, at that time, has the legal estate in the land to be benefited;

d) the assignee seeking to enforce the covenant has that same legal estate in the land. This rule has now been extended by s78 LPA 1925 in that for covenants made after 1925 it is sufficient to show that the person seeking to enforce the covenant is a 'successor in title' of the covenantee.

On the other hand, when the question relates to the burden of covenants it is clear that the burden of a positive covenant does not run at common law: *Austerberry* v *Oldham Corporation* (1885). The reasoning in this case is not entirely satisfactory, but the statement of the law by Lindley LJ is quite clear:

'... in the absence of authority it appears to me that we shall be perfectly warranted in saying that the burden of this covenant does not run with the land ... If the parties had intended to charge this land for ever, into whosesoever hands it came, with the burden of repairing the road, there are ways and means known to conveyancers by which it could be done with comparative ease: all that would have been necessary would have been to create a rentcharge and charge it on the tolls, and the thing would have been done. They have not done anything of the sort, and, therefore, it seems to me to show that they did not intend to have a covenant which should run with the land. That disposes of the part of the case which is perhaps the most difficult.'

During that statement Lindley LJ did point to one of the methods of circumvention of the rule which have become necessary - to use a rentcharge rather than a covenant, and this method remains available today by way of the estate rentcharge under s2 of the Rentcharges Act 1977. Other methods of enforcing the burden of positive obligations which have been suggested or have succeeded include:

a) using a lease rather than a conveyance of the fee simple;

b) chains of indemnity covenants;

c) use of positive easements rather than covenants - *Crow* v *Wood* (1971);

d) imposing covenants in a long lease then converting this long lease into the freehold under s153 LPA 1925;

e) the so-called benefit/burden rule established in *Halsall* v *Brizell* (1957), which obliges a person who wishes to take advantage of a facility such as roads or drainage to observe any corresponding obligation to contribute to the cost of providing or maintaining it.

Throughout these exceptions the problems of enforcing positive obligations appear to hinge on the financial issue of supervision where the spending of money is concerned. The law takes great care where the consequence of a direction will require the spending of money. No such problem arises in the case of negative or restrictive covenants. As a result, the burden of a restrictive covenant will run in equity based on the principle established in *Tulk* v *Moxhay* (1848). In order for the burden of the restrictive covenant to run the following conditions must be satisfied:

a) the covenant is negative in substance;

b) the covenantee must continue to own land capable of being protected by the covenant;

c) the covenant must touch and concern the dominant land; and

d) it must be the common intention of the parties that the burden of the covenant shall run with the land of the covenantor.

Thus the different rules depend on the nature of the covenant and appear to arise out of the attitude adopted by the courts as to their ability to supervise negative obligations and the difficulties that arise in enforcing and supervising positive obligations.

Are the differences justified? The fact that they exist indicates there must be justification in the eyes of the court. The question today is whether the continuation of the differences can be justified. There is no doubt that this distinction does create problems. This is neatly summarised by Megarry and Wade:

'(e) POSITIVE COVENANTS. It has been recommended that the law should provide for the running of positive as well as negative covenants. Apart from limited statutory exceptions, there is at present no satisfactory way of imposing positive obligations (eg to repair walls and fences) so as to bind successors in title where the property is freehold. There is no such difficulty with leasehold property, but the declining popularity of leasehold tenure makes the leasehold system less useful. This handicap on freehold property is illogical. It is particularly troublesome in the case of divided buildings, blocks of flats and building estates, where there is a need for permanent obligations to maintain the property and to contribute to the maintenance of common facilities and services, and where in the absence of binding covenants owners may be unable to obtain mortgages. Schemes for allowing such obligations to run with land have therefore been proposed ... Other countries have made statutory provision for this, including elaborate schemes of management which can be adopted for blocks of flats and similar developments. This is known in North America as the law of condominiums, and in Australasia as that of strata titles.'

Thus the short answer to the question as posed is, no! The differences are no longer justified.

In January 1984 the Law Commission published report No 127 - Transfer of Land: The Law of Positive and Restrictive Covenants. The report gives a comprehensive review of the present law and provides suggested solutions to the problems posed in this question. The report states at paragraph 4.16: '... there can be no doubt that the law of POSITIVE covenants is in urgent need of radical reform, and we are committed to a project designed to achieve this. The real question, therefore, is whether the law of restrictive covenants can stay as it is in the context of that project.' In the following paragraph 4.17 the Law Commission identify the real difficulty of reform in this area of Land Law. It is not enough merely to bring both covenants into line by using the present rules for restrictive covenants for the enforcement of positive covenants. They say:

'The real objection is that the existing law of restrictive covenants is not suitable for positive covenants in any case. Two of the main reasons for this are as follows:

a) ... a restrictive covenant requires people merely to refrain from doing something. But positive covenants require them actually to do something, and that something may be a burdensome and expensive thing ... Liability to perform a positive covenant ... cannot rest on all those interested in the burdened land.

b) The burden of a restrictive covenant runs only in equity, so that equitable remedies alone are available for its enforcement. This may not greatly matter in the case of a restrictive covenant because ... the remedy most often sought will be the equitable remedy of injunction, or damages in lieu. But legal remedies must be available for positive covenants. The idea of enforcing a simple covenant to pay money by means of equitable remedies is wholly artificial. And the normal remedy for breach of a covenant to carry out works must be legal damages (including, if appropriate, damages for consequential loss). This point goes to the heart of the conceptual nature of the covenant: legal remedies cannot be available unless the burden runs at law and it cannot do that unless it amounts to a legal - not an equitable - interest in land. The law for restrictive covenants is therefore fundamentally unsuitable ...'

The Law Commission concluded at paragraph 4.18:

'We hope that we have said enough to show that the law of restrictive covenants could not be retained and simply expanded so as to embrace positive covenants. Positive covenants demand a legal regime which is different in fundamental respects.'

'This requires a totally new "legal regime" and this is, in the opinion of the Law Commission, provided by the Land Obligation. This would be achieved by extending the process of law reform to include both positive and restrictive covenants and welding the two into a system which is both unified and more satisfactory': paragraph 4.20.

The Land Obligation would be a new interest in land 'whereby in appropriate circumstances obligations (whether positive or negative) may be imposed on one piece of land for the benefit of other land, and be enforceable by or on behalf of the owners for the time being of the one piece of land against the owners for the time being of the other': paragraph 4.21.

The new interest would be more like the easement and similar rules to easements would apply. Basically the new Land Obligation would be registerable, there would be limits on the persons who are liable for breach of the obligation, remedies should be made appropriate to the nature of the obligation and the provisions of s84 LPA 1925 should apply to enable the Land Obligations to be modified or discharged.

The Land Obligation is seen as a multi-faceted form of obligation suitable to all forms of land development. The major objective, however, is to do away with the problems raised in this question and provide '... for the first time, a means whereby the burden of positive covenants may be made to run with the servient land under English law.

Part V of the Law Commission Report No 127 explains the Land Obligation in detail and the report contains the draft of a proposed Bill to implement the recommendations of the Law Commission.

Tutorial comments

a) Be aware of the proposals of the Law Commission on the reform of the rules relating to both covenants and easements.

b) Consider the extent of the proposed 'Land Obligation'.

Question 3

Alan owned Blackacre and the adjoining Whiteacre, and in 1960 he sold Blackacre to Douglas who covenanted with Alan and his successors-in-title a) not to let the property fall into disrepair and b) not to use the property for business purposes.

On the assumption that the land is unregistered, consider how far these covenants will be enforceable

a) by a lessee of Whiteacre against Douglas;

b) by Alan against an adverse possessor of Blackacre; and

c) by a purchaser of Whiteacre against a purchaser of Blackacre.

University of London LLB Examination
(for External Students) Land Law June 1992 Q7

General comment

Not a difficult question for the candidate who is well-prepared. An understanding of how covenants affect successors-in-title other than purchasers is essential. The principles of registration must also be considered.

Skeleton solution

- Definition of restrictive covenant.
- Running of benefit to covenantee's successor - common law rules - *Smith and Snipes Hall Farm* v *River Douglas Catchment Board* (1949) - s78 LPA 1925.
- Limitation Act 1980.
- *Re Nisbet & Potts' Contract* (1905) - annexation - *Mill Lodge Properties Ltd* (1980).
- Running of benefit to covenantee's successor in equity - annexation - assignment - building scheme.
- Running of burden to covenantor's successor - *Tulk* v *Moxhay* (1848).
- Registration.
- Section 84 LPA 1925.

Suggested solution

A restrictive covenant is an agreement under seal whereby one party (the covenantor) agrees with another party (the covenantee) that he (the covenantor) will, or will not, do certain acts in relation to a defined area of land. The land owned by the covenantee will have the benefit of the covenant and that owned by the covenantor will have the burden. On the facts Alan, who owns Whiteacre, is the covenantee and Douglas, who owns Blackacre, is the covenantor.

Covenant (a) is a positive covenant because it requires the covenantor, or his successors, to maintain and repair Blackacre. Covenant (b) is negative in that it simply prohibits the use of Blackacre for business purposes.

a) *Lessee of Whiteacre*

A lessee of Whiteacre would be a successor-in-title to the original covenantee (Alan). In order to be able to enforce the covenants against Douglas (the original covenantor) the lessee must have obtained the benefit of the covenants. This he can do under the common law rules governing the running of the benefit. At common law four conditions have to be complied with in order for the benefit to run. Firstly, the covenants must 'touch and concern' the land. In *Smith and Snipes Hall Farm* v *River Douglas Catchment Board* (1949) this was said to be satisfied if the covenants affected mode of occupation, or directly affected the value of land. Covenant (b) clearly affects mode of occupation and (a) affects value. Secondly, the original covenantee must have had a legal estate in land. In this case Alan did have a legal estate in Whiteacre, presumably in the nature of fee simple.

Thirdly, the successor to the covenantee must have a legal estate in land, although not necessarily the same legal estate. This is also satisfied because the lessee would have a legal term of years in the land. In any event this requirement has been abrogated by s78 Law of Property Act (LPA) 1925 which states that a covenant relating to land of the covenantee shall be deemed to be made with the covenantee *and his successors-in-title and the persons deriving title under him or them*, and so extends to a lessee of the covenantee. Fourthly, there must be an intention that the covenants should run with the land. This too is covered by s78 which provides that such an intention is deemed to be present and does not admit of a contrary intention.

If the conditions are satisfied the benefit of both the positive covenant (a) and the negative one (b), will have run to the lessee enabling him to enforce them against Douglas.

It should be noted that it is not necessary to show that the burden of the covenants has run to Douglas as he is the original covenantor. Neither is it necessary to deal with registration because that would only be relevant when dealing with a purchaser of the burdened land (Blackacre).

b) *Adverse possessor of Blackacre*

An adverse possessor of Blackacre will have obtained Blackacre under the Limitation Act 1980, by showing 12 years' possession adverse to the paper owner (Douglas). In running up that time the adverse possessor must show factual possession and the intention to possess.

As the adverse possessor is not a purchaser of the servient land (Blackacre) he will be bound by any covenants which are annexed to the land: *Re Nisbet & Potts' Contract* (1905). This applies to both positive and negative covenants whether they are registered as D(ii) land charges or not. The covenants could be shown to be annexed in two ways, firstly, by way of express annexation and, secondly, by virtue of s78.

Express annexation will occur if certain conditions are satisfied. It must be possible to identify the land to be benefited from the wording of the covenants. In *Rogers* v *Hosegood* [1900] 2 Ch 388 the covenant was deemed to be annexed as it referred to the dominant land; however, in *Renals* v *Cowlishaw* (1878) the covenant was not annexed because it referred solely to 'heirs, executors, administrators and assigns'. It is not clear from the limited facts whether the dominant land is capable of being identified from the covenants themselves. Where the dominant land is sold off in plots it is also necessary to show that the covenants were annexed to each and every part of the estate rather than to the estate as a whole: *Re Selwyn's Conveyance* (1967). This is not the case here. It would also appear from *Re Ballard's Conveyance* (1937), that annexation can only occur where substantially the whole of the dominant land is capable of benefitting. There is nothing to suggest that Whiteacre is so large as to prevent this happening.

Alternatively, s78 LPA could operate to annex the covenants to the land. In *Federated Homes* v *Mill Lodge Properties Ltd* (1980) the court held that a covenant could be annexed to land by virtue of the section where the dominant land was identifiable and the covenants touched and concerned the land as per *Smith and Snipes*.

Consequently, provided there is effective annexation, Alan, the original covenantee, can enforce both covenants against the adverse possessor of Blackacre.

c) *A purchaser of Whiteacre and a purchaser of Blackacre*

In order for a purchaser of Whiteacre from Alan to enforce the covenants against a purchaser of Blackacre from Douglas, it must be shown that the benefit of the covenants has run to the former and the burden to the latter.

The purchaser of Whiteacre will be a successor-in-title to the covenantee, and the benefit of the covenants could run to him at common law or equity. The running of the benefit at common law has been dealt with in part a) above. This is not likely to be a successful way of enforcing the covenant as, with very limited exceptions (eg chain of indemnity covenants, long leases), the burden of covenants does not run at common law.

Consequently, it will be better for the purchaser to show that benefit and burden have run in equity. The benefit of the covenants can run in equity in four different ways, namely, annexation, assignment, building scheme and under s78 LPA 1925.

Annexation and s78 have already been dealt with under part b) above. Assignment is the process of transferring the benefit of the covenant to the covenantee's successor. In order for this to be achieved it has to be shown that the dominant land (Whiteacre) can be identified, directly or indirectly, in the assignment (see *Newton Abbot Co-operative Society* v *Williamson & Treadgold* (1952)), secondly, that the assignment was contemporaneous with transfer or conveyance, and thirdly, that there was a clear intention to assign.

A building scheme or scheme of development is governed by the rules laid down in *Elliston* v *Reacher* (1908), as amended: see *Re Dolphin's Conveyance* (1970) and *Baxter* v *Four Oaks Properties Ltd* (1965). Those rules require an intention on the part of the vendor to set up a building scheme in relation to a defined area of land. As long as that intention is manifest, the purchasers buy subject to the scheme of covenants which crystallises upon the first purchase. Under the scheme each purchaser can enforce, and have enforced against him, the negative covenants which make up the scheme.

Provided one of the four methods discussed above can be satisfied, the benefit of the covenants will have run to the purchaser of Whiteacre in equity.

The running of the burden of the covenants to the purchaser of Blackacre in equity is governed by the rule in *Tulk* v *Moxhay* (1848). Under *Tulk* four conditions have to be satisfied. Firstly, the covenants must touch and concern the land as per *Smith and Snipes* (discussed above). Secondly, the covenants must be negative in substance. Equity will not enforce positive covenants against a successor-in-title to the covenantor. The test to determine whether a covenant is negative is the 'hand in pocket test': *Haywood* v *Brunswick Permanent Benefit Building Society* (1881). If the covenant requires the covenantor to expend money it is positive and cannot be enforced against a successor-in-title. On the facts covenant (a) is positive and cannot be enforced against the purchaser of Blackacre from Douglas.

Thirdly, at the time the covenant was made the original covenantee must have retained land capable of benefitting from it. On the facts when the covenant was made in 1960 Alan, the original covenantee, retained land capable of benefitting (Whiteacre). Fourthly, there must have been an intention that the burden should run. This is provided for by s79 LPA 1925; in the absence of contrary intention the covenantor is deemed to covenant on behalf of himself and successors.

If these four factors are present the burden of covenant (b) will have run to the purchaser of Blackacre in equity. However, it is not enough to show that benefit and burden have run in equity - in order to be enforceable against the purchaser of Blackacre it must be shown that covenant (b) was properly protected by the registration of a D(ii) land charge by Alan (the original covenantee), against the name of Douglas (the original covenantor). If it was, the purchaser of Blackacre will be bound by it; if not, he will take free of it: see *Midland Bank Trust Co* v *Green (No 2)* (1981).

Even if benefit and burden have run in equity and covenant (b) was registered as a D(ii) charge, the purchaser of Blackacre may be able to rely on s84 LPA 1925 to modify or discharge the covenant. This can be done if he can show one of the following grounds: that the covenant is obsolete due to changes in the character of the neighbourhood, that it impedes the reasonable development of land, that it could be discharged without adversely affecting the covenantee or his successors, or there is agreement to do so.

8 EASEMENTS AND PROFITS À PRENDRE

8.1   Introduction

8.2   Key points

8.3   Recent cases and statutes

8.4   Analysis of questions

8.5   Questions

8.1   Introduction

Although they are often seen in the context of easements the specific rules relating to profits à prendre should not be overlooked and it is important to know where the rules differ as to these respective rights in alieno solo. The easement is said to be a privilege without a profit because it allows either the use of another person's land or controls the use of that land by the owner, but in neither case does it allow the taking of anything from that land. On the other hand the profit à prendre is a clear right to take something from the land of another person.

The flow chart on the opposite page illustrates the approach to be adopted once it has been established that the problem relates to a potential easement.

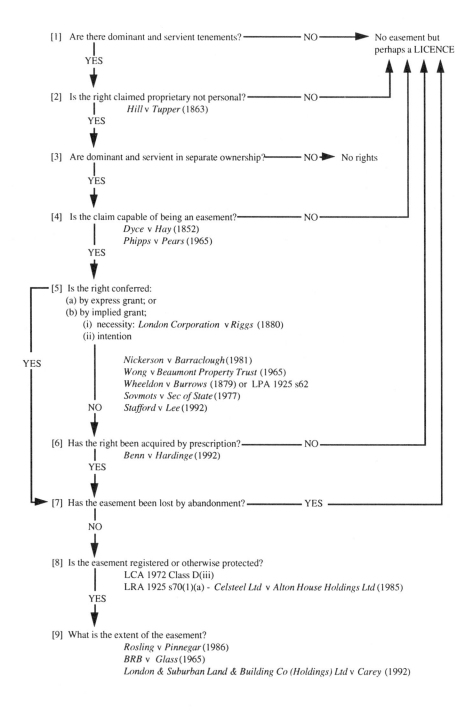

[1] Are there dominant and servient tenements? ——— NO ——▶ No easement but perhaps a LICENCE

YES

[2] Is the right claimed proprietary not personal? ——— NO
         Hill v *Tupper* (1863)

YES

[3] Are dominant and servient in separate ownership? ——— NO ▶ No rights

YES

[4] Is the claim capable of being an easement? ——— NO
         Dyce v *Hay* (1852)
         Phipps v *Pears* (1965)

YES

[5] Is the right conferred:
(a) by express grant; or
(b) by implied grant;
    (i) necessity: *London Corporation* v *Riggs* (1880)
    (ii) intention

YES

         Nickerson v *Barraclough* (1981)
         Wong v *Beaumont Property Trust* (1965)
         Wheeldon v *Burrows* (1879) or LPA 1925 s62
         Sovmots v *Sec of State* (1977)
NO   *Stafford* v *Lee* (1992)

[6] Has the right been acquired by prescription? ——— NO
         Benn v *Hardinge* (1992)

YES

[7] Has the easement been lost by abandonment? ——— YES

NO

[8] Is the easement registered or otherwise protected?
         LCA 1972 Class D(iii)
         LRA 1925 s70(1)(a) - *Celsteel Ltd* v *Alton House Holdings Ltd* (1985)

YES

[9] What is the extent of the easement?
         Rosling v *Pinnegar* (1986)
         BRB v *Glass* (1965)
         London & Suburban Land & Building Co (Holdings) Ltd v *Carey* (1992)

8.2 Key points

a) *Easements* - if legal is a legal interest - s1(2)(a) LPA 1925 - requires a deed or prescription to permanently bind the servient land.

   i) Essentials of an easement: *Re Ellenborough Park* [1956] Ch 131

- There must be a dominant and servient tenement

- Easement must accommodate dominant tenement: cf *Hill* v *Tupper* (1863) 2 H & C 121

- Dominant and servient owners must be different persons: cf quasi-easements

- Easement must be capable of forming subject matter of a grant. New types of easement may be created: *Crow* v *Wood* [1971] 1 QB 77 see also *Dyce* v *Lady Hay* (1852) 1 Macq 305 - the category of servitudes and easements must alter and expand with the changes that take place in the circumstances of mankind.

   ii) Easements distinguished from other rights

- Examples of easements - way, light, problems of storage - *Copeland* v *Greenhalf* [1952] Ch 488 and *Grigsby* v *Melville* [1974] 1 WLR 80 but see *Wright* v *Macadam* [1949] 2 KB 744.

- Compare easements with:

   - Licences - cannot exist as a legal interest - more flexible, revoke unilaterally

   - Quasi-easements - rights over own land

   - Other natural rights eg support of land

   - Restrictive covenants - wider eg right to view - but only BURDEN runs and must be NEGATIVE.

   - Customary rights - exercised by everyone within the custom.

   iii) Creation of easements

- Statute - Private Local Acts

- Express grant - deed

- Implied grant - easements of necessity (*Nickerson* v *Barraclough* [1981] Ch 426) and intended easements - *Wong* v *Beaumont Property Trust* [1965] 1 QB 173; *Stafford* v *Lee* (1992) The Times 16 November

   - Sale of quasi-servient tenement - must not derogate from grant - minimum implied by way of necessity or intended easement

   - Sale of quasi-dominant tenement: *Wheeldon* v *Burrows* (1879) 12 Ch D 31 - those easements which are continuous and apparent or necessary to reasonable user of property and in use at the time of the conveyance.

The facts of *Wheeldon* v *Burrows* (1879) may be demonstrated by this diagram:

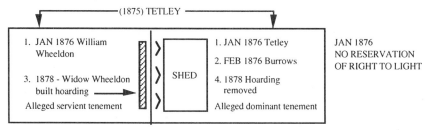

JAN 1876: sale of alleged servient tenement to William Wheeldon.

FEB 1876: sale of alleged dominant tenement to Burrows.

1878: widow Wheeldon erected hoarding to exclude light to shed.

Burrows knocked this down - successful action by widow in trespass because no right of access of light to shed windows had been reserved by Tetley in Jan 1876.

Thesiger LJ: '... Two propositions may be stated as ... the general rules. The first is that on the grant by the owner of a tenement of part of that tenement as it is then used and enjoyed there will pass to the grantee all those continuous and apparent easements (by which I mean quasi-easements) or [in other words] all those easements which are necessary to the reasonable enjoyment of the property granted, and which have been and are at the time of the grant used by the owners of the entirety for the benefit of the part granted. The second proposition is that, if the grantor intends to reserve any right over the tenement granted, it is his duty to reserve it expressly in the grant.' [Then mentioned the exception of 'cases of what are called ways of necessity'.] Thesiger LJ concluded: '... In the case of a grant you may imply a grant of such continuous and apparent easements or such easements as are necessary to the reasonable enjoyment of the property conveyed, and have in fact been enjoyed during the unity of ownership, but that, with the exception ... of easements of necessity you cannot imply a similar reservation in favour of the grantor of the land.' Quoted in Cheshire - underlined above.

- S62 LPA 1925 - must be a 'conveyance' - will pass all easements, rights and privileges.

- Presumed grant - prescription - long usage based on presumption that grant by deed was made at some time. Requirements for prescriptions at common law are:

  - Enjoyed as of right - *NEC VI, NEC CLAM, NEC PRECARIO.*

  - Continuous - enjoyed as and when required.

  - Used by a fee simple owner against a fee simple owner.

  - Must lie in grant.

  - Common law prescription - 1189.

  - Lost modern grant -*Tehidy Minerals Ltd* v *Norman* [1971] 2 QB 528.

  - Prescription Act 1832 ss1-4. The effect of the 1832 Act is that if a right has been enjoyed for a certain period of time before the action is brought the claim to the right shall NOT be defeated merely by proving the enjoyment began since 1189.

  - Easements other than light - s2

  - Profits - s1

  - Easement of light - s3

    Colls v *Home and Colonial Stores Ltd* [1904] AC 179
    Allen v *Greenwood* [1979] 2 WLR 187
    Carr-Saunders v *Dick McNeil Associates Ltd* [1986] 1 WLR 922

  - Note 'interruption': s4. Interruption to have effect must be submitted to or acquiesced in for one year after the party interrupted shall have notice thereof (and of the person making or authorising the same to be made).

    Flight v *Thomas* (1840) 11 Ad & E 688
    Reilly v *Orange* [1955] 2 QB 112
    Davies v *Du Paver* [1953] 1 QB 184

iv) Extinguishment of easements

- Release - deed

  - Express

  - Implied: *Moore* v *Rawson* (1824) 3 B & C 332 - unilateral act by dominant owner - 17 years non-user was evidence of intention to give up permanently.

- Unity of seisin

  Must have the fee simple in BOTH properties - if only a leasehold interest the easement is suspended.

v) Alterations to the respective tenements

- Alteration to the servient tenement - must NOT deprive of access as in *Celsteel Ltd* v *Alton House Holdings Ltd* [1985] 1 WLR 204

- Alteration to dominant tenement - may NOT destroy the easement by enlarging the dominant tenement from a flat to the whole house: *Graham* v *Philcox* [1984] 3 WLR 150. Remedy - INJUNCTION - as to the terms of the injunction see *Rosling* v *Pinnegar* (1987) 54 P & CR 124.

vi) Extent of easement

- RIGHT OF WAY

  (A) EXPRESS - matter of construction against grantor. Normally only a means of access to dominant tenement - common form: 'At all times and for all purposes' - and not confined to purpose for which land is used at time of grant. House to hotel - easement allowed in *White* v *Grand Hotel Eastbourne Ltd* [1913] 1 Ch 113: see *Rosling* v *Pinnegar* above, *Jelbert* v *Davis* [1968] 1 All ER 1182 and *National Trust* v *White* [1987] 1 WLR 907; *London & Suburban Land & Building Co (Holdings) Ltd* v *Carey* (1993) 62 P & CR 481.

  (B) IMPLIED - necessity. Limited to necessity at time right arose (*London Corporation* v *Riggs* (1880) 13 Ch D 798). Other cases - right measured by extent of enjoyment overall: if no major change in dominant tenement user is not limited by reference to numbers and a right of way to a little used caravan site may still be used when site holds more caravans (*British Railways Board* v *Glass* [1965] Ch 538), or a right of way for business purposes may expand as the business expands: *Woodhouse & Co Ltd* v *Kirkland (Derby) Ltd* [1970] 1 WLR 1185. If the character of the user remains constant - there is no objection to an increase in its intensity even if the dominant tenement is enlarged from a flat to the user for the whole house: *Graham* v *Philcox* [1984] 3 WLR 150. *British Railways Board* v *Glass* (1965) above, Harman LJ: 'A right to use a way for this purpose or that has never been ... limited to a right to use the way so many times a day or for such a number of vehicles so long as the dominant tenement does not change its identity.'

- RIGHT OF LIGHT - amount of light. Megarry & Wade:

  'The right ... to have access of light for all ordinary purposes to which the room may be put.' The ordinary purposes for which the premises might reasonably be expected to be used: *Carr-Saunders* v *Dick McNeil Associates Ltd* [1986] 1 WLR 922.

- RIGHTS OF WATER - includes right to take water from a river or pond and may draw extra water if for same purpose: *Cargill* v *Gotts* [1981] 1

All ER 682. Metered supply of water paid for by servient owner no easement: *Rance* v *Elvin* (1985) The Times 27 February.

- RIGHT OF SUPPORT - may extend to providing buttresses and even weather proofing a party wall (*Bradburn v Lindsay* [1983] 2 All ER 408), but general rule is that an easement should not involve expenditure: *Phipps v Pears* [1965] 1 QB 76; cf *Crow v Wood* [1971] 1 QB 77.

b) *Profits à prendre*

   i) Nature - may exist in gross.

   Distinguish from easements - different prescriptive periods under the Prescription Act 1832. Owner of the profit does have possessory rights over the land.

  ii) Classification

- As to ownership:
    - Several - enjoyed by one person
    - Profits in common - enjoyed along with others
- In relation to land:
    - Profit appurtenant - annexed to nearby dominant land
    - Profit appendant - annexed to land by operation of law
    - Profit pur cause de vicinage - two adjacent commons
    - Profit in gross - may be enjoyed severally or in common but no land owned
- By subject matter:
    - Pasture - 2(i)-2(iv) above. See Commons Registration Act 1965.
    - Turbary - to cut peat or turf for fuel
    - Estovers - to cut wood for fuel or repairs
    - Piscary - to take fish
    - Profit in the soil - to take gravel.

 iii) Acquisition and extinguishment - 30 or 60 years under s1 of the Prescription Act 1832.

 iv) Public rights similar to profits

- Public rights - eg to fish in sea or tidal waters - enjoyed by all members of the public.
- Rights of fluctuating bodies of persons - at common law not a legal person to whom a grant could be made. The common law rules could be avoided by showing long enjoyment AND right derives from the Crown

AND the beneficiaries act like a corporation: *Goodman* v *Mayor of Saltash* (1882) 7 App Cas 633.

- Presumed charter of incorporation
- Presumed charitable trust

8.3   Recent cases and statutes

Graham v *Philcox* [1984] 3 WLR 150

Rosling v *Pinnegar* (1987) 54 P & CR 124

Bridle v *Ruby*, below

Mills v *Silver* [1991] Ch 271

Benn v *Hardinge* (1992) The Times 13 October

Bridle v *Ruby* [1988] 3 All ER 64

Facts

Having erected the houses, the estate developers transferred the freehold of two adjoining properties to the predecessors in title of the plaintiff and the defendants. As originally drafted, the transfer of the plaintiff's house reserved to its owner a right of way over the defendants' driveway, but this reservation was deleted on execution of the transfer. However, the plaintiff and his predecessors in title used the defendants' driveway for 22 years in the mistaken belief that a right of way had been granted to them. Following a dispute, the plaintiff sought to establish his right of way.

Held

He was entitled to succeed as his mistaken belief about the legal origin of the alleged right of way did not prevent the user being as of right.

Parker LJ:

'It is not necessary to set out the detailed history of the user of an alleged right over the driveway... by Mr Bridle and his predecessors for it is accepted by the defendants that, unless such user cannot, by reason of mistake, avail Mr Bridle, he and his predecessors have established 22 years' user as of right and are entitled to succeed on the basis of the doctrine of lost modern grant, such being a judge-made fiction devised to cure the injustice caused by the difficulties of establishing a right by prescription at common law and, later, by prescription under the Prescription Act 1832.

I turn now to the contention that a lost modern grant will only be presumed where the state of affairs is otherwise unexplained. This proposition I accept. It is amply supported by authority: see eg *Gardner* v *Hodgson's Kingston Brewery Co Ltd* [1903] AC 229 at 239 and *Alfred F Beckett Ltd* v *Lyons* [1967] 1 All ER 833 at 845. The question, however, is whether a mistaken belief amounts to an alternative explanation within the meaning of the proposition. In my view it does not. What is contemplated by the proposition are such things as permission from time to time, neighbourly tolerance and the like. Another example lies in the *Kingston Brewery* case, where 15 shillings per year was paid. The alternatives were that the money was by way of a rent charge on the grant of a permanent way or successive payments for yearly licences. The latter, which would negative prescription, could not be excluded.

In the present case the origin of the user was when (Mrs Harvey's predecessor in title) put in his garage and began to use the driveway. The alternative to a grant might have been neighbourly tolerance or permission from time to time, but these are not relied on by the defendants and, even if they were, they would not in my view have prevailed, for the judge was clearly entitled on the evidence to reject these possibilities. It may be that others, including myself, might not have done so, but when the whole matter started with the building and use of a garage it was clearly open to the judge to conclude that the user was, in its origin, consistent only with a permanent permission and that thereafter nothing changed. As Lord Lindley said in the *Gardner* v *Hodgson's Kingston Brewery* case [1903] AC 229 at 239:

"A temporary permission, although often renewed, would prevent an enjoyment being 'as of right'; but a permanent, irrevocable permission attributable to a lost grant would not have the same effect."

There is no trace here of a temporary permission or a series of permissions.'

8.4 Analysis of questions

Most easement answers can begin with setting out the four essentials as confirmed in *Re Ellenborough Park* [1956] Ch 131. Thereafter the questions divide into either those relating to implied easements or those with a prescription element. Consider also the content of the easements in all aspects. Never forget profits à prendre are included in this chapter.

8.5 Questions

Question 1

a) 'For a claim by prescription (to an easement) it is not enough to show long user by itself; there must have been continuous user "as of right" before the court will go so far as to presume a grant, and even then the court will not presume a grant except in fee simple.' (Megarry and Wade, *The Law of Real Property*).

Explain and illustrate this statement.

b) For nineteen and a half years Alf has used a path across Bert's land as a short cut to the railway station. Last December Bert put up a fence to stop Alf, and has told Alf that he is hoping to sell his land to Jerry, a builder, who wishes to build a block of flats.

Advise Alf.

University of London LLB Examination
(for External Students) Land Law June 1985 Q8

General comment

It is always useful to show where there is a link between the two parts of the question. In this case the first part should provide the necessary introduction for the detailed requirements of part (b). The answer to part (b) would benefit from some form of diagram to show how the facts interact with the requirements of ss2 and 4 of the Prescription Act 1832.

Skeleton solution

a) *Meaning of 'prescription' - three methods of prescribing*:

    i)   common law - time immemorial 1189;

    ii)   lost modern grant;

    iii) Prescription Act 1832.

          Conclude - must show he has been in actual enjoyment of the right for a sufficient length of time - then essentials of an easement: *Re Ellenborough Park* (1956).

          Quotation

          •   continuous;

          •   as of right - nec vi - nec clam - nec precario;

          •   in fee simple.

b) *Main query - Does Alf own any land?*

    Consider four essentials in detail - *Re Ellenborough Park* above:

    i)   must be a dominant and servient tenement;

    ii)   easement must accommodate the dominant tenement;

    iii) dominant and servient owners must be different persons;

    iv) must be capable of forming the subject matter of a grant.

(See diagram in Suggested solution.)

s2 Prescription Act 1832 - Right of way 20 years

s4 Prescription Act 1832 - next before action brought and without interruption - must be submitted to or acquiesced in for ONE YEAR - there must be a full 20 year's user: *Reilly* v *Orange* (1955).

Crucial period for Alf is June to December when he has over 20 years' user and less than one year's interruption - the window of time is in his favour.

Any 'interruption' must be submitted to or acquiesced in: *Davies v Du Paver* (1953). If Alf does not own land which can benefit, he has a mere personal right - a licence - which can be terminated on reasonable notice: *Hill* v *Tupper* (1863).

Suggested solution

a) It is interesting to note that the quotation continues in these words: 'These fundamental conditions must first be discussed before considering the three methods of prescription ... '

For the purposes of this answer it may be better to define prescription and consider the 'three methods' mentioned above before considering the 'fundamental condition' set out in the question.

Prescription merely means long usage, but this is not sufficient in the case of easements and one early authority expanded the meaning of these words:

'Every species of prescription, by which property is acquired or lost, is founded on the presumption that he who has had a quiet and uninterrupted possession of anything for a long period of years, is supposed to have a just right, without which he would not have been suffered to continue in the enjoyment of it.'

The long usage is the pre-requisite out of which the courts will uphold the right, if possible, by presuming it had a lawful origin.

The original common law method of prescription required proof of enjoyment since time immemorial, 1189. This is rarely possible and enjoyment for some 20 years will raise the presumption of use since 1189. This method is, however, vulnerable to proof of impossibility of user at some intervening time, the obvious example being a claim to light for a building which was only built in the last century. To this the common law added the refinement of the lost modern grant where long user, again of some 20 years or so, would raise the presumption that the origin lay in a grant which has subsequently been lost. This is a recognised fiction described by Cheshire and Burns:

'The doctrine is plainly a fiction: it is a means to an end, and the end is that some technical ground may be found for upholding a right that has been openly enjoyed.'

See also *Tehidy Minerals Ltd v Norman* (1971). It continues to have a part to play in modern land law as was seen in *Bridle* v *Ruby* (1988).

To these methods must be added the Prescription Act 1832, which was designed to simplify and regularise prescription by establishing set periods of time of enjoyment which could form the basis of any claim. Lord Macnaghten described this in *Gardner* v *Hodgson's Kingston Brewery Co Ltd* (1903):

'The Act was an Act for shortening the time of prescription in certain cases. And really it did nothing more.'

This description of prescription provides the first fundamental principle that in order to be successful the claimant must show that he has been in actual enjoyment of the right claimed for a sufficient length of time to meet the requirements of the particular method of prescription.

A further pre-requisite is that the easement claimed must satisfy the four criteria originally propounded by Cheshire and given judicial approval in *Re Ellenborough Park* (1956). These are that there must be a dominant and servient tenement, the easement must accommodate the dominant tenement, the dominant and servient owners must be different persons and the easement in question must be capable of forming the subject matter of a grant.

Once these two matters are fully satisfied the detailed requirements of prescription set out in the question must be considered.

The first requirement is that the user must have been continuous. This means regular use for the full prescriptive period on the basis that the claimant has been able to take advantage of the right as and when he wanted. 'Frequent' is often used instead of continuous and there is no need to establish, say, daily user if the frequency of use indicates an assertion of continuous user. On the other hand, the gaps must not be excessive and a claim for user every twelve years to remove cut timber was rejected in *Hollins* v *Verney* (1884).

This continuous user must be 'as of right'. Megarry and Wade explain this by saying: 'the essence of this rule is that the claimant must prove not only his own user but also circumstances which show that the servient owner acquiesced in it as in an established right'. The basis of the right is often explained in the Latin as being 'nec vi, nec clam, nec precario'. To explain these in more detail:

Nec vi means without force. Force can mean both physical violence such as tearing down a fence or verbal protests which indicate the enjoyment is being challenged.

Nec clam means without secrecy. Thus a claim to a right of way which has only been enjoyed in the middle of the night to avoid any challenge would not be as of right. This was seen in *Liverpool Corporation* v *Coghill (H) & Sons Ltd* (1918) where waste material discharged secretly into the local authority's sewerage system was held not to be as of right.

Nec precario means without permission. Any form of permission will defeat the claim and may be recognised by annual payments. Normally permission granted will remain as a block to any claim, but circumstances can change and it is possible for an earlier permission to lapse. This could arise, in the words of Goff J in *Healey* v *Hawkins* (1968), where ' ... there is a change in circumstances from which revocation may fairly be implied.'

The question makes it clear that the consequence of prescription is a presumed grant, hence the stringent rules, above, which may lead to a rebuttal of the presumption. The quotation concludes: 'the court will not presume a grant except in fee simple'. This means that the user must be by or on behalf of a fee simple owner against a fee simple owner. It is possible to grant an easement expressly for a term of years, but under the rules of prescription only a legal fee simple can be acquired. A tenant cannot acquire a right of way over adjoining land of his landlord: see *Kilgour* v *Gaddes* (1904).

The effect of this is summarised by Cheshire and Burns:

'The rule is absolute that an easement claimed either by prescription at common law, under the doctrine of a lost modern grant or under the Prescription Act 1832 must be claimed in favour of the fee simple estate in the claimant tenement. An easement may be granted expressly for a lesser interest than a fee simple but it cannot arise by virtue of a presumed grant.'

b) Any claim for an easement must firmly satisfy the four essentials of an easement: this was confirmed by the Court of Appeal in *Re Ellenborough Park* (1956). The four essentials are:

   i)   There must be a dominant and servient tenement

      The question is silent on this point and although Alf has used the path across Bert's land we do not know whether Alf is a land owner in the neighbourhood. The rule demonstrates that the easement is a right in land for the benefit of other land and if Alf is merely making a personal convenience of the right across Bert's land he will have no claim for an easement.

   ii)   An easement must accommodate the dominant tenement

      This means that there must be some natural connection between the two tenements even though they need not be adjoining. It would be necessary to establish the 'direct nexus between the enjoyment of the right and the user of the dominant tenement'. In the words of Byles J in *Bailey v Stephens* (1862):

      'You cannot have a right over land in Kent appurtenant to an estate in Northumberland, for a right of way in Kent cannot possibly be advantageous to Northumberland land.'

      Thus it would be necessary to show that Alf did own land nearby which benefited from this short cut to the railway station.

   iii)   The dominant and servient owners must be different persons

      An easement is a right in alieno solo and it is not possible to have an easement over your own land. In this problem Alf is using the short cut across Bert's land.

   iv)   A right over land cannot be an easement unless it is capable of forming the subject matter of a grant

      This provision is used to show that new easements can be created provided they satisfy the other criteria. In this problem the right of way is a recognised form of easement and would be capable of forming the subject matter of a grant.

Having established the four essentials it must be emphasised that the remainder of the answer is based on the proposition that Alf does satisfy all four criteria and, in particular, that the short cut is from his land, across land owned by Bert, to the railway station.

The fence forms an 'interruption' to the user. Alf has enjoyed the use four nineteen and a half years and the fundamental problem is to establish what rights he has today. The problem may be illustrated by a linear diagram.

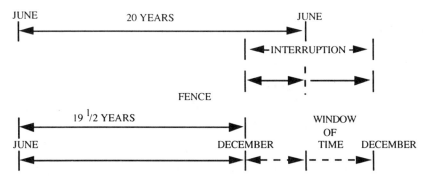

Under s2 of the Prescription Act 1832 if Alf can show 20 years' use before the action brought to establish his claim he cannot be defeated by showing the claim could not have existed since 1189. It is the last 20 years before the action that are decisive and this must be a period without 'interruption'. 'Interruption' is explained in s4 of the Prescription Act 1832 in that it must be submitted to or acquiesced in for one year in order to become a statutory interruption.

The problem facing Alf is that he does not have the basic twenty years' user. This is an essential pre-requisite, see *Reilly* v *Orange* (1955).

Alf must wait until June before he can pursue his claim. In the meantime he is vulnerable to a declaration on behalf of Bert or Jerry that no easement exists because the full twenty years have not elapsed. If no such declaration is made in June the initiative switches to Alf. He then has twenty years' user and less than one year's interruption and could successfully pursue his claim in the court. This may be described as the 'window of time' which operates in his favour. This state of affairs continues until December. After this the interruption will be seen to have been submitted to or acquiesced in which could defeat Alf's claim for an easement.

The advice to Alf is to hope neither Bert nor Jerry seek a declaration from the court that no easement exists. He could protest against the fence: this might prolong the period of interruption by showing that he has not submitted to or acquiesced in the interruption and so give him more time in which to pursue his claim. This is well illustrated by the words of Morris LJ in *Davies* v *Du Paver* (1953):

'The parties were breathing fury on each side of a newly erected fence. Could it be said that the challenging protests of the plaintiff must, as the August days passed, be deemed to have signified nothing, and that his former claims and assertions should be regarded as supplanted by submission and acquiescence? As time went by it might well be that silence and inaction could be interpreted as submission or acquiescence, but the date when submission or acquiescence begins must be determined as a question of fact, having regard to all the circumstances.'

Tutorial comments

a) Always be aware of the four essentials to an easement as a potential introduction to many easement questions (*Re Ellenborough Park* [1956] Ch 131).

161

b) In prescription questions always consider the value of a straight line showing the various dates supplied in the question. There should be a time when a valid claim can be supported - the 'window of time' in favour of the dominant owner.

Question 2

a) Outline the methods of acquiring easements.

b) Country Adventures plc bought Runndowne Manor from Lord Broke two years ago, and have since spent large sums in restoring it. Access is along a lane which also gives access to eight cottages and Home Farm, which is still owned by the Broke family trusts, and the conveyance of the Manor granted 'a right of way over and along the lane in common with all others similarly entitled'. Increasing numbers of visitors are being attracted to the house, and Country Adventures have just obtained planning permission to open a fun fair and garden centre in the grounds. Donald and Edith, owners of three of the cottages, and the Honourable Fulleigh Broke, who occupies the Farm, want to know whether they could obtain injunctions to restrict traffic to a level consistent with the use of the Manor as a private country house and sporting estate. What are their chances of success?

University of London LLB Examination
(for External Students) Land Law June 1987 Q9

General comment

This is a popular form of question. Part (a) provides an opportunity to summarise the methods of acquiring easements. In any event this should have been the basis for any revision of easements and could provide a useful mark-earner.

Part (b) covers a problem which is likely to trouble the courts with increasing regularity over the years. With the changes in life-style and leisure activities in recent years, it may well be found that rights of way become damaged and put at risk due to the amount of use to which they are put. If the right is 'for all purposes' in a rural environment this may well have intended all agricultural purposes but it was never expressly limited to agriculture alone. By not being so specific the owners of servient properties may find the right of way becoming especially onerous as even larger agricultural machines, other all purpose leisure vehicles, and caravans take advantage of the terms of the easement. It is welcome to see examiners asking the candidates to address their minds to problems which demonstrate that Land Law is a creature of the real world to which they can relate on a day to day basis.

Skeleton solution

a) Introduce with diagram (see Suggested solution).

1) *Statute* - rare: local authority using local legislation.

2) *Express grant* - ideally used for all easements - deed - but a written agreement may be used: *McManus* v *Cooke* (1887).

3) *Implied grant*

    a) Easement of necessity - at time of grant: *London Corporation* v *Riggs* (1880)

       Intended easement - to give effect to common intention: *Wong* v *Beaumont Property Trust Ltd* (1965).

    b) *Wheeldon* v *Burrows* (1879). Continuous and apparent or necessary to reasonable enjoyment of land and in use at time of the grant.

    c) Section 62 LPA 1925. Conveyance and no contrary intention. Includes privileges, easements and rights and must be diversity of ownership/occupation. *Sovmots Investments Ltd* v *Sec of State for the Environment* (1977).

4) *Presumed grant* - based on long enjoyment.

    a) Common law prescription. As of right (nec vi, nec clam, nec precario) between fee simple owners. Back to 1189.

    b) Lost modern grant. Fiction - prove enjoyment for minimum of 20 years: *Tehidy Minerals Ltd* v *Norman* (1971) and *Bridle* v *Ruby* (1988).

    c) Prescription Act 1832, makes proof easier.

       • s1 Profits à prendre 30/60 years.

       • s2 Easements, except light 20/40 years.

       • s3 Easements of light, 20 years only (not defeated by oral permission).

       • s4 Next before action brought and any interruption must be submitted to or acquiesced in for one year: *Davies* v *Du Paver* (1953).

b) BROKE FAMILY TRUST

    Introduce with diagram (see suggested solution).

    INJUNCTION sought by Hon F Broke and Donald/Edith to restrict traffic to a level consistent with the use of the Manor as a private country house and sporting estate. Runndowne Manor purchased two years ago and restored - increased visitors - further expansion reflected in planning permission.

    Term of EXPRESS right of way - not confined to use at time of grant, *White* v *Grand Hotel Eastbourne Ltd* (1913).

    But must not infringe rights of others entitled to use it - *Jelbert* v *Davis* (1968), quote Danckwerts LJ:

    'A use of the right of way which is so excessive that it renders the rights of such persons practically impossible.'

    Injunction is possible - not as complete as required - must be 'give and take' and so probably must accept some increase but not so much as to make their use of the lane impossible.

Use compromise formula of *Rosling* v *Pinnegar* (1987) - to regulate traffic to a reasonable user thus allowing others to continue enjoying existing rights.

See May LJ: ' ... a plaintiff was entitled to an injunction to prevent an unreasonable and excessive user of a way and any consequent nuisance.'

Suggested solution

a) The limits to part (a) may be demonstrated by the following diagram:

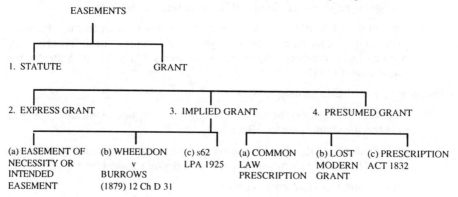

Each of the above will be dealt with in turn.

1) *Statute*

   The Inclosure Acts were early examples of easements created by statute. Many local authorities have the benefit of easements created by local legislation and this is, perhaps, the best example of the modern use of easements created by statute.

   Apart from this all easements may be said to be in grant which will be either express, implied or presumed.

2) *Express grant*

   This is the method by which all easements should be created which would then leave the only possible conflict as a question of interpretation of the expressed words. The grant should be by deed in order to create a legal easement, but equitable easements may be created by a document under hand or even orally, as in *McManus* v *Cooke* (1887). Any such informal easement in unregistered land created since 1925 must be protected by registration as a land charge Class D (iii): s2(5)(iii) LCA 1972.

3) *Implied grant*

   Under this heading may be found some three forms of easement.

   An easement of necessity arises where land which is entirely surrounded by other land is sold by the owner without expressly granting or reserving a right of way. The law will not allow the land to remain land-locked and unusable and allows the owner of the land-locked dominant tenement a right of way as an easement of necessity. The necessity relates to the time of the grant and the uses to which the land is put at that time: *London Corporation v Riggs* (1881).

A close relation is the intended easement which is implied to give effect to the common intention of the parties. This was illustrated by the need for ventilation to a basement café in *Wong v Beaumont Property Trust Ltd* (1965).

The rule in *Wheeldon v Burrows* (1879) states that where part of the land is sold the grantee obtains as an easement all those former quasi-easements which are continuous and apparent OR are necessary to the reasonable enjoyment of the land granted AND (in either case) are in use at the time of the grant. The main restriction to the more general application of the rule is the need to show that the easements are continuous and apparent or reasonably necessary to the land obtained.

If this claim is not available then s62 LPA 1925 may pass easements and other rights to the grantee unless the conveyance expressly negatives the application of s62 (see s62(4) LPA 1925). On the face of it s62 appears to be very widely drawn to include, inter alia, 'all ... privileges, easements, rights and advantages whatsoever.' There is, however, a serious limit to the application of s62 in that there must be some diversity of ownership or occupation prior to the conveyance. This restriction was confirmed by Lord Wilberforce in *Sovmots Investments Ltd v Secretary of State for the Environment* (1977):

'... when land is under one ownership one cannot speak in any intelligible sense of rights or privileges or easements being exercised over one part for the benefit of another. Whatever the owner does, he does as owner and, until a separation occurs, of ownership or at least of occupation, the condition for the existence of rights does not exist.'

4) *Presumed grant*

Prescription is based on long enjoyment from which the courts will infer 'that all those acts were done that were necessary to create a valid title': Cheshire. The rules are essentially common law rules to which statute has been added. The fundamental rules are that use must be as of right and must not be enjoyed forcibly, secretly or with permission (nec vi, nec clam, nec precario). Also the user must be continuous in the sense that the dominant owner can use the right as and when he wishes at sensible intervals of time. In addition, the claim must be made by one fee simple owner against another fee simple owner.

The three methods of prescription begin with this basic common law presumption that user has continued since time immemorial, that is to say 1189. The problem is that any proof that the use began since 1189 can defeat such a claim. To overcome this the courts created the concept of the lost modern grant. Once enjoyment of the right can be shown for a reasonable time of, say, 20 years, the court will presume an actual grant was made but that this grant has now been lost: *Tehidy Minerals Ltd v Norman* (1971).

Finally the Prescription Act 1832 has changed the emphasis. The Act relates to both profits à prendre (s1) and easements (ss2 and 3). In essence a claim for 20 or 30 years for easements (other than easement of light) or profits à prendre will mean it cannot be defeated by showing the right began after 1189. If the respective enjoyment is 40 or 60 years then any claim can only be defeated by proof of written consent. The easement of light has only one time period of 20 years after which it becomes absolute unless it is enjoyed with written consent.

All claims are also subject to s4 of the 1832 Act by which the time periods are related to the time next before the action is brought. Also s4 defines interruption to any of the time periods as being a period of a year which has been submitted to or acquiesced in after the party interrupted had notice of the interruption: *Reilly* v *Orange* (1955), *Davies* v *Du Paver* (1953).

b) BROKE FAMILY TRUST

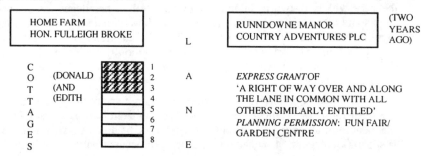

INJUNCTION sought by Hon. Fulleigh Broke, Donald and Edith to restrict traffic to a level consistent with the use of the Manor as a private country house and sporting estate.

PLANNING PERMISSION obtained to open a fun fair and garden centre in the grounds of the restored Runndowne Manor.

In considering the chances of success it will be assumed that the lane is still owned by the Broke family to give access to Home Farm which is also owned by the Broke family trust but is presently occupied by the Honourable Fulleigh Broke.

Two years ago Lord Broke sold Runndowne Manor to Country Adventures plc. The Manor must have been in a poor condition because the purchasers have 'since spent large sums in restoring it'. The restoration work has been successful to the extent that 'increasing numbers of visitors are being attracted to the house'. This has given Country Adventures plc even greater ambitions and they 'have just obtained planning permission to open a fun fair and garden centre in the grounds' of Runndowne Manor. This will certainly increase the potential number of visitors and the traffic along the lane which gives access to both Runndowne Manor and Home Farm and the eight cottages which, presumably, adjoin the farm.

The access to the Manor is controlled by the terms of an express grant in the conveyance of the Manor. This grants 'a right of way over and along the lane in common with all others similarly entitled'. Where a grant is made in such general terms it is not confined to the purpose for which the land is used at the time of the grant. Thus the right of way may stand more traffic than would serve a dilapidated manor house. It was held in *White* v *Grand Hotel Eastbourne Ltd* (1913) that an unrestricted right of way to a public road granted to the owner of a private house was not to be limited to the circumstances existing at the time of the grant. Thus when the private house became the Grand Hotel, Eastbourne, the owners of the hotel were entitled to a right of way for the general purposes of the hotel.

On the other hand the right of way must not be used so as to infringe the rights of others entitled to use it. In *Jelbert* v *Davis* (1968) agricultural land was conveyed to Jelbert in 1961 'together with the right of way at all times and for all purposes over the driveway retained by the vendor leading to the main road in common with all other persons having the like right'. In 1966 Jelbert obtained planning permission to use part of the land as a tourist caravan and camping site for not more than 200 caravans or tents from April 1st to October 31st in each year. The defendants, two neighbouring landowners, objected to the proposed use of the driveway for caravan traffic and put up notices warning off caravans and campers. The Court of Appeal held that the words of the grant of the right of way were wide enough to entitle him to use it when the use of the land was changed for a different kind of vehicle for different purposes, but not in such a manner as to cause substantial interference with the use of the right of way by other persons entitled to its use, and it was clear that use for 200 caravans or camping units was excessive. Danckwerts LJ summarised the attitude of the courts when asked to interpret express grants of this nature:

'... it is plain that the easement so granted is in such wide terms that the use by the plaintiff of it for caravans is permissible: but it is an easement which on its terms is a right which is to be used "in common with all other persons having the like right". That includes the defendants. A use of the right of way which is so excessive that it renders the rights of such other persons practically impossible, therefore, is not justified. The difficulty is to fix the limit in respect of such use. The test must be whether the interference is so substantial as to interfere with the rights of other persons in an unreasonable manner. It cannot be right that the others should be swamped by the traffic created by the plaintiff so as to amount to a legal nuisance. It is impossible to quantify this in figures, particularly as the problem relates to the future. These people are neighbours and share the right of way and there must be give and take and accommodation. Time will show what is practicable, and in the interests of both parties a practical solution must be found or a deadlock will result.'

So too in our problem Donald and Edith together with the Honourable Fulleigh Broke are advised to seek the necessary injunction. It may not be restricted to the use when sold and it may be too ambitious to hope it is only limited to a private country house and sporting estate. On the other hand, the proposed use by Country Adventures plc must not be 'so excessive that it renders the rights of such other persons practically impossible' which suggests the chances of some success are good. They must, however, be prepared to allow some increase in the traffic as was recently seen in *Rosling v Pinnegar* (1987) where May LJ set out the terms of an express grant as 'for all purposes' but 'in common with' all the owners of land adjoining a lane which served both a house recently opened to the public known as Hammerwood House and other properties on the same lane. He went on to say: '... it was clear that the mere fact that the house was now open to the public for part of the year attracting traffic along the lane, whereas not very long ago the house had been derelict and generated practically no traffic, was no breach by the appellant of the terms of the grant, and therefore the cross-appellants were not entitled to the injunction which they had sought restraining the appellant from opening the house to the public altogether.' The decision of the Court of Appeal was to confirm the grant of an injunction which would set out in detail the amount of traffic which was permitted and so prevent an unreasonable and excessive use of the right of way.

This suggests that Donald, Edith and the Honourable Fulleigh Broke would also expect to obtain an injunction which would regulate the traffic to a reasonable use thus allowing these other users of the lane to continue to enjoy their existing rights. In the words of May LJ:

'... a plaintiff was entitled to an injunction to prevent an unreasonable and excessive use of a way and any consequent nuisance.'

Tutorial comments

a) The diagrammatic presentation of easements should help to formulate the essay.

b) Note the extent of any claimed easement and the remedies available if this is exceeded - *Rosling v Pinnegar* (1987) 54 P & CR 124.

Question 3

Pat was the owner of Blackacre and Whiteacre, two adjoining pieces of land. In 1978 Pat leased Blackacre to his friend Mick for ten years at a rent for the purpose of growing vegetables and Pat covenanted to keep the fence which separated the two properties in a good state of repair. In 1980 Mick asked Pat if he could store his tools in a shed on Whiteacre and Pat agreed. In 1982 Mick asked Pat if he and his friends could play football on Whiteacre on Sundays and Pat agreed. In 1988 Pat died, leaving his entire estate to Rob. Rob has now refused to allow Mick to store his tools or to play football on Whiteacre, and Rob has also refused to repair the boundary fence.

Advise Mick.

University of London LLB Examination
(for External Students) Land Law June 1991 Q8

General comment

Another fairly standard question on easements which should have caused no problems to most students with a reasonable grasp of the subject. The areas covered included rights capable of existing as easements and acquisition of easements by implied grant.

Skeleton solution

Does Mick have rights against Rob? - Are storage and the right to play football possible easements? - Four main characteristics of easements - Storage must not amount to exclusive possession - Playing football does not seem to accommodate use of dominant tenement - If rights can be easements, have they been acquired as such - LPA 1925 s62 requirements - Fencing: covenant in lease - Binding on Rob due to s142 LPA and privity of estate - Conclusion: probably Mick can use shed, have fence repaired but not play football.

Suggested solution

If Mick has a legal right to store his tools and play football on Whiteacre, he will be able to enforce his rights against Rob. If these privileges were merely enjoyed by permission of Pat, Rob will not be bound by them.

Mick will need to show that these rights are capable of existing as easements and that he has acquired them as legal easements. There are four essentials of an easement. There must be a dominant and servient tenement, the easement must accommodate the dominant tenement, the dominant and servient tenements must not be both owned and occupied by the same person and the easement must be capable of forming the subject-matter of a grant. The right of storage was recognised as an easement in *Wright* v *MacAdam* (1949), but it is clear from the decisions in *Copeland* v *Greenhalf* (1952) and *Grigsby* v *Melville* (1974) that if the right claimed is so extensive as to amount to exclusive or joint user of the servient tenement it cannot exist as an easement. It seems that this is a question of degree and further information should be sought on the extent of the right claimed by Mick. It seems unlikely that the right he claims could amount to exclusive or joint user of the shed as he is only storing his tools there, but it may depend on the size of the shed and the number of his tools.

The right to play football is not one of the recognised types of easement. There is a dominant and servient tenement and both are not owned and occupied by the same person. Does the 'easement' accommodate the dominant tenement? In *Hill* v *Tupper* (1863) a right to put boats on a canal was not recognised as an easement on the ground that the right was not beneficial to the land itself but merely to Hill's business which he conducted on the land. The right was a personal licence. On the other hand in *Re Ellenborough Park* (1956) it was held that a right to enjoy a park as a communal garden did accommodate the neighbouring houses. In this case Mick grows vegetables on Blackacre and it is difficult to see that the right to play football on Whiteacre accommodates the use of Blackacre for growing vegetables. If this is wrong it is necessary to consider whether the right is capable of forming the subject-matter of a grant. The nature and extent of the right claimed must be capable of exact description. Again in *Re Ellenborough Park* a right to wander at large over the servient tenement was considered sufficiently precise. The list of easements is not closed, but a new category of easement must conform to the four essential characteristics. A new easement is unlikely to be recognised if it would require expenditure by the servient owner, or if it is negative in character - *Phipps* v *Pears* (1965). This right does not require expenditure and is not negative, nor does it amount to a claim to joint or exclusive user of Whiteacre. However it is suggested that on balance the right to play football would not be accepted as an easement in this case.

Even if these rights, or some of them, are capable of existing as easements, Mick can only enforce them against Rob, if he has acquired them as legal easements. If the 1988 lease to Mick included an express grant of these rights then the terms of the lease (providing it is a legal and not an equitable lease) will be binding on Rob. If there has been no express grant, Mick will need to rely on implied grant. The right to have the fence kept in repair was contained in the original 1978 lease and may have been repeated in the new lease. Provided that the covenant to keep the fence in good repair was contained in the 1988, as well as in the 1978, lease, Mick as tenant can enforce the covenant against Rob as the assignee of the reversion. There is privity of estate between the parties and the burden of the covenant passes to Rob by LPA 1925 s142 since it has reference to the subject matter of the lease

The other two rights were originally enjoyed by permission only and there is no indication that an express grant was made. It is provided in s62 LPA 1925 that, subject to a contrary intent being expressed, every conveyance of land passes with it 'all liberties, privileges, easements, rights, and advantages whatsoever ... enjoyed with the land'. This section has been held to create easements out of rights previously enjoyed by permission. In *Goldberg* v *Edwards* (1950), a right of way enjoyed by revocable licence was turned into an easement by a subsequent grant of a lease. There must be diversity of ownership or occupation for s62 to operate - *Long* v *Gowlett* (1923). In this case Mick enjoyed the right to store his tools and play football by permission before the new lease was granted and unless a contrary intention was expressed in the new lease, these rights may have been transformed into easements by s62. However s62 will not apply if the rights claimed cannot exist as easements and if the right to play football cannot exist as an easement at all, it will not become one by virtue of s62.

Thus if these rights can exist as easements and have been acquired as such by Mick either by express or implied grant, Mick may enforce them against Rob. If the right to play football is not an easement, it will be a licence and on these facts it will be a bare licence. The licence will not be binding on Rob. If the right of storage is not an easement, it might be either a lease or a licence. In order to be a lease, there must be exclusive possession, which seems unlikely and there does not seem to be a certain term agreed, nor is it a periodic tenancy as no rent is payable. It is more likely that this right, if not an easement, is a licence and not binding on Rob. It seems likely that the covenant to keep the fence in good repair is part of the lease itself and it will then be binding on Rob.

Question 4

Alf and Bert own adjoining farms and from January 1972 Alf has used a rough track leading from his farm over Bert's land to the public road. The surface of the track made it only suitable for use by farm vehicles and when the weather was bad, the track was hardly passable at all. Alf and Bert were friends, and Bert never objected to Alf's use of the track. However, in 1990 Alf and Bert quarrelled and when, in April 1991, Alf began work paving the track with a view to making it suitable for passage by all kinds of vehicles, Bert wrote to Alf withdrawing 'the permission I gave you to use the track' and erected a fence barring access to the track from Alf's farm.

Advise Alf.

University of London LLB Examination
(for External Students) Land Law June 1992 Q3

General comment

Not a particularly difficult question on easements. The key issues to deal with are whether there is permission or acquiescence on the part of Bert, whether the limited time during which the path was useable is relevant and whether Alf can improve the path. Candidates who are aware of *Mills* v *Silver* (1991) should not be unduly troubled by this question.

Skeleton solution

- Definition of easement.

- Characteristics of easement - *Re Ellenborough Park* (1956).

- Acquisition of easements generally.

- Prescription - acquiescence or permission - *Dalton* v *Angus* (1881) - nec vi, nec clam, nec precario - Prescription Act 1832 - 20 years' user - *Mills* v *Silver* (1991).

- Maintenance or improvement of easements - *Mills* v *Silver* (1991).

Suggested solution

An easement is a right in or over the land of another - it is a right 'in alieno solo'. Alf wishes to know whether he can continue to make use of the track across Bert's land. In order to be able to do so he must show that the track has the characteristics of an easement, and has been acquired as such.

The characteristics of an easement were laid down in *Re Ellenborough Park* (1956) as follows. Firstly, there must be a dominant and servient tenement. The dominant tenement has the benefit of the alleged easement and the servient the burden. In this case Alf's farm is the dominant tenement and Bert's the servient.

Secondly, the easement must 'accommodate' the dominant tenement. In *Re Ellenborough Park* the court said that an easement would do so if it made the dominant tenement a 'better and more convenient property', eg if it increased the value of that property. It was also said in that case that there must be a sufficient nexus between the

171

enjoyment of the easement and the dominant tenement; in other words the servient and dominant tenements must be proximate, but not necessary adjoining or adjacent, so as to enable the dominant tenement to derive a realistic benefit from the easement. On the facts it is clear that the nexus test is satisfied as the farms are adjoining, and it could also be argued that the use of a path over Bert's land increases the value of Alf's farm. In addition it must be shown that the easement accommodates the land (Alf's farm) as opposed to the person (Alf), as an easement is more than a mere personal right: see *Hill* v *Tupper* (1863) and *Moody* v *Steggles* (1879). As paths are the most common type of easement it may be safe to assume that the easement accommodates the land.

Thirdly, the dominant and servient land must be owned and occupied by different persons. This is clearly satisfied as Bert owns the servient land and Alf the dominant. Finally, the easement must be capable of forming the subject matter of grant - it must be a right which could have been granted by deed. For this to be satisfied there must be a capable grantor and grantee, and as there is nothing to suggest that Bert or Alf are subject to some incapacity at law there would be a grantor and grantee respectively. The right claimed as an easement also needs to be sufficiently definite and not a claim of privacy or view, as well as being in the nature of a recognised easement. Again these requirements are satisfied as a path in the nature of a right of way is one of the oldest recognised easements.

Thus the path across Bert's land is capable of being an easement in the form of a right of way in favour of Alf. However, whether Alf actually has an easement depends on whether he has acquired it in a manner recognised by law.

An easement can be acquired in several ways, most of which can be discounted here. There is no suggestion of an express grant of an easement by Bert in favour of Alf, nor is there likely to be an easement of necessity in the absence of Alf's farm being 'land-locked': see *Wong* v *Beaumont* (1965) and *Nickerson* v *Barraclough* (1980). Similarly, in the absence of a conveyance between Bert and Alf, s62 Law of Property Act 1925 and the doctrine in *Wheeldon* v *Burrows* (1879) cannot apply. Therefore, if Alf has acquired an easement at all he will have done so by prescription.

A prescriptive easement can be acquired in three ways - common law prescription, lost modern grant, and under the Prescription Act 1832. All three are based on acquiescence and it is necessary to show that the servient owner knows of the use over his land by the dominant owner, has the power to stop it or sue in respect of it, and fails to do: *Dalton* v *Angus* (1881). On the facts it would appear that these factors are satisfied as Bert knows of Alf's use of the track and only takes steps to stop it in 1991. All three types of prescription are also based on longer user as of right, without force, secrecy or permission (nec vi, nec clam, nec precario). These factors will now be considered in respect of the different types of prescription.

In order to successfully plead common law prescription, Alf would have to show that the path has been used across Bert's farm since time immemorial - 1189. Although the rule is deemed to be satisfied if the use can be shown to have existed throughout the memory of the oldest living inhabitant of the area, such a plea will fail even if the farms had existed since that time in view of the fact that the path has, apparently, only existed since 1972. Alf may have more success in pleading lost modern grant. This is essentially a fiction whereby 20 years' user or more as of right was presumed to arise from the grant of a deed which had since been lost: *Tehidy Minerals v Norman* (1971). The difficulty for Alf here would be that he could not show 20 years' user as of right. Obviously until April 1991 there is 19 years and four months' user as of right, but since then user has been prevented by virtue of the fence across the path.

Alf's strongest case lies in pleading the Prescription Act 1832. Under s2 and s4 of the Act, 20 years' user as of right next before some suit or action without interruption must be shown. Several points must be considered here: is there 20 years' user in view of the fact that the path is not passable when the weather is bad?; has Alf used as of right?; and is there an interruption?

As to the first point, it was settled in *Mills v Silver* (1991) that an easement in the form of right of way could come into existence notwithstanding the fact that the path in question could only be used in dry weather. As to the second point, Bert will no doubt seek to argue that he had given Alf permission to use the path back in January 1972 as indicated in his letter of April 1991; however, a distinction must be drawn between acquiescence which is the basis of prescription (*Dalton v Angus*) and permission. If there was true permission Alf cannot claim an easement, but if there was acquiescence or toleration it is not open for Bert to seek to grant permission ex post facto by his letter of April 1991.

The 20 year period can, of course, be defeated by an interruption provided that it lasts for at least one year and is known to the dominant owner who submits to it. Although it is reasonable to assume Alf knows of the existence of the fence, it is not clear whether he has submitted to it. In any event it will not be a valid interruption because the year of interruption will expire in April 1992, whereas the 20 years' user will expire four months earlier in January 1992, thereby enabling Alf to claim the easement.

Hence, Alf appears to have acquired a legal easement over Bert's farm by virtue of the Prescription Act 1832, which will entitle him to get a mandatory injunction requiring Bert to remove the fence. However, the easement is limited to the right to pass and re-pass along the track. In other words it does not give Alf the right to improve the track, merely to repair it, and insofar as Alf has commenced improvements by paving the track he has committed a trespass which will enable Bert to recover damages from him (see *Mills v Silver*).

Question 5

Rita, Sara and Tina occupy three adjacent large workshops. Sara owned the middle workshop and also Tina's workshop, which had been let to Tina, and her father before her, for a total of thirty years, under a series of leases. Rita owns her workshop.

Ever since the first lease was granted, Tina's father, and then Tina herself, walked through the yard of the middle workshop to reach their end workshop, as this is quicker than going along the road. Sara never said anything about this and Tina doesn't know

173

if she was aware of the fact or not. In 1978, Sara agreed to Tina's request to use a lean-to shed at the rear of Sara's workshop, and Tina had used it, on and off, ever since, for storage.

Rita and her staff have also walked over the yard to Sara's workshop to reach Rita's workshop 'for as long as anyone can remember'.

In 1988, Tina bought the freehold of her workshop from Sara. The conveyance made no mention of the use of the shed, but Tina still uses it.

Sara has now sold her workshop to VAX Developments Ltd, who have a proposal to redevelop the site. They have told Rita and Tina to keep off the land and have demanded that Tina clear out the shed and hand over the key.

Advise Rita and Tina.

University of London LLB Examination
(for External Students) Land Law June 1990 Q5

General comment

Not a difficult question for the student who has his wits about him and appreciates that Tina, prior to 1988, was a tenant so there cannot be a prescriptive right in her favour. Thereafter, the question simply requires the application of the rules relating to the characteristics of, and acquisition of, easements.

Skeleton solution

Introduction - definition of easement

Characteristics of an easement

- *Re Ellenborough Park* (1956)

- dominant and servient land

- different ownerships

- must accommodate dominant land

- must be capable of forming the subject matter of grant

Cases: Hill v *Tupper* (1863); *Moody* v *Steggles* (1879); *Wright* v *Macadam* (1949); *Grigsby* v *Melville* (1974); *Copeland* v *Greenhalf* (1952); *Attorney-General of Southern Nigeria* v *John Holt* (1915)

NB The problem of storage rights

Acquisition

Rita - prescription

- common law

- lost modern grant - *Tehidy Minerals* v *Norman* (1971)

- Prescription Act 1832

Tina - s62 LPA 1925 - *Goldberg* v *Edwards* (1950)

NB Tina was a tenant prior to 1988 and so no prescriptive easement in her favour.

Binding on VAX Developments Ltd

Prescription and s62 LPA 1925 give rise to legal easements - no need to register as legal rights bind in rem.

Suggested solution

As easement is a right in or over the land of another, in other words a right in or over Blackacre which exists for the benefit of Whiteacre. Three issues arise for discussion here, firstly whether the rights claimed by Rita and Tina over Sara's land are capable of being easements; secondly, whether they have validly been acquired as easements; and thirdly, whether they are capable of binding VAX Ltd which has purchased Sara's land.

Rita is claiming the right to walk over Sara's land and Tina is claiming both that right and the right to store tools in the shed on Sara's land. In order to be easements these rights must satisfy the requirements of an easement laid down in *Re Ellenborough Park* (1956). First there must be a dominant tenement which benefits from the easement and a servient tenement which takes the burden of it. In respect of Rita her land is the dominant tenement and Sara's the servient. In respect of Tina her land is the dominant land and Sara's the servient.

Secondly, the dominant and servient tenements must be in different ownership which is the case here. Thirdly, the right must accommodate the dominant tenement in the sense of a benefit to the land itself and not in the nature of a purely personal right for Tina and Rita. In Rita's case the right to walk over Sara's yard is not a personal right akin to a license (see *Hill* v *Tupper* (1863)) but benefits Rita's land itself in the sense that it makes that land a better and more convenient property (see eg *Moody* v *Steggles* (1879)). The same could be said in respect of Tina's claim to walk across Sara's yard. As regards Tina's claim to store tools in Sara's shed, there may be a difficulty in the sense that this could be seen as a purely personal benefit for Tina (*Hill* v *Tupper* (1863)), although rights to storage have been recognised as easements (see *Wright* v *Macadam* (1949)).

Fourthly, the right claimed must be capable of forming the subject matter of a grant, ie it must have been capable of being granted by deed. There appear to be no difficulties in respect of the legal capacity of grantor and grantee, and so far as Rita's and Tina's claim to walk across Sara's yard it falls within the categories of recognised easements being in fact a right of way. Tina's claim to store tools in Sara's shed is more problematic. As a general rule if it amounts to a claim to exclusive possession of Sara's shed it will not be recognised as an easement (see *Copeland* v *Greenhalf* (1952) and *Grigsby* v *Melville* (1974)). However, rights of storage have been recognised as valid easements (see *Wright* v *Macadam*), particularly when the claim concerns a right to store trade or business assets on another's land as is the case here (see *Attorney-General of Southern Nigeria* v *John Holt* (1915)). On balance it would appear that the rights claimed by Rita and Tina are capable of being easements.

Dealing first with Rita, there is no indication of an express grant of an easement of a right of way in favour of her land, or an implied grant via s62 Law of Property Act 1925 or under the doctrine of *Wheeldon* v *Burrows* (1872). Furthermore, as the path across Sara's land is a short cut and it is possible to get to Rita's land by using the road, it is clearly not an easement of necessity. However, Rita may have acquired an easement by prescription, as the path across Sara's land has been used for as long as anyone can remember. Provided there has been user for at least twenty years an easement can be acquired under common law prescription or lost modern grant or the Prescription Act 1832.

Twenty years user will raise a presumption of user since time immemorial, time immemorial being arbitrarily fixed at 1189 for these purposes. This is liable to be deflated by showing that at some intervening time there has been an impossibility of user, which is more than likely here as it is extremely unlikely that the workshops have been in existence for a substantial period of time. That notwithstanding a claim under lost modern grant may well succeed (see *Tehidy Minerals Ltd* v *Norman* (1971)) giving rise to a legal easement. Whilst a prescriptive easement under lost modern grant is likely to have been acquired, Rita may also be able to rely on the Prescription Act 1832 by showing twenty years user as of right, nec vi, nec claim, nec precario (without force, without secrecy and without permission), there being no evidence of an effective interruption. Whether Rita acquires the prescriptive easement under the doctrine of lost modern grant or under the Act of 1832, it will be a legal easement which will be binding on the purchaser of Sara's land, VAX Developments Ltd, without the need for registration.

Turning to Tina and her claim in respect of a right of way and a right of storage, two points must be stressed at the outset. Firstly, there has not been an express grant of those rights in the conveyance of 1988, and secondly, the rights cannot be claimed by way of prescription because prior to 1988 she was a leaseholder and prescription can only apply in favour of one freeholder against another. Similarly, there is nothing to suggest an easement of necessity.

Tina's best chance of acquiring the rights as an easement will be under s62 LPA 1925 or under the doctrine in *Wheeldon* v *Burrows*. The former method is the most likely given that prior to 1988 Tina was Sara's tenant and hence there was the necessary diversity of occupation as required by s62 LPA 1925. Provided that the conveyance was by deed and did not contain any provision to the contrary, and that the right of way and storage were being used at the time of conveyance then the conveyance will carry out those rights and crystallize them into legal easements. In this way the right of storage, even though originally only a licence, attains the status of a legal easement (see *Goldberg* v *Edwards* (1950)). There is a remote possibility of the rights being acquired as easements under *Wheeldon* v *Burrows* in favour of Tina's *father* although there is no evidence of this. On the assumption that the requirements of s62 LPA 1925 are not, Tina will have acquired legal easements which will bind VAX Developments Limited without the need for registration.

To conclude, it appears that Rita has a legal easement on the form of a right of way which is binding on VAX Developments Ltd and she can continue to use the way across VAX's land, and in fact could obtain both a declaration of her right and an, injunction to restrain VAX Developments Ltd from interfering from her exercise of it. Provided the storage of tools satisfies the requirements of *Re Ellenborough Park*, Tina will have acquired legal easements in respect of storage and a right of way under s62 LPA 1925 which bind VAX Developments Ltd. Like Rita, Tina can obtain a declaration and injunction in support of these rights.

9 MORTGAGES

9.1	Introduction
9.2	Key points
9.3	Recent cases and statutes
9.4	Analysis of questions
9.5	Questions

9.1 Introduction

Most Land Law examinations will contain a question on mortgages. There are four essential areas for revision: the form of the mortgage, the rights of the mortgagor, the remedies of the mortgagee and the question of priorities. Knowledge of these four topics should provide material for most answers on mortgages. Some questions can be rewarding in terms of effort spent on revision and any question within the general theme of once a mortgage always a mortgage provides ample opportunity to both display knowledge of the extensive case law on this theme and the method to use these cases by way of comparison inter se. The Law Commission's proposals for the reform of mortgages should also be understood.

9.2 Key points

a) *Nature of mortgage* - a conveyance of land in order to secure a loan. It is only a security for a loan.

b) *Form of a legal mortgage of freehold land*: s85 LPA 1925

    i) Pre-1926 - conveyance of fee simple or long lease

    ii) Post-1925

       • Demise for a term of years absolute subject to a proviso for cesser on redemption;

       • Charge by deed expressed to be way of legal mortgage - s87 LPA 1925 - now the most popular method of creating legal mortgages.

    iii) Second and subsequent mortgages - possible as either legal or equitable mortgages today.

c) *Form of a legal mortgage of leasehold land*

    i) Pre-1926 - assignment or sub-lease

    ii) Post-1926:

       • Mortgage by sub-demise - usually less last 10 days

- Charge by deed expressed to be by way of legal mortgage

iii) Second and subsequent mortgages - plus one day on the earlier mortgage

d) *Equitable mortgages*

   i) Mortgage of an equitable interest - eg tenant for life's own interest under a strict settlement

   ii) Mortgage of a legal estate not made by deed - must satisfy s2 Law of Property (Miscellaneous Provisions) Act 1989

   iii) Mortgage by deposit of title deeds - with INTENTION to secure a loan

   iv) Equitable charge: *First National Securities Ltd* v *Hegerty* [1984] 3 All ER 641 - a valid charge on H's severed beneficial interest - and *Thames Guaranty Ltd* v *Campbell* [1984] 2 All ER 585 - not effective as an equitable charge because only one co-owner had charged the interest.

e) *Rights of mortgagor*

   i) His rights of redemption

   ii) Once a mortgage always a mortgage: Lord Eldon in *Seton* v *Slade* (1802) 7 Ves 265

   Samuel v *Jarrah Timber Corporation* [1904] AC 323; cf *Reeve* v *Lisle* [1902] AC 461

   Fairclough v *Swan Brewery Co Ltd* [1912] AC 565 - 20 years less last 6 weeks; cf *Knightsbridge Estates Trust Ltd* v *Byrne* [1939] Ch 441 - fee simple - 40 years

   Esso Petroleum Co Ltd v *Harpers Garage (Stourport) Ltd* [1968] AC 269 - 2 mortgages - one tie clause was for 21 years, and the other for $4^{1}/2$ years

   Consumer Credit Act 1974

   Cityland & Property (Holdings) Ltd v *Dabrah* [1968] Ch 166

   iii) The equity of redemption must not be clogged:

   Noakes v *Rice* [1902] AC 24 - buy beer for full period of lease - 26 years whether mortgage repaid or not; cf *Biggs* v *Hoddinott* [1898] 2 Ch 307 - 5 years - for as long as money due on the mortgage

   iv) Collateral advantages to the mortgagee:

   Kreglinger v *New Patagonia Meat and Cold Storage Co Ltd* [1914] AC 25

   Index linking: *Multiservice Bookbinding Ltd* v *Marden* [1978] 2 WLR 535

   v) Who may exercise the right to redeem? - mortgagor and any assignee of equity of redemption

   vi) Notice of intention to redeem - legal date - or 6 months' notice or 6 months' interest in lieu of notice

vii) Price of redemption - must pay principal + interest + costs

viii) Loss of the right of redemption - release of equity of redemption to mortgagee, sale by mortgagee, foreclosure

ix) Discharge of the mortgage: s115 LPA 1925 - statutory receipt signed by mortgagee, naming person who pays

x) Mortgagor's right to a sale - s91 LPA 1925

xi) Mortgagor's right to compel transfer instead of himself redeeming - s95 LPA 1925

xii) Mortgagor's right to bring actions - because he is in possession

xiii) Mortgagor's right to lease: s99 LPA 1925 - agricultural/occupation 50 years - building 999 years - best rent - possession within 12 months - condition for re-entry if rent in arrear for 30 days

xiv) Mortgagor's right to accept surrender of lease: s100 LPA 1925

xv) Mortgagor's right to cut timber

xvi) Mortgagor's right to inspect the title deeds

xvii) Upon redemption mortgagee must deliver title deeds to person next entitled: s96(2) LPA 1925. Registration not enough, mortgagee must have ACTUAL NOTICE of later mortgages

f) *Consolidation of mortgages*: s93 LPA 1925

The right of a person who holds two or more mortgages granted by the same mortgagor on different properties to refuse in certain circumstances to be redeemed as to one unless he is also redeemed as to the other. Consolidation is part of the price paid by the mortgagor for the court's assistance to recover his property.

i) Definition

ii) Four conditions:

- Rights reserved in one mortgage deed;

- Both mortgages created by same mortgagor;

- Legal date for redemption passed on all mortgages;

- At one time all mortgages vested in one person and all equities in another.

Theme of consolidation is he who seeks equity must do equity.

g) *Rights and remedies of the mortgagee*

Remedies

i) Right to take possession: *Four-Maids Ltd v Dudley Marshall (Properties) Ltd* [1957] Ch 317 - before ink is dry on the mortgage - *White v City of*

London Brewery Co (1889) 42 Ch D 237, s36 Administration of Justice Act 1970 *and* s8 AJA 1973 - *Quennel* v *Maltby* [1979] 1 WLR 318 - remedies only available if used bona fide to enforce the security and NOT for some ulterior motive such as avoiding the Rent Act

ii) Right to sue the mortgagor personally

iii) Power of foreclosure

iv) Power of sale: s101 LPA 1925

Tse Kwong Lam v *Wong Chit Sen* [1983] 3 All ER 54

Distinguish when the power of sale arises from when it becomes exercisable

v) Power to appoint a receiver: s101 LPA 1925, s37 Supreme Court Act 1981.

Rights

vi) Power to insure the property

vii) Undue influence by or on behalf of the mortgagee.

- The effect of seeking to avoid the practical consequences of *Williams & Glyn's Bank Ltd v Boland* [1980] 3 WLR 138 To avoid the consequences of an overriding interest under s70(1)(g) LRA 1925 many lenders require occupiers to sign a form consenting to the mortgage and postponing the interests of the occupier to the mortgagee.

- Problems of such method of avoidance - has undue influence been used in obtaining the signature of the occupier?

- Solution of the courts - *National Westminster Bank plc* v *Morgan* [1985] AC 686 - House of Lords said that before a transaction could be set aside on the grounds of undue influence must show it constituted a manifest disadvantage to the person seeking to avoid it. Not so here, because the loan saved the home from possession by original mortgagee.

Kingsnorth Trust Ltd v *Bell* [1986] 1 All ER 423 - Court of Appeal - undue influence exerted by husband in obtaining wife's signature to a second mortgage. Court emphasised importance of independent legal advice. Conclusion: any document postponing rights of an occupier in favour of mortgagee should only be signed in the presence of a solicitor. *Morgan* case applied in:

Cornish v *Midland Bank plc* [1985] 3 All ER 513 - Court of Appeal - mortgage NOT set aside because the only relationship between plaintiff and bank was customer/bank. No unfair advantage had been taken of plaintiff and no presumption of undue influence arose. But damages awarded for negligent misstatement of the effect of the mortgage. Again *National Westminster Bank plc* v *Morgan* case considered in:

Woodstead Finance Ltd v *Petrou* (1986) *The Times* 23 January - where evidence showed rate of interest to be high (42.5% per annum) but normal, terms not manifestly disadvantageous to borrower. In absence of undue influence or breach of fiduciary duty by lender, a wife who stood surety for her husband's loan was liable when he defaulted.

See also *Midland Bank plc* v *Shephard* [1988] 3 All ER 17

h) *Priorities of mortgages*

   i)   Pre-1925 - 'When the equities are equal, the first in time prevails'

   ii) Post-1925 - note s2 LCA 1972, s97 LPA 1925 and s4 LCA 1972. In any conflict it is suggested that s4 LCA 1972 will prevail.

i) *Tacking of mortgages* - prior but NOT subsequent mortgagees

   Rights of prior mortgagees after 1925 under s94 LPA 1925

   i)   Arrangement with subsequent mortgagees - s94(1)(a)

   ii) First mortgage imposes obligation on mortgagee - s94(1)(c)

   iii) Where prior mortgagee no notice of intervening mortgages - s94(1)(b)

        Note s94(2). Registration is NOTICE except if prior mortgage made expressly for securing a current account or further advances

j) *Priority as to mortgages of registered land*

   Three methods of creating mortgages of registered land.

   i)   Registered charge - s26 LRA 1925 - order of registration is order of priority - s29 LRA 1925

   ii) NOTICE (s106(3)(c)) or CAUTION (s106(3)(a)). This new s106 LRA 1925 substituted by s26 AJA 1977 - only takes effect in equity until becomes a registered charge. Protected as a MINOR INTEREST by an ordinary notice or caution

   iii) Deposit of land certificate - s66 LRA 1925. *Barclays Bank Ltd* v *Taylor* [1974] Ch 137 - notice of deposit to registrar who enters a NOTICE on the register which operates as a CAUTION under s54.

9.3   Recent cases and statutes

National Westminster Bank plc v *Morgan* [1985] 2 WLR 588

Kingsnorth Trust Ltd v *Bell* [1986] 1 WLR 119

Woodstead Finance Ltd v *Petrou* (1986) The Times 23 January

Midland Bank plc v *Shephard* [1988] 3 All ER 17

City of London Building Society v *Flegg* [1987] 2 WLR 1266 - House of Lords

Kingsnorth Finance Ltd v *Tizard* [1986] 2 All ER 54

Law Commission Working Paper no 99 - 'Land Mortgages' (1986)

Parker-Tweedale v *Dunbar Bank plc* (1989) The Times 29 December

Target Home Loans v *Clothier* (1992) The Times 7 August

9.4 Analysis of questions

As indicated in the Introduction, this is one subject where the questions generally fall into a number of clearly identifiable areas. There might be exceptions such as rights of a mortgagor leading into remedies of the mortgagee or remedies of the mortgagee becoming mixed with the rules of priority. In addition, the registered land aspect is important and the significance of the decision in *Williams & Glyn's Bank Ltd* v *Boland* [1980] 3 WLR 138 should not be understated. It is important for the positive statements on s70(1)(g) LRA 1925 and because of the steps now taken by the institutional lenders to avoid the practical consequences of the decision.

9.5 Questions

Question 1

Distinguish between a legal mortgage of land, an equitable mortgage of land and an equitable charge over land.

How is each of them created at the present day?

University of London LLB Examination
(for External Students) Land Law June 1980 Q6

General comment

For some reason, candidates are reluctant to attempt questions on mortgages. This question may have overcome this reluctance in the minds of a number of candidates, although some may have had difficulty in establishing the true relationship between the equitable mortgage of land and the equitable charge over land.

Skeleton solution

Define 'mortgage' - Lindley MR in *Santley* v *Wilde* (1889): '... a conveyance of land ... as a security for the payment of a debt or the discharge of some other obligation for which it is given.'

Legal mortgage of land - deed necessary and secure legal estate

Before 1926:

Either: conveyance/assignemnt of freehold/leasehold estate

or   mortgage by demise or sub-demise

After 1925:

Either: demise/sub-demise for a term of years absolute (s85 LPA 1925)

or   charge by deed expressed to be by way of legal mortgage (freehold/leasehold): s87

Any attempt to convey/assign operates as a mortgage by demise: ss85(2) and 86(2)

Grangeside Propeties Ltd v Collingwoods Securities Ltd (1964)

If title deeds not obtained as security - register as land charge Class C(i) - puisne mortgage

Equitable mortgage of land - four types:

a) Deposit of title deeds - with intention to secure a loan - bank overdraft. No deed/writing is necessary - but is often required. No land charge.

b) Agreement to create a legal mortgage - must satisfy s2 LP(MP)A 1989 - money must be advanced. No deeds deposited - register as land charge Class C(iii) general equitable charge.

c) Security itself only equitable - beneficial interest of tenant for life under SLA. Conveyance of whole interest to mortgagee - protect by notice to trustees of the settlement. Section 137(2) LPA 1925 - *Dearle* v *Hall* (1828).

d) Equitable charge over land - where any land is appropriated to discharge of a debt. No proprietary interest in chargee but may have debt realised by sale. *Cedar Holdings Ltd* v *Green* (1979) - no charge - no interest in 'land'. *Williams and Glyn's Bank Ltd* v *Boland* (1980): Lord Wilberforce said *Cedar Holdings* was wrongly decided. *First National Securities Ltd* v *Hegerty* (1984) - valid equitable charge over husband's equitable interest - severed to become tenancy in common. Megarry and Wade: 'It is sufficient if an intent that the property should constitute a security can be gathered.'

Suggested solution

A mortgage was defined by Lindley MR in *Santley* v *Wilde* (1899) as:

'... a conveyance of land or an assignment of chattels as a security for the payment of a debt or the discharge of some other obligation for which it is given.'

The Law of Property Act 1925 made a number of changes in the law relating to mortgages including the manner in which mortgages are created. Before 1926, a mortgage of the fee simple or the leasehold interest was effected by a conveyance or assignment respectively to the mortgagee with a proviso that the interest be re-conveyed or re-assigned upon redemption. This is no longer possible by virtue of the effect of ss85(1) and 86(1) of the Law of Property Act 1925. The Law of Property Act 1925 provides that a legal mortgage of the fee simple must be effected by either:

a) a demise for a term of years absolute (usually, but not necessarily, 3,000 years) subject to cessor on redemption (s85(2) LPA 1925); or

b) a charge by deed expressed to be by way of legal mortgage which gives to the mortgagee the same protection, powers and remedies as if a term of 3,000 years had been created in his favour (s87(1)(a) LPA 1925).

In the case of leaseholds, a legal mortgage can now only be effected by either:

a) a sub-demise for a term of years absolute, less by one day at least than the term vested in the mortgagor and subject to a proviso for cessor on redemption; or

b) a charge by deed expressed to be by way of legal mortgage which gives the mortgagee the same protection, powers and remedies as if a sub-term less by one day than the term vested in the mortgagor had been created in his favour (ss86(1) and 87(1)(b) LPA 1925).

The Law of Property Act 1925 ss85(2) and 86(2) contain provisions to cover the attempt to create mortgages by the pre-1926 method. If a person purports to convey a fee simple by way of mortgage the transaction operates as a demise of the land to the mortgagee for a term of years absolute. A first mortgagee will take a term of 3,000 years from the date of the mortgage. A second or subsequent mortgage will take a term one day longer than the term vested in the next prior mortgagee. In the case of leaseholds, any purported assignment by way of mortgage takes effect as a sub-demise. If it is a first mortgage, it takes effect as a sub-demise for the residue of the term vested in the mortgagor, less ten days. The term taken by second or subsequent mortgagees will be one day longer than the term vested in the next prior mortgagee. This procedure was illustrated by *Grangeside Properties Ltd v Collingwoods Securities Ltd* (1964) in which a leasehold owner purported to assign his property as security for a loan. It was held that the transaction was in substance a mortgage and, therefore, took effect as a sub-lease.

The legal mortgage must be created by a deed being within a demise, sub-demise or charge expressed to be by way of legal mortgage. The deed will contain four main clauses:

a) A personal covenant to repay the loan and interest;

b) A demise of the mortgaged property;

c) A proviso for cesser of the term on redemption or discharge of the charge upon repayment of the loan;

d) Covenants including covenants to pay all outgoings and for repair and insurance of the property.

The charge expressed to be by way of legal mortgage is becoming increasingly popular as the common form of legal mortgage today. It is shorter because there is no need for the conveyance of any estate in the land to the mortgagee. It has an advantage where freehold and leasehold property form the security as one deed can be used to include both forms of security. If the properties are leasehold, the legal charge will not be a breach of any covenant in the lease against sub-letting.

Under the Land Registration Act 1925, a legal mortgage of registered land is usually made by 'registered charge'. The charge must be by deed and must be registered in the name of the mortgagee as proprietor of the charge. A registered charge, unless it contains a demise of the land, takes effect as a charge by way of legal mortgage. The mortgagor will surrender his land certificate to the Land Registry who will issue a charge certificate to the registered chargee, retaining the land certificate in the registry.

A legal mortgage of land requires that the mortgagor has a legal estate in the land and these are set out in s1(1) of the Law of Property Act 1925 - the fee simple absolute in possession or the term of years absolute. The mortgage must be by deed and this deed must contain either a demise of the land for a term of years absolute, or a charge expressed to be by way of legal mortgage.

Any mortgage which does not comply with all these conditions is an equitable mortgage. All mortgages of an equitable interest after 1925 (eg the life interest of a tenant for life under the Settled Land Act 1925) are equitable mortgages whether they are made by deed or not. A mortgage of a legal estate not made by deed in either of the forms required by the Law of Property Act 1925 must be an equitable mortgage. An equitable mortgage may be defined negatively to include any mortgage which is not a legal mortgage, either because the subject matter is not a legal estate or, if it is a legal estate, because the mortgage is not made in either of the two ways in which a legal mortgage can be made after 1925.

Four types of equitable mortgage may be identified, one of which will form the third type of security required to be described by the question itself.

The first type of equitable mortgage arises where title deeds to the land are deposited with the lender by way of security. This type of transaction occurs when a customer borrows money from a bank by way of overdraft and deposits his title deeds or land certificate as security for repayment of the loan. No mortgage deed or writing is necessary, although a bank often requires a memorandum under seal which, in effect, makes this a mortgage by deed.

The deposit of the title deeds is an agreement to execute a legal mortgage, but in addition to the actual deposit parol or written evidence must be evinced to prove that the deposit was intended to be by way of security. The mere deposit of deeds by a customer with a bank does not alone constitute an equitable mortgage in respect of an overdraft. If the intention is present, equity will imply an agreement to execute a legal mortgage of the land to which the deeds relate. This is enforceable by specific performance, provided the contract satisfies s2 of the Law of Property (Miscellaneous Provisions) Act 1989. The action is for specific performance of the borrower's implied undertaking to execute a legal mortgage and the successful lender then has all the rights and remedies of a legal mortgagee.

The second type of equitable mortgage arises where there is an express agreement to create a legal mortgage with or without any deposit of the title deeds. This is an application of the maxim: 'Equity regards that as done which ought to be done'. If a borrower agrees that in consideration of money advanced to him he will execute a legal mortgage in favour of the lender, an equitable mortgage is created which can be enforced by specific performance. The pre-requisite is that the money has, in fact, been advanced. If a deed is subsequently executed in accordance with the agreement, this will convert the transaction into a legal mortgage where the other requirements of a legal mortgage are also fulfilled. The agreement must now satisfy the provisions of s2 of the Law of Property (Miscellaneous Provisions) Act 1989.

The third type of equitable mortgage arises where the security itself is only an equitable interest, as in the case of a tenant for life under the Settled Land Act 1925 mortgaging his own life interest. This method of effecting a mortgage has not changed with the Law of Property Act 1925. The mortgage will be effected by a conveyance of the mortgagor's whole interest to the mortgagee subject to a proviso for re-conveyance on redemption. The assignment must be in writing, signed by the mortgagor and the mortgagee should protect himself by giving written notice of it to the owner of the legal estate - *Dearle v Hall* (1828). The better opinion is that such a transaction is not capable of registration under the Land Charges Act 1972.

The fourth type of equitable mortgage, and the third part of the question, comprises the equitable charge. This arises where, without any transfer of ownership or possession, property is appropriated to the discharge of a debt or other obligation. No special form of words is required. There is no proprietory interest in the chargee, but he is entitled to have the debt realised by a judicial sale of the property.

The nature of the equitable charge was described by Kindersley VC in *Matthews* v *Doodday* (1861):

'Suppose a man signed a written contract, by which he simply agreed that he thereby charged his real estate with £500 to A, what would be the effect of it? It would be no agreement to give a legal mortgage, but a security by which he equitably charged his land with payment of a sum of money and the mode of enforcing it would be by coming into a court of equity to have the money raised by sale or mortgage ... the thing would be an equitable charge and not a mortgage.'

An abortive attempt to establish an equitable charge was seen in *Cedar Holdings Ltd* v *Green* (1979).

A husband and wife were the joint legal and beneficial owners of land. After their divorce, the husband and a woman posing as his wife purported to execute a legal mortgage in favour of the plaintiffs. This was ineffective, but did it operate as a charge in equity over the husband's beneficial interest? The Court of Appeal held it did not. By virtue of the statutory trust for sale he had an interest in the proceeds of sale and the mortgage was expressed to be a charge on the land alone. All the husband held was an equitable interest in the proceeds of sale and not an interest in land.

But this decision was considered by Lord Wilberforce in *Williams and Glyn's Bank Ltd* v *Boland* (1980) where it was said to be wrongly decided. The question was considered by the Court of Appeal in *First National Securities Ltd* v *Hegerty* (1984) where a valid equitable charge over a husband's equitable interest was held to exist. The forging of his wife's signature was held to be an act of severance converting his equitable joint tenancy into a tenancy in common. As a consequence his equitable undivided share was now subject to an equitable charge. Megarry and Wade comment: 'It is sufficient if an intent that the property should constitute a security can be gathered.'

In conclusion, it should be noted that registered land may also be mortgaged off the register in any way applicable to unregistered land. The mortgagee has no protection against subsequent dealings in the land unless he preserves his priority by entering a caution on the register.

See s26 Administration of Justice Act 1977.

Tutorial comments

a) Consider why the legal charge has become so popular today.

b) Does the equitable charge have a future after *Thames Guaranty Ltd* v *Campbell* [1984] 2 All ER 585?

Question 2

In 1983 Jack and Jill, husband and wife, purchased the fee simple of 'The Wine Bar' where they have sold drinks and snacks. The title is unregistered and the conveyance was made to Jack alone. The purchase price was £40,000; Jack and Jill each provided £10,000 and the X Wine Co Ltd lent £20,000 on the security of a legal mortgage from Jack. In the mortgage Jack covenanted:

a) that for ten years he would purchase all wines and spirits for 'The Wine Bar' from the X Wine Co Ltd;

b) that the mortgage should be irredeemable for ten years; and

c) that after the expiration of the ten years the X Wine Co Ltd should for a further five years have the right of first refusal at market price, if Jack should decide to sell 'The Wine Bar'.

Profits from the business have been falling and Jack believes this has been caused by the poor quality and selection of the wines supplied by the X Wine Co Ltd.

Advise Jack:

i) whether he is bound by any of the above mentioned covenants;

ii) whether, if he falls into arrears with payments of mortgage interest, the X Wine Co Ltd will be able to obtain possession of, and sell, 'The Wine Bar'.

University of London LLB Examination
(for External Students) Land Law June 1986 Q6

General comment

Interesting combination of two of the popular areas for mortgage questions. This involves material relating to both the rights of the mortgagor and the remedies of the mortgagee. In answering part (ii) it will be necessary to look at some details of the possession procedure in order to do justice to this half question. The candidates may have found a little confusion due to the covenants and the question being designated (i) to (iii) and (i) to (ii) respectively. An (a) and (b) would have been helpful.

Skeleton solution

i) *Purchase wine for ten years from X Wine Co Ltd*

'Once a mortgage always a mortgage' - Lord Eldon in *Seton* v *Slade* (1802)

Clog on the right of redemption - *Biggs* v *Hoddinott* (1898) - collateral advantage - *Kreglinger* v *New Patagonia Meat and Cold Storage Co Ltd* (1914)

Restraint of trade - *Esso Petroleum Co Ltd* v *Harper's Garage (Stourport) Ltd* (1968)

Conclusion - Jack is bound by the covenant

Mortgage is irredeemable for ten years

Redemption illusory? *Fairclough* v *Swan Brewery Ltd* (1912); cf *Knightsbridge Estates Trust Ltd* v *Byrne* (1939)

Conclusion - probably is reasonable on the facts

Right of first refusal between 10-15 years

Not an option to purchase, if so would be void - *Samuel* v *Jarrah Timber and Wood Paving Corporation* (1904)

A right of pre-emption and valid - *Kreglinger* v *New Patagonia Meat and Cold Storage Co Ltd* (1914)

See also *Bradley* v *Carritt* (1903). Will also be valid.

Conclusion - all three covenants appear valid on the given facts

ii) *Possession before ink is dry on the mortgage - Four-Maids Ltd* v *Dudley Marshall (Properties) Ltd* (1957)

Must be valid grounds for possession - *Quennell* v *Maltby* (1979)

Rules of strict accountability - *White* v *City of London Brewery* (1889)

Sale - has power of sale arisen? If not consider rules of foreclosure with sale in the alternative under s91(2) LPA 1925, *Twentieth Century Banking Corporation Ltd* v *Wilkinson* (1977)

Upon sale must obtain true market value - *Cuckmere Brick Co Ltd* v *Mutual Finance Ltd* (1971)

Method of sale - auction, but note reservations of Lord Templeman in *Tse Kwong Lam* v *Wong Chit Sen* (1983)

Conclusion - if Jack is in arrears on mortgage interest court may order sale instead of foreclosure, in which case obtain true market value

Suggested solution

i) In answering part (i), reference must be made to part (ii). In this problem we have a covenant that Jack would purchase all wines and spirits for 'The Wine Bar' from X Wine Co Ltd for ten years. In addition covenant (b) makes the mortgage irredeemable for ten years. The general theme relating to the rights of the mortgagor was expressed by Lord Eldon in *Seton* v *Slade* (1802):

'Any stipulation which may deprive the mortgagor of his equitable right to redeem or prevent him getting back his property on payment of the loan in substantially the same state as when the mortgage is made is void in equity. There must be no clog or fetter on the exercise by the borrower of the right to redeem, ie once a mortgage, always a mortgage.'

In this case the purchase of the wines and spirits is not a 'clog or fetter' on the right of redemption because it will only extend for the period of the mortgage. As in the decision of the Court of Appeal in *Biggs* v *Hoddinott* (1898) this would not be an unconscionable bargain induced by fraud or undue influence nor did it fetter the mortgagor's right to redeem. This is a collateral advantage which would be valid because it did not fall within the excluding criteria expressed by Lord Parker in *Kreglinger* v *New Patagonia Meat and Cold Storage Co Ltd* (1914). It was not:

'(1) ... unfair and unconscionable; or (2) in the nature of a penalty clogging the equity of redemption; or (3) inconsistent with or repugnant to the contractual and equitable right to redeem ...'

In addition a mortgage is subject to the common law doctrine of restraint of trade and a postponement of the right to redeem which is not, by itself, excessive or oppressive may become so if it is accompanied by an excessive restraint upon the mortgagor's business activities. In *Esso Petroleum Co Ltd* v *Harper's Garage (Stourport) Ltd* (1965) the House of Lords confirmed that restraint of trade principles did apply to mortgages and that a restriction of twenty-one years upon a mortgagor garage proprietor to sell, under a solus agreement, the petrol of the mortgagee petrol company was unreasonable. The normal constraint rules in respect of restraint of trade will apply and an agreement will only be enforced if it is reasonable between the parties and reasonable in the public interest. A second tie of only $4^{1/2}$ years was upheld in the *Esso Petroleum* v *Harper's Garage (Stourport) Ltd* case and a tie for four years and seven months in a mortgage was enforced in *Texaco Ltd* v *Mulberry Filling Station Ltd* (1972). The varying circumstances do make it difficult to express a clear opinion. If the mortgage and tie are separate and independent transactions then a tie for almost twenty years may be valid as it was in *Rosemex Service Station* v *Shell-Mex and BP Ltd* (1969). If the solus agreement forms part of a lease-back arrangement then apparently an agreement to buy petrol for 21 years will be valid in those circumstances: *Alec Lobb Garages Ltd* v *Total Oil (Great Britain) Ltd* (1985).

In this problem, Jack will probably be bound by the covenant unless the quality of the wine is so bad that it breaks the general provisions of consumer legislation.

The question of the mortgage being irredeemable for ten years has already been mentioned. Generally a provision postponing the exercise of the equity of redemption is not void provided it does not make redemption illusory or, in the light of ALL the terms of the bargain between the parties, it is not in fact oppressive or unconscionable. The illusory nature of such a provision was seen in *Fairclough* v *Swan Brewery Co Ltd* (1912) where redemption of a mortgage of leasehold property would only take place six weeks before the expiry of the lease. Lord Macnaghten said:

'For all practical purposes this mortgage is irredeemable ... It was made irredeemable in and by the mortgage itself.'

On the other hand, a mortgagor who receives independent advice and is not directly under any commercial pressure from the mortgagee may agree not to redeem for any length of time provided the mortgagee also agrees not to call in the mortgage for the same period. In *Knightsbridge Estates Trust Ltd* v *Byrne* (1939) a period of 40 years postponing redemption was held to be reasonable. The commercial nature of the transaction prevailed as is seen in the words of Sir Wilfred Greene MR who indicated that to hold the provision valid would mean:

'that an agreement made between two competent parties, acting under expert advice and presumably knowing their own business best, is one which the law forbids them to make on the ground that it is not "reasonable" ... A decision to that effect would ... involve an unjustified interference with the freedom of businessmen to enter into agreements best suited to their own interests and would impose upon them a test of reasonableness laid down by the courts without reference to the business realities of the case'.

The Master of the Rolls concluded that there were two main criteria, one that redemption is not made illusory and secondly that the terms are not oppressive or unconscionable and one of the features in deciding this may be the length of postponement. He concluded that something more than mere unreasonableness is necessary to satisfy this second criterion.

On the basis of the *Knightsbridge Estates Trust Ltd* v *Byrne* decision it must be decided that the second covenant is reasonable.

The third covenant is a variation on a familiar theme. Any attempt to impose an option to purchase at the time of the mortgage is automatically void: *Samuel v Jarrah Timber and Wood Paving Corporation Ltd* (1904). This is following the major theme that pervades this area that once a mortgage always a mortgage. On the other hand, a right of pre-emption does not come within this rule. The reason is that the mortgagor does not surrender any initiative when he grants a right of pre-emption. It is up to the mortgagor to decide if he is going to sell. If he decides not to sell the mortgagee is not able to force him to sell. There is no complete authority on the point but reference should be made to the general review of collateral advantages in *Kreglinger v New Patagonia Meat and Cold Storage Co Ltd* (1914). The rules as to collateral advantages were expressed by Lord Parker and the three points he made have been mentioned earlier. The major distinction between the terms of *Kreglinger* and our problem is that the agreement to purchase the sheepskins in *Kreglinger* was to last for the same period as the mortgage, five years. It was held that the agreement in relation to the sheepskins was valid even though the mortgage was redeemed earlier. On the other hand, an attempt to bind the whole of the property of the mortgagor for a period after the redemption of the mortgage was held void in *Bradley* v *Carritt* (1903). It is not easy to reconcile the cases on this principle. The courts will take into account the bargaining powers of the two parties; the circumstances of the loan, commercial or private; and the nature and duration of the restriction on the mortgagor's right to deal freely with his property. The fact that it is to endure beyond redemption does not necessarily make it invalid.

In the problem the right of pre-emption is to last from the tenth to the fifteenth year. It may be that the mortgage will continue for this period because the only restriction is not to redeem within the first ten years. As the sale is entirely dependent on Jack's decision and as the sale will then be at 'market price', presumably the then market price, this covenant appears to be valid. In particular it does not fall under any of Lord Parker's three requirements set out above.

Thus all three covenants appear to be valid on the given facts.

ii) If the mortgagor falls into arrears with the mortgage repayments the X Wine Co Ltd have a number of remedies available. We are asked to concentrate on the taking of possession and selling 'The Wine Bar'. In the words of Harman J in *Four-Maids Ltd* v *Dudley Marshall (Properties) Ltd* (1957), this right to possession is available to the mortgagee '... before the ink is dry on the mortgage unless there is something in the contract, express or implied, whereby he has contracted himself out of that right. He has the right because he has a legal term of years in the property'. X Wine Co Ltd must obtain a court order before taking possession and the court may refuse an order if it is inequitable to grant it: *Quennell* v *Maltby* (1979).

If X Wine Co Ltd do take possession then, until sale, they may use the income in lieu of interest payments and any surplus may be used to reduce the capital debt. A mortgagee in possession is subject to the rules of strict accountability and may become liable to the mortgagor, Jack, for any loss due to negligence in not making full use of the property to obtain the maximum potential income therefrom: *White* v *City of London Brewery Co Ltd* (1889).

The power of sale arises when the mortgage money becomes due, which is the legal date of redemption. In theory if the mortgagee purports to sell before that date the result will be a transfer of the mortgage. In this case the legal date for redemption is unclear except that the mortgage is irredeemable for ten years, making the legal date for redemption, at least, 1993. However it has been held in *Twentieth Century Banking Corporation Ltd* v *Wilkinson* (1977) that where there is no express proviso for redemption then the mortgagor has only an equitable right to redeem. If so, this right may be ended by an order for foreclosure if the mortgagor is in breach of the covenant to pay mortgage interest, as expressed in our question. If so, the court has power under s91(2) LPA 1925 to order sale instead of foreclosure and so sale may be effected by this method even though the power of sale may not have arisen for the purposes of s101(1) LPA 1925. This decision of Templeman J is not without its critics but would, in this case, enable X Wine Co Ltd to seek an order of the court for sale under s91(2) LPA 1925.

If X Wine Co Ltd do sell they are not trustees of the power of sale and may sell as and when they please. The only obligation is that they must sell correctly and make a genuine sale. Once they decide to sell they must obtain the best price available on that date. This obligation was expressed by Salmon LJ in *Cuckmere Brick Co Ltd* v *Mutual Finance Ltd* (1971):

'... a mortgagee in exercising his power of sale does owe a duty to take reasonable precautions to obtain the true market value of the mortgaged property at the date on which he decides to sell.'

Arguably the best way to ensure that the true market value is obtained is to put 'The Wine Bar' to auction. Then clearly at the fall of the hammer that is the true market value at that moment on that day. In the *Cuckmere* case itself an auction was used, but the mortgagee's agent failed to disclose certain planning permissions in the auction particulars which would have enhanced the value of the property. When the hammer fell the price was not the true market value. As a result the mortgagee was liable for the difference between the actual price realised and the price which would have been realised if those planning permissions had been included in the auction particulars. Further cautionary words were expressed by Lord Templeman in *Tse Kwong Lam* v *Wong Chit Sen* (1983):

'On behalf of the mortgagee it was submitted that all reasonable steps were taken when the mortgagee, with adequate advertisements, sold the property at a properly conducted auction to the highest bidder. The submission assumes that such an auction must produce the best price reasonably obtainable, or, as Salmon LJ expressed the test, the true market value. But the price obtained at any particular auction may be less than the price obtainable by private treaty and may depend on the steps taken to encourage bidders to attend. An auction which only produces one bid is not necessarily an indication that the true market value has been achieved.'

Subject to these important reservations, and on the basis that Jack has fallen into arrears with payment of mortgage interest, the X Wine Co Ltd could seek possession and sell 'The Wine Bar'. In effecting the sale, by whatever method of sale is chosen, they must obtain the true market value.

Tutorial comments

a) Consider the classification of the rights of the mortgagor.

b) Consider the five major remedies of the mortgagee.

c) Questions may be set which combine the effect of these rights with the remedies as seen here.

Question 3

'Once a mortgage always a mortgage and nothing but a mortgage. The meaning of that is that the mortgage shall not make any stipulation which will prevent a mortgagor, who has paid principal, interest, and costs, from getting back his mortgaged property in the condition in which he parted with it.' (per Lord Davey)

Explain this statement and consider the extent to which it remains true today.

University of London LLB Examination
(for External Students) Land Law June 1991 Q7

General comment

Most students were probably relieved to find this question on mortgages rather than a problem on priority of mortgages and students with a reasonable knowledge of the relevant case law should have had no difficulty in dealing adequately with this question.

Skeleton solution

Quotation from *Noakes* v *Rice* (1902): facts - Basic principle: once mortgage paid off, mortgagor should be in same position as before the mortgage - *Bradley* v *Carritt* (1903)

- Contrast *Kreglinger* (1914): why was the collateral stipulation held binding? - Importance of freedom of contract, don't willingly interfere in businessmen's arrangements - Must be independent bargain - Collateral advantage must not be harsh or unconscionable.

Suggested solution

The quotation is taken from the case of *Noakes* v *Rice* (1902) and the issue raised is that of the validity of collateral advantages in mortgages. The mortgagee may wish to secure some collateral benefit to himself during the mortgage and even wish to secure the continuance of that benefit after the mortgage debt itself has been paid off. The traditional approach of the courts has been to hold that collateral benefits may not continue after redemption of the mortgage, but that approach has been to some extent modified in order to conform to modern business requirements.

In *Noakes* v *Rice* itself, the mortgage included a covenant that the mortgagor would only purchase liquor from the mortgagee and this obligation was expressed to endure even after the redemption of the mortgage. The mortgagor claimed to be able to pay off the mortgage and be free of the covenant and it was held that he should be able to do so. The House of Lords held that whilst a mortgage may provide for a collateral advantage, provided that the collateral advantage was not oppressive or unconscionable and did not clog or fetter the equity of redemption, the collateral advantage must come to an end when the loan was paid off. It was said that a mortgage must not be converted into something else and since the collateral stipulation is part of the mortgage transaction, it must necessarily end with the mortgage. The mortgagor had mortgaged a free house and was entitled to recover a free house and not a tied house when he had repaid the mortgage.

The same principle can be seen in the slightly later decision of *Bradley* v *Carritt* (1903). In that case the mortgagor mortgaged his shares which gave him a controlling interest in the company and the mortgage provided that the mortgagor would use his best endeavours to appoint the mortgagee as the company's broker and would pay him the commission the mortgagee would have earned as broker, were he not actually appointed as broker. Some time after the mortgage had been paid off, the shares were sold and the mortgagee lost his appointment as broker. He then sued the mortgagor for his lost commission. It was held that he could not do so as the stipulation was void. It amounted to a clog on the equity of redemption. If it had been valid, it would have been difficult for the mortgagor ever to have sold his shares without rendering himself liable for it was only if he retained his controlling interest in the company that he could ensure that the mortgagee was appointed as broker.

The leading case in which a collateral stipulation was held to remain binding after redemption is *Kreglinger* v *New Patagonia Meat Co* (1914). The loan was made on terms that the mortgagee would not call in the principal for five years provided that all interest payments were made on time, but the mortgagor was free to repay within the five years if he wished. The loan was secured by a floating charge and it was provided that the mortgagor would only sell its sheepskins to the mortgagee for a five year period, although the mortgagee agreed to pay the market price for the sheepskins. The loan was repaid within the five year period and the mortgagor claimed to be able to sell its sheepskins to persons other than the mortgagee. It was held that the term was still binding. The House of Lords held that the granting of the collateral advantage was a separate contract independent of the mortgage contract and since it did not amount to a clog on the equity of redemption, it remained valid after the mortgage itself was paid off.

It was true that the mortgagor was still restricted in the conduct of its business after the mortgage was at an end, but the House of Lords was clearly unwilling to intervene in a transaction freely contracted by businessmen, when there had been no inequality of bargaining power and no oppression of the mortgagee. One difference between the *Kreglinger* case and *Bradley* v *Carritt* and *Noakes* v *Rice* is that in *Kreglinger* the collateral advantage was only to last five years from the making of the mortgage. In *Bradley* v *Carritt,* had the collateral advantage remained valid the mortgagor would have been permanently unable to sell his shares, and in *Noakes* v *Rice* the 'tying' was intended to remain effective throughout the duration of the lease of the premises.

Thus broadly Lord Davey's statement remains true but if there is a stipulation in the mortgage which is independent of it, that stipulation may remain binding on the mortgagor after he has repaid the mortgage, even if it does affect the way he may deal with the mortgaged property. There is no doubt that the courts will be less willing to regard such collateral advantages as independent of the mortgage if there is a personal loan than if there is a business transaction between parties of equal bargaining power. The *Kreglinger* doctrine allows the courts a measure of flexibility and perhaps reflects the fact that the mortgagor is not necessarily now the traditional oppressed figure of the last century.

Question 4

In 1990 Henry bought a house to live in with his girlfriend, Joanna. The house was conveyed into Henry's sole name, but he agreed orally with Joanna that she was to have a 50% beneficial interest in the house. The purchase price was £50,000; Henry provided £5,000 from his savings, Henry's father lent him a further £15,000 and Henry borrowed the remaining £30,000 from the Savewell Bank in whose favour he executed a charge of the property expressed to be by way of legal mortgage. In 1991 Henry lost his job and began to fall badly into arrears with his mortgage repayments. Joanna has now left him and the bank is pressing him to repay his debt even though he is confident that he will find a well paid job within the near future.

Henry would like to know:

a) what his position would be if the bank applied to the court for a possession order;

b) whether he would have any remedy if in the exercise of its power of sale the bank sold the house by private contract for less than its market value; and

c) how the proceeds of sale would be disposed of.

Advise Henry.

University of London LLB Examination
(for External Students) Land Law June 1992 Q4

General comment

A question which coupled the law of mortgages and trusts. As regards the bank seeking possession mention must be made of the Administration of Justice Acts. The case of *Cuckmere Brick* must be discussed in the context of the low sale price, and s105 Law of Property Act (LPA) 1925 as regards the distribution of proceeds. In dealing with the distribution of proceeds it is necessary to see whether Henry's father and Joanna can claim an interest in the house, and, consequently, in the proceeds. Constructive trusts, resulting trusts and proprietary estoppel should be considered in this context.

Skeleton solution

- Definition of mortgage.

- *Four-Maids* v *Dudley Marshall* (1957).

- Possession a prelude to sale - dwelling house - s36 Administration of Justice Act 1970 - s8 Administration of Justice Act 1973.

- *Cuckmere Brick Co Ltd* v *Mutual Finance Ltd* (1971) - mortgagee's duty of care on sale - negligence.

- Section 101 LPA 1925 - s103 LPA 1925 - distribution of proceeds: s105 LPA 1925.

- Interest for father - loan - *Re Sharpe* (1980).

- Interest for Joanna - constructive or resulting trust.

Suggested solution

A mortgage is a security for a loan and can be either legal or equitable. In this case Savewell Bank have a legal mortgage in the form of a charge over the property. As legal mortgagee the bank have certain powers, namely of sale, to take possession, to foreclose and to appoint a receiver.

a) *Possession*

The bank are entitled to take possession of the house 'before the ink is dry on the mortgage' (*Four-Maids* v *Dudley Marshall* (1957)), unless they have expressly or impliedly excluded their right to do so (*Birmingham Citizens' Permament Building Society* v *Caunt* (1962)). Should the bank wish to rely on these broad rights, possession will only be granted if it is equitable to do so: *Quennell* v *Maltby* (1979). In reality however, possession is usually sought for two different reasons. Firstly, if the mortgagee does not wish to realise his security he may seek possession of the land with a view to intercepting the rents and profits from the land, and recovering his interest. Such a move is attended by liability on the basis of wilful default, in the sense that the mortgagee will be liable to the mortgagor not for the income he actually generates from the land, but for the income he *could* have generated from the land: *White* v *City of London Brewery* (1889).

The second use of possession is as a prelude to sale, as the mortgagee will wish to obtain possession in order to sell with vacant possession. This appears to be the case here. In these circumstances there are several remedies open to Henry as the action concerns a dwelling house. Under s36 Administration of Justice Act 1970, the court may adjourn or suspend or postpone proceedings if the mortgagor could, within a reasonable time, pay off the arrears. The fact that Henry is confident that he will find a well paid job in the near future is a relevant consideration. On the assumption that the mortgage is an instalment mortgage, the court may treat as the sums owing only those instalments which are actually in arrear, even though the mortgage may require the whole of the outstanding balance to be paid upon default: s8 Administration of Justice Act 1973.

In the circumstances then it would be open to Henry to apply to the court under the Administration of Justice Act 1970 to postpone or suspend any order for possession sought by the bank.

b) *Sale at less than market value*

In the first place the bank, as mortgagee, has an absolute discretion as to the mode and time of sale. It can choose to sell by way of private treaty (as in this case) or by way of auction, and it is not obliged to wait until the market improves. However, once the bank decides to sell it is subject to certain duties. First, and foremost, it is clear from *Cuckmere Brick Co Ltd* v *Mutual Finance Ltd* (1971) that a mortgagee is not a trustee for the mortgagor in respect of the power of sale. He is, however, a trustee in respect of how that power is exercised and accordingly owes a duty of care to the mortgagor or guarantor to obtain the best price upon sale: *Standard Chartered Bank* v *Walker* (1982). Failure to do so will render the mortgagee liable to the mortgagor for the difference between the price he obtained and the price he could have obtained (*Cuckmere*).

c) *Proceeds of sale*

As the mortgage is by way of legal charge made by deed after 1881, the power of sale has arisen in favour of the bank (s101 LPA 1925), and in view of the fact that Henry is badly in arrear, one of the conditions making the power exercisable under s103 LPA 1925 has been satisfied. Upon sale being concluded the proceeds of sale will be distributed in accordance with s105 LPA 1925. Under that section, in the absence of any prior encumbrance, the costs and expenses of sale will be defrayed first, then the bank will take the mortgage monies owing to it, any balance will be paid to subsequent mortgagees if any, and if not, to the mortgagor (Henry). Should there be any prior encumbrances they will be paid first.

Assuming the proceeds of sale are sufficient to satisfy the mortgage debt and leave a balance, that balance is paid to the mortgagor (Henry). The question is whether Henry's father and Joanna are entitled to a share of that balance.

It is likely that the father will be entitled to a share in the balance by virtue of the loan he made to Henry. As it is a loan, it negatives any presumption of advancement or gift between father and son, and, according to *Re Sharpe* (1980) and

Hussey v *Palmer* (1972), would give the father an interest in property pending repayment of the loan. In the circumstances Henry's father will be entitled to the repayment of his £15,000 loan.

On the other hand it is unlikely that Joanna will be able to claim a share in the proceeds. In the first place she has not made any direct financial contribution to the purchase of the house either by way of deposit or mortgage instalments, so as to establish a beneficial interest in her favour under a resulting or constructive trust (*Lloyds Bank* v *Rosset* (1990)). Secondly, although she may be able to point to the oral agreement that she should have 50 per cent share in the house, she does not appear to have acted to her detriment upon that agreement so as to raise an interest under a trust or by way of estoppel in her favour: *Lloyds Bank* v *Rosset* and *Grant* v *Edwards* (1986).

10 REGISTRATION

10.1   Introduction

This is a comprehensive area of Land Law with two clearly distinct spheres of operation. In registered land the rules of the Land Registration Acts must be seen both in their own right and as possibly coming within questions relating to settlements, co-ownership, easements, mortgages or adverse possession. In unregistered land the effect of the Land Charges Act 1972 on the equitable doctrine of notice is of particular importance.

When applying these rules the first question to ask is: 'Which system or doctrine to apply?' Use the following sequence.

a)   i)   Is title registered? [registration of title]

   ii)   Consider use of direct words - 'title to which is registered', or indirect - by reference to owner as 'registered proprietor'.

b)   If so - apply Land Registration Act 1925. Only may be registered interest: minor interest: overriding interest. Do not use the doctrine of notice: Lord Wilberforce: *Williams and Glyn's Bank Ltd* v *Boland* [1980] 3 WLR 138.

c)   i)   If title not registered: [registration of land charges/incumbrances]   Does the Land Charges Act 1972 apply? S2 LCA 1972

   ii)   Class C(i)   Puisne mortgage   Class D(ii)   Restrictive covenant
         Class C(iii)   General equitable charge   [created after 1925]
         Class C(iv)   Estate contract   Class D(iii)   Equitable easement

   iii)   Void against a purchaser if not so registered: s4 LCA 1972

d)   If interest not capable of entry on land charges register then apply the equitable doctrine of notice. Is the person a bona fide purchaser for value of the legal estate without notice?

   Pre-1926 restrictive covenants or licence by estoppel - proprietary estoppel

   Ives (E R) Investments Ltd v *High* [1967] 2 QB 379

e)   i) Examination context

     ii) If nothing is said in the particular question then assume the title to the land is not registered and use 3 and 4 above in that same sequence.

10.2   Key points

Note meaning of 'registration' in the context of both registered and unregistered land. The purpose of the LRA is to register title to land at the Land Registry to create a 'mirror' of the land itself.

a) *Registration of title* - Land Registration Acts 1925-1988. By the Registration of Title Order 1989, all of England and Wales became subject to compulsory registration of title with effect from 1 December 1990.

    i) Introduction

      Essential characteristics of registered title may be summarised as follows:

- Abolishes need for repeated examinations of title

- Establishes a record of proprietors

- Ability to cure certain defects of title. Section 13(c) LRA 1925: 'If the registrar, upon the examination of any title, is of the opinion that the title is open to objection, but is nevertheless a title the holding under which will not be disturbed, he may approve of such title ...'

- Provision of reliable plan

- Issue of land certificate to registered proprietor to replace title deeds

- Provides short, simple forms as transfers, mortgages or other dealings

- Search system to check entries on the register

- Quick detection of conveyancing mistakes

- Insurance fund to compensate for mistakes

- Complete privacy for registered proprietors - but see s1 LRA 1988

      But Cheshire concludes:

      'Registered conveyancing is not ... a new system of land law.'

      In other words, the normal substantive law of real property applies to registered land.

      Advantages of system

- Cheaper by reducing legal costs for dealing with registered land

- Simplicity of the system

- State guarantee of the title to the land

      Conclusion - Cheshire:

'The conveyancing of registered land is different in principle and practice. Once the title to land is registered, its past history is irrelevant. The title thenceforth is guaranteed by the state, and a purchaser can do no other than rely on it.'

Megarry and Wade: 'Its great merits are that it eliminates repetitive and unproductive work in conveyancing and provides financial compensation in some cases where otherwise an innocent party would suffer loss.'

ii) *Principles of registration* - registered land only

- Classification of rights - registered interests - overriding interests - minor interests

- The register - 3 parts - property - proprietorship - charges

- When registration necessary - s123 LRA 1925 - freehold or grant/assignment of lease over 21 years. There are 2 months to register - fail to register and vendor holds as bare trustee for purchaser.

Problems may arise in dealing with leases in registered land. This may be illustrated by the following diagram:

LEASES IN REGISTERED LAND

TERM	RENT	FREEHOLD REGISTERED	NATURE OF LEASEHOLD TITLE/ INTEREST	LRA 1925 and LRA 1986
More than 21 years	Yes/No	Yes	Absolute leasehold	ss8(1) & 123 (s2 LRA 1986)
More than 21 years	Yes/No	No	Good leasehold	ss8(1) & 123 (s2 LRA 1986)
Legal 21 years or less	Yes	Yes	Overriding interest	s70(1)(k)
Legal 21 years or less	No	Yes	Overriding interest	s70(1)(k) (s4 LRA 1986)
Equitable 21 years or less + 'actual occupation'	Yes/	Yes	Overriding interest	s70(1)(g) + *City Permanent Building Society* v *Miller* [1952] Ch 840
Legal, not exceeding 3 years, because in writing or oral, taking effect in possession under s54(2) LPA 1925	Best rent	Yes	Overriding interest (a 'right' protected by 'actual occupation')	s70(1)(g) NOT s70(1)(k) because although the loan is legal it is not granted

- Classes of registered title:
  - Absolute
  - Qualified
  - Possessory
  - Good leasehold
- Conversion of titles - s1 LRA 1986

iii) Classification of interests

- NB - overriding interests: LRA s70(1) - note, in particular
- s70(1)(a) - *Celsteel* v *Alton House Holdings Ltd* [1985] 2 All ER 562; revsd in part [1986] 1 All ER 608
- s70(1)(f) - Limitation Act 1980

- s70(1)(g) -*Williams and Glyn's Bank Ltd* v *Boland* [1980] 3 WLR 138 and *Lloyds Bank plc c* v *Rosset* [1990] 2 WLR 867

- s70(1)(k) - *City Permanent Building Society* v *Miller* [1952] Ch 840 and s4 LRA 1986 - must be granted.

- Minor interests - notice - caution - inhibition - restriction.

- Rules of notice should not apply to registered land - cf *Peffer* v *Rigg* [1978] 3 All ER 745

iii) Indefeasibility of title

- Rectification of title: s82 - note s82(3) to give effect to an overriding interest

- Compensation: s83

But see *Re Chowood's Registered Land* [1933] Ch 574 as to the limits of the availability of this compensation.

b) *Registration of incumbrances* - Land Charges Act 1972 - unregistered land only

i) Registration of land charges

- Object - to enable a purchaser of land to discover easily the incumbrances affecting that land

- Matters registrable under LCA 1972:

  - Pending actions - action relating to land - 5 years and renewable

    Selim Ltd v *Bickenhall Engineering Ltd* [1981] 1 WLR 1318

  - Annuities - created before 1926

  - Writs and orders affecting land - *Clayhope Properties Ltd* v *Evans* [1986] 1 WLR 1223, s6 LCA 1972

  - Deeds of arrangement - control of debtor's property given for benefit of creditors

  - Land charges:

    Class A - charge imposed on application of person who has incurred expenditure relating to land

    Class B - charge imposed automatically by statute

    Class C

    1) Puisne mortgage - legal mortgage/legal estate/no deeds

    2) Limited owner's charge - equitable charge of tenant for life who
    Brenda has discharged a liability out of his own funds

3) General equitable charge - equitable mortgage/legal estate/no deeds

   Effect of failing to register is void against a purchaser for value - s4 LCA 1972

4) Estate contract - contract to convey legal estate/option to purchase. *Pritchard* v *Briggs* [1980] Ch 338, *Midland Bank Trust Co Ltd* v *Green* [1981] AC 513, *Philips* v *Mobil Oil Co Ltd* [1989] 3 All ER 97.

EDWARD

Class D

1) Charge of Commissioners of Inland Revenue - unpaid inheritance tax

2) Restrictive covenant - created after 1925 and not between landlord and tenant

3) Equitable easement: *Shiloh Spinners Ltd* v *Harding* [1973] AC 691. Created after 1925 - construe narrowly.

   CALVIN

   Effect of failing to register (Class C(iv) and Class D) is void against any purchaser of the legal estate for money or money's worth - s14(6) LCA 1972

Class E - annuities created before 1926, registered after 1925

Class F - rights of occupation under Matrimonial Homes Act 1983 - confers rights of occupation on spouse who has no estate/interest in the property. (NB - in registered land this is a minor interest protected by a notice: s2(8) 1983 Act)

- Effect of registration - s198 LPA 1925 - deemed ACTUAL notice. This is the only form of notice to use when the interest is capable of being registered: s199(1) LPA 1925

- Effect of failure to register - s4 LCA 1972 - see above - generally void against a purchaser

- Effect of search - conclusive in favour of a purchaser

- Unregistrable matters eg licences by estoppel - equitable doctrine of NOTICE: *Ives (E R) Investments Ltd* v *High* [1967] 2 QB 379 and *Kingsnorth Finance Ltd* v *Tizard* [1986] 1 WLR 783. Consider actual notice, constructive notice, *Hunt v Luck* [1902] 1 Ch 428 and imputed notice - *Kingsnorth Finance Ltd* v *Tizard*

ii) Registration of local land charges: s1 Local Land Charges Act 1975

- Location - District Council/London Boroughs

- Interests registrable - public rights - prohibitions on use of land. Only private matter is a light obstruction notice

- Effect of failure to register - purchaser bound by charge but is entitled to compensation from the local authority.

- Effect of search: s10 Local Land Charges Act 1975 - search is no longer conclusive.

iii) Companies Register - land charge created by company for securing money

iv) Agricultural Credits Acts 1928-1932 - register at the Land Charges Register if charge made in favour of a bank on farming stock and other agricultural assets as security for a sum advanced to farmer.

10.3   Recent cases and statutes

Celsteel Ltd v *Alton House Holdings Ltd* [1985] 2 All ER 562; revsd in part [1986] 1 All ER 608

Paddington Building Society v *Mendelsohn* (1985) 50 P & CR 244

City of London Building Society v *Flegg* [1986] 2 WLR 616

Clayhope Properties Ltd v *Evans* [1986] 1 WLR 1223

Kingsnorth Finance Co Ltd v *Tizard* [1986] 2 All ER 54

Ashburn Anstalt v *WJ Arnold & Co* [1988] 2 All ER 147

Abbey National Building Society v *Cann* [1990] 2 WLR 832

Lloyds Bank plc v *Rosset* [1990] 2 WLR 867

Land Registration Act 1986

Land Registration Act 1988

See also Registration of Title Order 1989

10.4   Analysis of questions

The questions appear in a number of guises. There may be specific questions on the protection of third party rights in registered and unregistered land, inviting a discussion which must include references to the equitable doctrine of notice. There may be questions on overriding interests under s70(1)(g) LRA 1925. Questions on registered land may also form part of a question on another area of Land Law where the examiner adds this dimension by including a phrase such as 'would your answer differ if the title to the land were registered?'

10.5   Questions

Question 1

To what extent, as regards both unregistered and registered land, does the law strike a satisfactory balance between the interests of a purchaser and the interests of other persons who have some commercial rights in the property?

University of London LLB Examination
(for External Students) Land Law June 1986 Q2

General comment

A question to probe the decision in *Williams and Glyn's Bank Ltd* v *Boland* [1980] 3 WLR 138 as it again comes under closer scrutiny. Many students are reluctant to attempt the essay style questions; those who do are often pleasantly surprised at the amount of material they are able to assemble. In the end the familiar problem of time may emerge as the greatest threat to good marks on this question.

Skeleton solution

Introduction

Unregistered land

Doctrine of Notice:

Actual	-	knowledge possessed
Constructive	-	*Hunt* v *Luck* (1902)
	-	*Midland Bank Ltd* v *Farmpride Hatcheries Ltd* (1981)
Imputed	-	*Kingsnorth Finance Co Ltd* v *Tizard* (1986)

Land Charges Act 1972 s2 and s198 LPA 1925

Conflict between s97 LPA 1925 and s4 LCA 1972

Conclusion

Registered land

s70(1) LRA 1925	-	s70(1)(a): *Celsteel Ltd* v *Alton House Holdings Ltd* (1985); revsd in part (1986)
	-	s70(1)(f): *Re Chowood's Registered Land* (1933)
	-	s70(1)(g): *Williams and Glyn's Bank Ltd* v *Boland* (1980)
		City of London Building Society v *Flegg* (1986)
		Lloyds Bank plc v *Rosset* (1990)
Undue influence	-	*National Westminster Bank plc* v *Morgan* (1985)
Problem case	-	*Paddington Building Society* v *Mendelsohn* (1985)

Conclusion

Suggested solution

The diverse interests which can exist in land do give rise to conflicts. These conflicts are, surprisingly, not only of a financial nature and the dispute may be as to the binding nature of some obligation or as to who, in fact, has the true title to the land. This is one area where the 1925 property legislation has not provided a complete answer. Many of the reforms helped particularly in the sphere of settlements and the rules relating to third party rights in general, but areas of uncertainty remain which inevitably create problems between the interests of a purchaser and the interests of other persons who have some commercial rights in the property. These problems differ when the title to the property is not registered and when it is registered. It will be better to deal with these as two distinct aspects of the answer and, then, conclude by considering if a satisfactory balance has been struck.

Unregistered land

The major problem here relates to the risk of the purchaser acquiring a property over which third party rights exist. Before 1926 the equitable doctrine of notice would protect the bona fide purchaser for value of the legal estate without notice. This phrase may be briefly analysed as the purchaser must have good faith with no fraud being present. As a 'purchaser' he must acquire his interest in any way apart from operation of law. 'Value' includes any form of consideration and need not be full value. Thus purchaser must acquire the legal estate in order to obtain the protection of the equitable doctrine of notice. Finally, there must be no notice of any third party right when the purchaser acquires his interest. Notice may take the form of actual knowledge in the purchaser. There is also constructive notice which is knowledge the purchaser would have obtained if proper inquiries had been made. Constructive notice is the subject of a number of alternatives including the knowledge which would have been acquired if existing knowledge of some existing incumbrance had been properly investigated

Alternatively, the purchaser may have deliberately refrained from making enquiries in which case he will have constructive notice of those facts which a prudent purchaser would have discovered upon making appropriate enquiries: *Re Cox and Neve's Contract* (1891). In any event the prudent purchaser should investigate the land itself because if the land is occupied by any person other than the vendor the purchaser will have constructive notice of the interest of that occupier. *Hunt* v *Luck* (1902) will still apply in such circumstances. If that person in occupation of the land deliberately withholds information about his interest then that person will be estopped from relying on the defence that the purchaser had constructive notice arising from the occupation: *Midland Bank Ltd* v *Farm Pride Hatcheries Ltd* (1981). The third form of notice is imputed notice which is the actual or constructive notice of an agent obtained in the course of the transaction. Such notice is then imputed to the principal. This creates problems for surveyors or estate agents who visit premises in order to effect a valuation for their principal. Any knowledge acquired by such agent during the valuation will be knowledge in the principal even if the agent fails to disclose fully the information he has received: *Kingsnorth Finance Co Ltd* v *Tizard* (1986).

The equitable doctrine of notice was, to some extent, replaced by the Land Charges Act 1925, now LCA 1972. Section 2 LCA 1972 sets out a number of interests which must be registered as land charges, including puisne mortgages (Class C(i)), general equitable charges (Class C(iii)), estate contracts (Class C(iv)), restrictive covenants created after 1925 (Class D (ii)), equitable easements created after 1925 (Class D(iii)) and the rights of a spouse under the Matrimonial Homes Act 1983 (Class F). The general effect of failing to register any such interest is that it is void against a purchaser - s4 Land Charges Act 1972. If the Land Charges Act 1972 set out a comprehensive list of third party rights it would mean that a search in the Land Charges Register would be conclusive in favour of a purchaser. If the interest was revealed it would bind the purchaser; if not it would not bind the the purchaser. Unfortunately this is not the case.

The Land Charges Act 1972 does not provide such a comprehensive list and the earlier rules of notice continue to apply to remedy these deficiencies in the legislation. With the possible exception of mortgages, it is true to say that where the LCA 1972 does apply it works satisfactorily to protect third party interests which have been correctly entered on the register. The problem with mortgages is entirely an academic one relating to competing mortgages not protected by the deposit of title deeds. Each of such mortgages of the legal estate should be protected by registration as a land charge (either Class C(i) or Class C(iii)) in order to bind third parties. There is a potential conflict between the effect of s97 LPA 1925 and s4 LCA 1972. This conflict has never been the subject of any litigation but has occupied the minds of a number of authors over the years. Suffice it to say that if every person who has an equitable interest does what they are supposed to do at the appropriate time a problem will never arise. The collective wisdom of the commentators on the problem suggests that any conflict will be resolved by the application of s4 LCA 1972.

A more worrying practical problem is the failure of the LCA to keep pace with changes in Land Law generally. It is true that recognition of the rights under the Matrimonial Homes Act 1983 is provided for, but other rights and interests remain completely outside the LCA. The LCA itself does have exceptions including restrictive covenants created before 1926 and any restrictive covenants between landlord and tenant. In addition a body of other interests has been shown to be outside the legislation. These include equitable rights of entry (*Shiloh Spinners Ltd v Harding* (1973)), the beneficial interests of a wife who has contributed towards the purchase price (*Caunce* v *Caunce* (1969)) and licences by estoppel: *Ives (E R) Investments Ltd v High* (1967).

Do the above rules establish a satisfactory balance in unregistered land? The answer is probably no because of the continuing existence of the equitable rules of notice. This can create a minefield for the purchaser and may not always give any compensatory benefit to the interests of the persons who have some commercial rights in the property. This may be seen in the conflict within the legislation itself arising from s97 LPA 1925 and s4 LCA 1972.

Registered land

The theory is that because this is the more recent system of conveyancing lessons should have been learnt to avoid many of the problems which exist in unregistered land. There is no doubt that if the system had achieved the target set by the Land Registry Act 1862 'to give certainty to the title to real estates' no problems would arise. The objective is that the title should mirror the reality on the ground by including in the register all the interests of other persons who have some commercial rights in the property. This objective has not been achieved for two major reasons - the irony is that both reasons are derived from the LRA 1925 itself. The first is the ability to rectify the register given to either the court or the registrar by s82 LRA 1925. The second problem arises from the overriding interests in s70(1) LRA 1925.

Much of the litigation on registered land appears to hinge on the interpretation of these twelve overriding interests in s70(1). Many cover areas of potential conflict but there is no doubt that the courts do find it difficult to interpret these provisions. Section 70(1)(a) appears to clearly exclude equitable easements from the collection of third party rights mentioned therein. In *Celsteel Ltd* v *Alton House Holdings Ltd* (1985), Scott J was able to include equitable easements in s70(1)(a) by the use of rule 258 of the Land Registration Rules 1925. He found that a right of way (clearly an equitable easement in the circumstances) was 'a right enjoyed with the land' for the purposes of rule 258 and as this affected the registered title it was an overriding interest which did not need to be protected by notice on the register.

Section 70(1)(f) provides that '… rights acquired or in course of being acquired under the Limitation Acts …' are also overriding interests. If a title is subsequently acquired subject to rights under the Limitation Act 1980 then the person who has the benefit of the 1980 Act rights may seek rectification to give effect to that overriding interest under s82(3) LRA 1925. It might be thought that the purchaser would then seek indemnity under s83 LRA 1925. It has been held that any loss suffered by the purchaser was on account of his own faulty conveyancing in not discovering the true position rather than because of the rectification itself: *Re Chowood's Registered Land* (1933).

It is s70(1)(g) LRA which has provided most litigation. The Act protects 'the rights of every person in actual occupation of the land or in receipt of the rent and profits thereof, save where enquiry is made of such person and the rights are not disclosed'. The 'actual occupation' is the key to the interpretation of s70(1)(g). If such occupation is proved then the 'rights' of the occupier will be protected. These protected rights have been held to include an estate contract (*Bridges* v *Mees* (1957)), the right to buy the freehold reversion of a lease (*Webb* v *Pollmount* (1966)), the right of a beneficiary under a bare trust (*Hodgson* v *Marks* (1971)) and the rights of a beneficiary under a trust for sale: *Williams and Glyn's Bank Ltd* v *Boland* (1981). This final case related to the rights of a wife who had contributed to the purchase of the matrimonial home and had thus become an equitable tenant in common, but the title to the property was in the husband alone. The 'right' of the wife prevailed against the mortgagee as an overriding interest under s70(1)(g) LRA 1925. Apparently this 'right' will prevail even when there are two trustees for sale who could give a valid receipt and thus allow the overreaching rules of s2(1)(ii) LPA 1925 to apply: *City of London Building Society* v *Flegg* (1986). On the other hand the court is prepared to impute an intention that a contributor clearly intended that her interest should be postponed to the interest of a mortgagee and so prevent the exercise of s70(1)(g) LRA 1925 in her favour: *Paddington Building Society* v *Mendelsohn* (1985).

It is not easy to conclude as to the state of the balance between the purchaser and the interests of other persons who have some commercial right in the property when the title to the land is registered.

Many applauded the decision in *Williams and Glyn's Bank Ltd* v *Boland* (1981). On the other hand the institutional lenders, representing the interests of those with commercial rights in the property, had to take dramatic action to discover or eliminate problems of persons holding 'rights' in the land. This, is turn, has led to further allegations of undue influence against those lenders leading to cases such as *National Westminster Bank plc* v *Morgan* (1985) and *Woodstead Finance Ltd* v *Petrou* (1986).

The major threat to *Williams and Glyn's Bank Ltd* v *Boland* may now be posed by the implications of the decision in *Paddington Building Society* v *Mendelsohn* because if the courts are prepared to impute an intention that the contributor does not intend to seek priority over the mortgagee then the problems of the mortgagee are eased considerably.

The conclusion must be a plea for a return to some certainty in this area of the law. The House of Lords in *Williams and Glyn's Bank Ltd* v *Boland* and the Law Commission both concluded that the onus is on the conveyancer to take more care. The institutional lenders responded by taking more care to the extent that other complaints have been made against them. The position appeared to be relatively certain in that enquiries and disclaimers were seen to be the solution to the conveyancing problems posed by *Williams and Glyn's Bank Ltd* v *Boland*. Now we are confronted by the realisation that the problem may never have existed if *Paddington Building Society* v *Mendelsohn* is correct. Until certainty returns it may be that the balance between the purchaser and the holder of third party rights is something of a lottery which depends not only on equity 'rights' but other 'rights' which may be imputed in the circumstances of the case. Not a happy position for either party.

Tutorial comments

a) Consider the effect of the decision of the House of Lords in *Lloyds Bank plc* v *Rosset* [1990] 2 WLR 867.

b) Is there any real justification for saying that the decision in *Williams and Glyn's Bank Ltd* v *Boland* was a 'damp squib'?

Question 2

a) In January 1987 Charles, who was registered proprietor with absolute freehold title of The Bungalow, granted by deed a lease for 5 years of The Bungalow to Derek. In the lease there was a provision that Derek could buy the freehold at any time during the lease for £10,000.

Earlier this year Charles sold The Bungalow to Edward, and in April 1989 Edward was registered as proprietor of The Bungalow.

Derek lived in The Bungalow from January 1987 until May 1989, when he moved out and allowed his daughter Fiona to move in. Derek now wishes to exercise his option to purchase the freehold. Advise Edward whether he is bound by (i) the lease (ii) the option to purchase.

b) Would your answer be different if the title were unregistered?

University of London LLB Examination
(for External Students) Land Law June 1977 Q9

General comment

Registration of title is to be found in both the Land Law and the Conveyancing syllabus and a grasp of the general principles is essential for Land Law purposes. This question selects one of the difficult areas of registration of title and is a good problem. Once again the student who has been selective in his revision may be found wanting in making the comparison between registered and unregistered conveyancing.

Skeleton solution

THE BUNGALOW

(See diagram in suggested solution.)

Is Edward bound by (i) lease (ii) option to purchase?

a) *Registered land*

    i)   5 year legal lease is not registrable: s19(2) LRA 1925

    ii)   Derek has two overriding interests:

- s70(1)(k) LRA 1925 (s4 LRA 1986) - 'Leases granted for a term not exceeding 21 years' by deed will be 'granted'

- s70(1)(g) LRA 1925 - legal lease a 'right' protected by his 'actual occupation' at date Edward became registered proprietor.

    iii)   Fiona not protected because not in occupation at that time:

        Strand Securities Ltd v Caswell (1965)

    iv)   Derek continues to be protected by s70(1)(k): Edward bound by lease

    v)   Even though Derek is not in occupation may still exercise the option:

        London and Cheshire Insurance Co Ltd v *Laplagrene Property Co Ltd* (1971)

        If occupation at date of registration: not lost if then ceases occupation.

    vi)   Option to purchase is a 'right' within s70(1)(g) LRA 1925:

        Webb v *Pollmount Ltd* (1966)

b) *Unregistered land*

    i)   Legal lease. Good against the world: cf *Hunt* v *Luck* (1902)

    ii)   Option to purchase - land charge Class C(iv) s2(4)(iv) LCA 1972. Must register as estate contract: *Pritchard* v *Briggs* (1980)

    iii)   Void against Edward as purchaser for money/moneys worth of a legal estate in land if not registered: s4(6) LCA 1972

        Midland Bank Trust Co Ltd v *Green* (1981). Even if in a legal lease:

        Taylor Fashions Ltd v *Liverpool Victoria Trustees Co Ltd* (1982)

Suggested solution

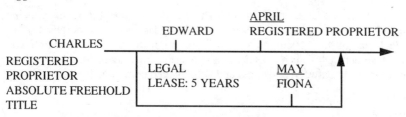

DEREK: Option to purchase freehold at any time £10,000

a) Charles is the registered proprietor with absolute freehold title of The Bungalow. So far as the legal estate is concerned the effect of an absolute freehold title is that Charles holds a fee simple absolute in possession subject only to entries in the register, overriding interests and minor interests of which he has notice.

The lease of The Bungalow for five years granted to Derek in January 1987 is not registerable as s19(2) of the Land Registration Act 1925 prohibits the registration of any lease granted for a term of 21 years or less. Although this lease is not registerable the interest of Derek is protected as one of two alternative forms of overriding interest under s70(1) of the LRA 1925. Overriding interests are defined in s3(xvi) LRA 1925 as 'all the incumbrances, interests, rights, and powers not entered on the register but subject to which registered dispositions are by this Act to take effect'. Thus the legal estate in registered land is always vested in the registered proprietor subject to any overriding interests.

If Derek pays rent then he is protected under s70(1)(k) of the LRA 1925, as amended by s4 LRA 1986, which declares that 'Leases granted for a term not exceeding twenty-one years' are overriding interests and, therefore, bind even the absolute freehold title.

If Derek does not pay rent he is now still protected by these amended provisions of s70(1)(k) LRA 1925.

In addition his legal lease is 'a right' protected by the provisions of s70(1)(g) LRA 1925.

'The rights of every person in actual occupation of the land or in receipt of the rents and profits thereof, save where enquiry is made of such person and the rights are not disclosed.'

This right of occupation would protect Derek during the period in early 1989 when Charles sold The Bungalow to Edward. This overriding interest also protects a transferee who has gone into possession before the transfer is registered but, apparently, not if after registration. Although such a lease is not registerable Edward will be bound by it. It will not matter whether Derek pays rent or occupies The Bungalow rent-free - s70(1)(k) LRA 1925: now applies to both circumstances due to the amendments introduced by the LRA 1986. This is emphasised by the opening words of s70(1) which state - 'All registered land shall, unless under the provisions of this Act the contrary is expressed on the register, be deemed to be subject to such of the following overriding interests as may be for the time being subsisting in reference thereto ...' The effect is that not only is Edward bound by the overriding interest but Derek has the benefit of it by being allowed to continue in occupation under the lease.

After Edward was registered as proprietor of The Bungalow in April 1989 Derek allowed his daughter Fiona to move into The Bungalow. The nature of Fiona's interest in the property could be critical if one relied exclusively on *Strand Securities Ltd v Caswell* (1965), where a lessee who allowed his step-daughter and her family to occupy his flat on their own account, without sharing occupation, was held not to have an overriding interest under s70(1)(g) of the LRA 1925. Lord Denning MR, referring to the step-daughter, stated:

'She was a licensee rent free and I fear that it does not give him (step-father) protection ... it is quite clear that if (the step-daughter) had paid a token sum as rent, or for use and occupation to the (lessee/step-father) he would be "in receipt of the rents and profits" and his rights would be protected under s70(1)(g). Again if (the lessee/step-father) put his servant or caretaker into the flat, rent free, he would be protected because his agent would have actual occupation on his behalf.'

In *Hodgson v Marks* (1971) the Court of Appeal held that a person could be 'in actual occupation of the land' within s70(1)(g) even though the vendor was or appeared to be also in occupation.

In this problem we must look at the date Edward registered his title being April 1989. At this time Derek was living in The Bungalow. It was held in *London and Cheshire Insurance Co Ltd v Laplagrene Property Co Ltd* (1971) that if a person had an overriding interest within s70(1)(g) by virtue of his actual occupation at the date of registration he does not lose the priority and protection thereby gained merely through subsequent cessation of occupation. It appears that occupation on the material date of Edward's registration is sufficient to establish the overriding interest.

Brightman J set out the reasoning thus:

'I can see nothing ... which causes a paragraph (g) overriding interest, subject to which a disposition was made, to be extinguished merely because the owner of the right ceases occupation after that disposition but before there has been any other material dealing with the land. The extinction of the overriding interest in such a case, for the fortuitous benefit of the proprietor of the land, seems to me both unsupported by the wording of the Act and an unreasonable result. A right exists as an overriding interest for the very good reason that the owner of the right is in occupation of the land, ought to have been asked to define his rights by the intending transferee or grantee, but is ignored and has no inquiry made of him. In such circumstances it is reasonable to provide that the transferee or grantee takes subject to the right as an overriding interest. The transferee or grantee has no one but himself to blame for that result. If the overriding interest were extinguished when the owner of the right went out of occupation, that would be a windfall for the transferee or grantee. He would be freed from a burden for no good reason that I can discern.'

The fact that Fiona is now in occupation apparently need not trouble us further as it is established that Derek was in occupation at the date of the registration of Edward's interest who is thus bound by that overriding interest. This is supported by the fact that it is Derek who now wishes to exercise the option to purchase the freehold and who thus retains some form of control over the occupation.

Edward is concerned that the lease contains a provision that Derek could buy the freehold at any time during the lease for £10,000. It has been established that Derek's occupation at the time of registration creates an overriding interest under s70(1)(g) and it appears that such protection extends to any interest of the person in occupation and also that all his rights associated with that occupation are also protected. The test for determining the nature of the rights was stated by Russell LJ, in a dissenting view in the Court of Appeal subsequently adopted by the House of Lords in *National Provincial Bank Ltd* v *Ainsworth* (1965), as follows:

'It seems to me that s70 in all its parts is dealing with rights in reference to land which have the quality of being capable of enduring through different ownerships of the land, according to normal conceptions of title to real property.'

The decisive case on this matter is *Webb v Pollmount Ltd* (1966) where it was held that an option to purchase the reversion granted by a lease of registered land bound a purchaser of that reversion - Edward in our problem - as an overriding interest within s70(1)(g), the lessee being in actual occupation, as Derek was at the date of registration, even though the option has not been protected by notice or caution on the register. Ungoed-Thomas J said:

'Thus, for a right to be within s70(1)(g), it must be an "interest in the land" "capable of enduring through different ownerships of the land according to normal conceptions of title to real property" ... An option to purchase is an interest in the land in respect of which it is exercisable, whether contained in a lease or not ... My conclusion, therefore, is that ... the option to purchase appears to be an overriding interest.'

The option to purchase will, therefore, be binding on Edward and Derek will be able to exercise his option to purchase the freehold.

b) There is a marked difference in the results of these events where the title to the land is unregistered.

A lease by deed for five years is not registerable as a land charge. As a legal lease it is good against the world and the rules of notice play no part where the lease is legal. At the time of Edward's purchase in early 1989 Derek was in occupation and Edward would have either actual or constructive notice of Derek's lease of The Bungalow. But this need trouble us no further as the legal lease stands on its own feet.

The rules relating to overriding interests are not carried through to unregistered land and when Derek leaves the property to allow Fiona into occupation it is the fact of the lease which will predominate and not the nature of Fiona's occupation. Edward will be subject to the lease for the full term of 5 years, irrespective of the present occupier of The Bungalow, unless Derek is in breach of an absolute covenant in the lease not to assign, sub-let or part with the possession of The Bungalow under any circumstances.

The option to purchase is an 'estate contract' within s2(4)(iv) of the Land Charges Act 1972 as was confirmed by *Pritchard* v *Briggs* (1980). By s4 of the Land Charges Act 1972 any such estate contract which is not registered before a subsequent sale is void against a subsequent purchaser of that land. Even if Edward knew of the option to purchase he is not bound by it if Derek has not registered this against Charles before the sale of The Bungalow to Edward in early 1989. As a result Edward must wait until the lease determines in January 1992 by effluxion of time after which, subject to the provisions of the Rent Act 1977, he will be entitled to take possession of The Bungalow as owner of the freehold estate.

Lord Wilberforce summarised the position in *National Provincial Bank Ltd* v *Ainsworth* (1965) at p1261:

'... there is a difference as to the nature of the rights by which a purchaser may be bound between registered and unregistered land...'

Even though the option is contained in a legal lease it must be the subject of separate registration as a land charge Class C(iv): *Taylor Fashions Ltd* v *Liverpool Victoria Trustees Co Ltd* (1982).

Tutorial comments

a) Note the different treatment of legal leases in registered and unregistered land.

b) Overriding interests may overlap between s70(1)(g) and s70(1)k) LRA 1925.

Question 3

In 1980 Mr and Mrs Hall purchased a cottage as their matrimonial home. The price of the cottage was £60,000, of which Mr Hall provided £30,000, Mrs Hall provided £20,000, and Mrs Hall's mother, Norma, provided £10,000 as a wedding gift for the couple. The cottage (the title to which was not registered) was conveyed into Mr Hall's sole name. In 1987 Mr Hall mortgaged the cottage to the Quickfix Bank in order to raise some money to invest in his brother's construction business. Mrs Hall knew about the mortgage, but, when the bank's representative came to inspect the cottage prior to granting the mortgage, she was away on a week's holiday. Recently Mr Hall has started to default on his mortgage payments and the bank is threatening to bring possession proceedings with a view to selling the cottage.

Advise Mrs Hall as to her position. If the cottage was sold, how would the proceeds of sale be distributed?

University of London LLB Examination
(for External Students) Land Law June 1991 Q4

General comment

It is to be hoped that not too many students talked about overriding interests here as the question clearly states that title is not registered. Although the problems raised by the issues in the question are well-known, there is often a tendency to overlook unregistered land and the doctrine of notice and concentrate on registered land and overriding interests.

Skeleton solution

Does Mrs Hall have an equitable interest and if so, is it binding on the bank? - Legal title in Mr Hall but presumption of resulting trust applies - Does Norma have an interest or did she intend a gift? - What are the original equitable interests? - Unregistered land, so enforceability depends on notice - *Caunce* v *Caunce* (1969), *Boland* (1981) - What are requirements for purchaser without notice: see *Kingsnorth Finance* v *Tizard* (1986) - If no notice, bank not bound by Mrs Hall's interest - If bank has notice, does Mrs Hall's consent to mortgage mean that she cannot assert her interest against bank? - How should proceeds of sale be divided?

Suggested solution

Mrs Hall needs to establish whether she has an equitable interest in the cottage and if so, whether her interest is binding on the bank as mortgagees. Mr Hall has the sole legal title as the cottage was conveyed into his name alone. However as Mrs Hall provided part of the purchase price there will be a presumption that the cottage is held on trust for the parties in proportion to their respective contributions. Mr Hall provided one half of the purchase price, Mrs Hall one third and the remaining one sixth came from Mrs Hall's mother. It seems unlikely that Mrs Hall's mother has an equitable interest in the cottage since she provided £10,000 as a wedding gift for the couple and therefore there will not be a trust in her favour. Is Mrs Hall entitled to a one third or some larger share?

It may well be that the intention of the parties was that they would be jointly entitled and that Mrs Hall has a half share in equity. She might argue that the gift from her mother was primarily to her although expressed as a gift to the couple, and thus that her contribution is one half of the purchase price. In any event her contribution is at least £25,000 out of £60,000 and it is suggested that the court is likely to find that the couple are entitled to half shares in equity. Is Mrs Hall's interest binding on the bank? She could have registered a Class F land charge to protect her right of occupation under the Matrimonial Homes Act but it seems that she did not do so, or the bank would not have granted the mortgage. Her equitable interest exists behind a trust and its enforceability depends on the old doctrine of notice. Mrs Hall needs to show that the bank had actual, constructive or imputed notice of her rights.

In *Caunce* v *Caunce* (1969) the house was conveyed into the name of the husband alone although the wife was entitled to a half share in equity. Unknown to the wife the husband mortgaged the house to Lloyd's Bank. It was held that the bank took free of the wife's equitable interest as a purchaser for value of a legal estate without notice. This decision was criticised by the House of Lords in *Williams & Glyn's Bank* v

Boland (1981) concerning registered land, when it was held in similar circumstances that the wife had an overriding interest binding on the bank under s70(1)(g) LRA 1925. It is clearly not desirable to have the rights of the parties dependent on whether or not the land is registered. The later decision of *Kingsnorth Finance Trust* v *Tizard* (1986) is also relevant. In this case the house was again conveyed into the sole name of the husband, although the wife claimed an equitable interest by virtue of her contribution. The marriage broke down and Mrs Tizard started to sleep at her sister's house on some nights. However she still slept at the matrimonial home on her husband's frequent absences and always went there early in the morning to get the children's breakfasts and ensure they were ready for school. She returned there in the afternoon and prepared the evening meal and went away if her husband came back. She kept most of her clothes there. Mr Tizard applied for the mortgage and arranged that his wife and children would be away when the valuer called to inspect one Sunday afternoon. Although on the application form he had described himself as single, he told the valuer that he was married but separated. The valuer's evidence was that he saw signs of occupation by Mr Tizard and the children but not by anyone else.

It was held that Mrs Tizard's interest was binding on the mortgagee as on the facts it was not a purchaser without notice. Mrs Tizard was still in occupation although she did not always sleep there, but in the case of unregistered land occupation in itself is not decisive. The reference to a separated wife, especially since Mr Tizard had previously said he was single, and the presence of the children should have alerted the valuer to make further enquiries. If the mortgagee carried out a proper inspection and did not find a person in occupation, or any evidence of occupation by that person, the mortgagee would have no notice of the rights of that person. An inspection at a time arranged by the mortgagor was not necessarily enough, but it depended on the circumstances of the case. Here the inspection had not been adequate.

In this case Mrs Hall was away on holiday when the inspection was made. It is not known whether the bank knew that Mr Hall was married, or whether there were any children. In *Kingsnorth* the court considered that the mortgagee should be alert for signs of occupation by other persons but that it was not necessary to open drawers and cupboards. It is suggested that if the bank knew that Mr Hall was married, or should have seen signs of occupation by Mrs Hall on the inspection, or had detected Mr Hall in making contradictory statements, the bank probably had notice of her rights. However if Mr Hall claimed to be single and there were no signs of occupation by anyone else, it may be that the bank can claim to be without notice of the rights of Mrs Hall.

A further problem is that Mrs Hall apparently knew of the mortgage, although she may not have known of its extent. There have been a number of cases where a wife has signed mortgage documents and later claimed that the mortgage was not binding on her. There is no presumption of undue influence between husband and wife. In *Cornish* v *Midland Bank* (1985) a wife was held entitled to damages for negligent advice when the bank failed to advise her of the full meaning and effect of a mortgage, but the mortgage itself was not set aside as the bank had not taken an unfair advantage. In *Kingsnorth Trust* v *Bell* (1986) the mortgagee could not enforce the mortgage against the wife as her signature was obtained by the husband's misrepresentations. The mortgagee had instructed the husband to obtain his wife's signature and so was liable for any misrepresentations he made. The mortgagee should have insisted the wife had independent legal advice.

This problem is rather different as Mrs Hall has not signed anything. If the bank had no notice of her occupation it will not be bound by her rights, but if it had notice, will Mrs Hall be unable to enforce her rights as she knew of the mortgage? In *Abbey National Building Society* v *Cann* (1990) the defendant claimed an equitable interest in a house purchased by C with the aid of a mortgage. The claim in the House of Lords failed on other grounds but the Court of Appeal held that the defendant's claim failed because she knew that C was going to raise part of the purchase price by a mortgage and therefore had impliedly authorised C to grant a charge over the property having priority to her interest. Although she claimed that the mortgage was greater than she had been informed, she could not complain against the mortgagee that C had exceeded his authority since the mortgagee could not be aware of any limitation. The bank could argue here that as Mrs Hall knew of the mortgage, she had authorised Mr Hall to grant the mortgage in priority to her interest and was bound by it. It would be useful to know whether Mrs Hall knew of the extent of the mortgage.

If the house is sold, the mortgage must be discharged. As discussed above it is not clear whether the mortgage is binding on Mrs Hall's share as well as on Mr Hall's share. The balance of the proceeds will be divided between Mr and Mrs Hall. It has been suggested that originally they were jointly entitled in equity. If Mrs Hall had been in full agreement to the mortgage and fully aware of its extent, it is suggested that the balance will be divided equally. If she had been misled by Mr Hall she may be entitled to claim her share of the equity and have the mortgage discharged out of Mr Hall's share alone.

Question 4

'The purpose of section 70(1)(g) of the Land Registration Act 1925 was to make applicable to registered land the same rule for the protection of persons in actual occupation of land as had been applied in *Hunt* v *Luck*.'

Explain this statement and consider the extent to which it is accurate.

University of London LLB Examination
(for External Students) Land Law June 1992 Q5

General comment

A question which requires candidates to state what the rule in *Hunt* v *Luck* (1902) is, how it applies and then to compare it with s70(1)(g). The similarities and the differences between the two principles should be teased out. This is not a question for the student who either does not know what *Hunt* v *Luck* says or is unable to analyse it.

Skeleton solution

• Explanation of *Hunt* v *Luck* (1902) - explanation of doctrine of notice.

- Elements of s70(1)(g) LRA 1925.
- Need to investigate the land.
- Enquiries of persons on the land.
- Overreaching.

Suggested solution

The rule in *Hunt* v *Luck* (1902) is intimately connected with the common law doctrine of notice. At common law the purchaser of land was bound by any equitable interest in land of which he had actual, constructive or imputed notice. The rule in *Hunt* can be expressed as follows; a purchaser of land must make enquiries of any person in possession of the land and if he fails to do so then any title he acquires will be subject to that of the person in possession. In short, the purchaser would be caught by constructive notice. In its original formulation the rule was only applicable to the interests of a tenant in possession, but was later extended to cover the interests of any person in possession.

Section 70(1)(g) applies in the context of the Land Registration Act 1925 and is one of the categories of overriding interest. As such it will not appear on the land certificate thereby shattering the 'mirror principle', and, as an overriding interest it is capable of binding a purchaser. In order for s70(1)(g) to be made out a person must be in actual occupation of the land (see *Epps* v *Esso Petroleum Co Ltd* (1973)) with an interest in land capable of binding subsequent owners of the land, in other words, a proprietary interest as opposed to a personal one (*Williams & Glyn's Bank* v *Boland* (1981)). Additionally he must not have concealed that interest upon enquiry being made of him.

In *Strand Securities* v *Caswell* (1965), Lord Denning described s70(1)(g) as carrying the rule in *Hunt* forward into registered land. Insofar as the person in actual occupation must have an interest in land, s70(1)(g) and *Hunt* are the same. Similarly both recognise that the presence of the vendor on the land does not exclude the possibility of occupation by another. In *Hunt* the occupation was that of the lessee, in *Boland* it was that of the wife although Lord Wilberforce said that the rule could apply in favour of any person in actual occupation.

However, there are marked differences. Whereas *Hunt* is based on, and requires some investigation of the land, s70(1)(g) will bind a purchaser whether he knows of the existence of the right or not and whether he could have discovered it or not; it does not require any search or investigation of the land and is not in any way based on the doctrine of notice.

Secondly, like *Hunt*, if enquiry is made under s70(1)(g) and the rights are not disclosed (as a result of active concealment on the part of the person who claims them), the purchaser will take free of them. But, unlike *Hunt*, s70(1)(g) neither requires nor presupposes any enquiry being made in the first place.

Thirdly, unlike *Hunt*, the overriding interests of a person in actual occupation of land under s70(1)(g) can be overreached by a purchaser. In order to do so the purchaser must comply with the provisions of s2 LPA 1925, viz, he must take a conveyance from

219

trustees, the interest must be of a type which is capable of being overreached and he must pay the capital monies to two trustees or a trust corporation: see *City of London Building Society* v *Flegg* (1988) and contrast *Boland.* The fact that s70(1)(g) is capable of being overreached serves to highlight the fact that a search or investigation of the land is not pre-supposed for the purposes of that section.

Fourthly, s70(1)(g) protects not just the person in actual occupation but also the recipient of rents and profits from the land. In this respect it is wider than the rule in *Hunt.*

Therefore there is limited truth in the statement. Both *Hunt* and s70(1)(g) deal with the interests of a person in occupation, but the former is rooted in the doctrine of notice - the latter is not and is capable of being avoided by way of overreaching.

Question 5

'The protection of a party with an equitable interest in a property who is not also a holder of a legal estate should not vary, as it does, with the chance of whether title is registered or not.'

How accurate is the assertion in this statement? To the extent it is accurate, do you agree with the criticism?

University of London LLB Examination
(for External Students) Land Law June 1990 Q3

General comment

The question looks at the forms of protection afforded the owner of an equitable interest behind a trust or settlement in the Land Charges system and the Land Registration system. A straightforward question for the student who is organised and knows his stuff.

Skeleton solution

Introduction

Unregistered Land:

Limited category of registered incumbrances (A-F)

Non-registrable but overreachable interests, ie those behind a trust for sale or strict settlement.

Impact of the Doctrine of Notice when failed to overreach

Actual	-	knowledge possessed
Constructive	-	*Caunce* v *Caunce* (1969)
Imputed	-	*Kingsnorth Finance Co Ltd* v *Tizard* (1986)

Registered land:

Minor interests - entered on Register to protect the interest

           - Notice

           - Caution

           - Restriction

           - Inhibition

Overriding interests s70(1)(g) - *Abbey National* v *Cann* (1990); *Hodgson* v *Marks* (1971); *Williams & Glyn's Bank* v *Boland* (1981); *Lloyds Bank* v *Rosset* (1990); *City of London Building Society* v *Flegg* (1987).

Conclusion

Suggested solution if B Not married

The systems of registration embodied in the Land Charges Act (LCA) 1925 and the Land Registration Act (LRA) 1925 were the consequence of the conveyancing difficulties caused by the feudal system of landholding and the common law doctrine of notice. The feudal system permitted the fragmentation of land into many estates and interests, both legal and equitable. Consequently, the equitable interests would bind a purchaser unless he could show that he was a purchaser without notice, actual, constructive or imputed. The systems of registration were aimed at replacing the Doctrine of Notice with a system of registration so that a purchaser would only be bound by an equitable interest if validly registered. However, the two systems achieve this to different degrees and afford the owner of a beneficial interest behind a trust for sale varying protection.

The owner of such an interest cannot register it as an encumbrance for it does not fall within the categories of registrable interest, classes A to F. Those classes of encumbrance permit only the registration of what may, for convenience, be termed 'commercial equitable interests', whereas the interest under discussion is in the nature of a 'family equitable interest'. The impact of the limited range of registrable incumbrances is that no protection in the form of registration is offered the holder of an equitable interest behind a trust.

However, the LCA 1925 provides such a person with some indirect protection through the requirements of overreaching. Whilst such an interest is not registrable, the LCA 1925 treats it as overreachable and provided the purchaser correctly overreaches by complying with s2 LPA 1925 he will take the property free of the equitable interest, and the holder of that interest will have a corresponding right in the capital monies (the proceeds of sale). The 'indirect' protection referred to comes into play when the purchaser fails to validly overreach, eg because he does not take a conveyance from trustees for sale or does not pay the capital monies to two trustees or a trust corporation. In at eventuality the purchaser will be bound if he has knowledge, actual, constructive or imputed, of the equitable interests, as is clear from the case *Kingsnorth*

Finance v *Tizard* (1986) where the court held that if there are signs of another occupant then a further investigation should be carried out and that a purchaser would be bound by notice of any such interest he would have discovered if he had carried out that further investigation properly, or at all. On the other hand if the purchaser does not have 'notice' he will take free of the equitable interest which is then extinguished (see Stamp J's restricted approach to notice in *Caunce* v *Caunce* (1969)).

Therefore it is clear that as far as the Land Charges scheme is concerned there is no effective direct protection by registration for the holder of such an equitable interest. If he is protected at all it is as a consequence of the purchaser's failure to overreach whereupon the common law Doctrine of Notice comes into play.

By marked contrast the Land Registration Act 1925 (LRA 1925), which deals with the registration of title, provides the holder of such an interest with substantially more protection. First, and foremost, such an interest can be 'entered on' the register as a minor interest, notwithstanding it is an interest behind a trust.

There are three possible forms of minor interest that are relevant here and which differ according to their effect, viz, notice, caution and restriction. The fourth type, an inhibition, is used mainly in the context of bankruptcy proceedings. The effect of a notice is that the purchase is bound by the interest protected in that way. Consequently, it provides the best method of protection for the holder of an equitable interest, but paradoxically is the most difficult to obtain in view of the fact that the land certificate must be produced before a notice can be entered on the register.

A caution on the other hand can be entered on the register without the land certificate being produced. It is, however, somewhat less effective in that it merely entitles the cautioner (the person with the equitable interest who has entered on the caution) to be warned in advance of any anticipated dealings with the property. The cautioner thereafter has to justify the existence of the caution or it will be removed. A restriction, like the caution, is not dependent on possession of the land certificate and is designed to prevent the property from being dealt with until certain conditions are complied with. A common form of restriction would be that the property is not to be sold without consultation with and/or the consent of the holder of the equitable interest.

Furthermore, the LRA 1925 provides a second tier of protection for the holder of an equitable interest by way of the overriding interests in s70(1)(a-l). In particular the holder of an equitable interest in the form of an equitable lease or behind a trust or settlement can rely on the overriding interest in s70(1)(g) LRA 1925.

Section 70(1)(g) protects the rights of any person in receipt of rents and profits from land or in actual occupation of land, save where enquiry is made of such a person and those rights are not revealed. In order to establish an overriding interest within s70(1)(g) a claimant must show (i) actual occupation, (ii) the existence of a right to be protected, and (iii) that such a right was not concealed upon enquiry. As far as actual occupation is concerned a literal approach is followed (see *Hodgson* v *Marks* (1971)), and it is possible to be in actual occupation even though absent provided there is the requisite intention to return (*Chokkar* v *Chokkar* (1984)). Where a person acquires an equitable interest in property which is subsequently mortgaged, in order to establish an overriding interest under s70(1)(g) against the mortgagee that person must have been in actual occupation at the time the mortgage was completed (see *Abbey National* v *Cann* (1990)).

The type of right needed for the application of s70(1)(g) is a proprietary right which subsists in reference to land and is capable of binding subsequent purchasers of the land (see Lord Wilberforce in *Williams & Glyn's Bank Ltd* v *Boland* (1981)). An equitable right behind a trust for sale or settlement, provided it is correctly acquired (see Lord Bridge in *Lloyds Bank* v *Rosset* (1990)), is sufficient as is clear from *Boland* itself as is an equitable lease.

Should actual occupation and a proprietary right be shown the overriding interest will only protect the holder of the equitable interest if he does not attempt to conceal it from the purchaser if asked whether he has such an interest, and if the purchaser does not validly overreach by complying with s2 Law of Property Act (LPA) 1925. If the purchaser does comply with s2 LPA 1925 then he will have effectively overreached the overriding interest and will take the property free of it (in the absence of a validly registered notice) leaving the holder of the interest with a corresponding interest in the proceeds of sale (*City of London Building Society* v *Flegg* (1987)). If the purchaser fails to overreach, eg because he does not take a conveyance from trustees or only pays the capital money to one trustee, then the overriding interest will prevail and he will be bound by the equitable interests (*Williams & Glyn's Bank Ltd* v *Boland*).

To summarise, the LRA 1925 provides the holder of an equitable interest with two forms of protection, that of the minor interest and that of overriding interests, and it is evident from *Williams & Glyn's Bank Ltd* v *Boland* that these are not mutually exclusive forms of protection but rather complimentary forms so that failure to 'enter on' a minor interest does not preclude the existence of an overriding one.

By way of conclusion, it is beyond doubt the degree of protection offered a holder of an equitable interest behind a trust depends on whether title is registered or not. As seen above, if title is registered two forms of protection are provided for by the LRA 1925 itself; if on the other hand, title is not registered the LCA 1925 itself provides no protection directly and only in the event of non-compliance with the overreaching requirements does a form of indirect protection, the common law Doctrine of Notice, come into play.

11 ADVERSE POSSESSION

11.1 Introduction

11.2 Key points

11.3 Recent cases and statutes

11.4 Analysis of questions

11.5 Questions

11.1 Introduction

An area of increasing importance in Land Law and now justifiably recognised by most examining bodies as being the legitimate subject for Land Law questions. The problem area remains the question of leases and their different treatment in registered and unregistererd land. This requires a need to distinguish the effect of the two decisions in *Fairweather* v *St Marylebone Property Co Ltd* [1963] AC 510 and *Spectrum Investment Co* v *Holmes* [1981] 1 All ER 6.

The pursuit of a claim may be demonstrated by the flow chart on the opposite page.

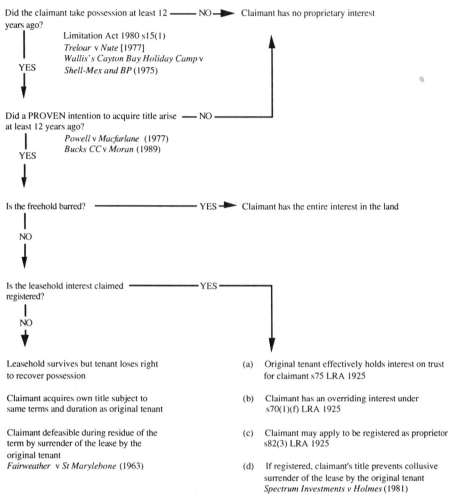

Did the claimant take possession at least 12 ——— NO ➤ Claimant has no proprietary interest
years ago?

    Limitation Act 1980 s15(1)

    Treloar v *Nute* [1977]

    Wallis's Cayton Bay Holiday Camp v
YES   *Shell-Mex and BP* (1975)

Did a PROVEN intention to acquire title arise ——— NO
at least 12 years ago?

    Powell v *Macfarlane* (1977)

    Bucks CC v *Moran* (1989)
YES

Is the freehold barred? ——————————— YES ➤ Claimant has the entire interest in the land

NO

Is the leasehold interest claimed ————— YES
registered?

NO

Leasehold survives but tenant loses right to recover possession	(a) Original tenant effectively holds interest on trust for claimant s75 LRA 1925
Claimant acquires own title subject to same terms and duration as original tenant	(b) Claimant has an overriding interest under s70(1)(f) LRA 1925
Claimant defeasible during residue of the term by surrender of the lease by the original tenant *Fairweather* v *St Marylebone* (1963)	(c) Claimant may apply to be registered as proprietor s82(3) LRA 1925
	(d) If registered, claimant's title prevents collusive surrender of the lease by the original tenant *Spectrum Investments v Holmes* (1981)

The case law of 1989 adds some interest to the subject.

11.2 Key points

a) i) Effect - s15(1) of the Limitation Act 1980: 'No action shall be brought ... to recover land after the expiration of 12 years from the date on which the right of action accrued ...'

   ii) Time runs from when another person takes adverse possession [see 1st Schedule, para 1 - 'Date of the dispossession or discontinuance']

b) i) Meaning of adverse possession - takes away but does not give. Possession inconsistent with the title of the true owner.

ii) *Wallis's Cayton Bay Holiday Camp Ltd v Shell-Mex & BP Ltd* [1974] 3 WLR 357

iii) Leaseholds - time only runs against reversioner when lease ends. Unregistered land.

iv) *Fairweather* v *St Marylebone Property Co Ltd* [1963] AC 510. But surrender lease then landlord may evict squatter: cf *Spectrum* below - in registered land.

c) i) Title acquired by adverse possessor.

ii) Title of former owner extinguished but not transferred to squatter. Possession must be adverse and not under a contract. *Hyde* v *Pearce* [1982] 1 All ER 1029

iii) Thus remedy barred and owner cannot recover through legal proceedings. Section 17 LA 1980. But no transfer of title.

iv) Exception - registered land: title not extinguished but proprietor deemed to hold on trust for adverse possessor. Section 75 LRA 1925. Cf *Fairweather* above; *Spectrum Investment Co* v *Holmes* [1981] 1 All ER 6.

[If squatter registers his rights not defeated by subsequent surrender of lease by original tenant to landlord]

d) i) No hypothetical licence

ii) Licence suggested by Lord Denning MR in *Wallis's* case (above) but now denied by s15(6) and Schedule 1, Part 1, para 8(4) LA 1980.

iii) Effect: does adverse possession = trespass to land? Presume yes.

e) Proof of intention: *Powell* v *McFarlane* (1977) 38 P & CR 452, *Buckinghamshire County Council* v *Moran* [1989] 2 All ER 225

Note the potential comparison between the effects of adverse possession in registered and unregistered land.

f) i) Effect of registered land

ii) s70(1)(f) LRA 1925 - overriding interest

iii) s75 LRA 1925 - rectification of the register s82 LRA 1925

iv) *Re Chowood's Registered Land* [1933] Ch 574

11.3 Recent cases and statutes

Mount Carmel Investments Ltd v *Peter Thurlow Ltd* [1988] 3 All ER 129

Boosey v *Davis* (1988) 55 P & CR 83 (below)

Buckinghamshire County Council v *Moran* [1989] 2 All ER 225 (below)

Morrice v *Evans* (1989) The Times 27 February (below)

Bladder v *Phillips* [1991] EGCS 109

Marsden v *Miller* (1992) The Times 23 January

Boosey v *Davis* (1988) 55 P & CR 83 Court of Appeal

Facts

The plaintiffs claimed that, by virtue of their adverse possession, they had acquired a possessory title to certain of the defendants' land opposite their home. They had used the land to graze goats when it provided forage, cleared scrub to facilitate the grazing and erected a fence to reinforce a fence erected by the defendants' predecessors in title: they had the necessary intention to dispossess the defendants.

Held

The plaintiffs' claim could not succeed as the facts were not sufficient to constitute adverse possession.

Nourse LJ:

' ... Assuming that there has been adverse possession, it is not in dispute that the requisite period of twelve years under s15(1) of the Limitation Act 1980 is satisfied ...

We have been referred to a number of authorities which throw light on what is necessary in order to acquire a possessory title to land. The requirements were well stated by Lord Denning MR in *Wallis's Cayton Bay Holiday Camp Ltd* v *Shell-Mex and BP Ltd* [1974] 3 WLR 387:

" ... Possession by itself is not enough to give a title. It must be *adverse* possession. The true owner must have discontinued possession or have been dispossessed and another must have taken it adversely to him. There must be something in the nature of an ouster of the true owner by the wrongful possessor ..."

Accordingly, we have to decide whether the facts found ... were sufficient in law to constitute adverse possession. The two alternatives posed by Lord Denning are either a discontinuation of possession or dispossession. In the present case there is no finding of a discontinuation of possession on the part of the defendants or their predecessors in title. The question therefore is whether there has been a dispossession. It is a question of fact and degree. A number of different matters must be considered including the condition of the land, the intention of the dispossessor and the quantity and quality of his acts of user ...

On a view of the facts as a whole, and making every allowance ... for the finding as to the intention of the plaintiffs, ... I conclude that the facts found ... were not sufficient in law to constitute adverse possession. It seems to me to be impossible to say that there was, to echo the words of Lord Denning, something in the nature of an ouster of the defendants.'

Buckinghamshire County Council v *Moran* [1989] 2 All ER 225 Court of Appeal

Facts

A plot of land had been conveyed to the plaintiffs in 1955. To the south the plot was separated by a laurel hedge; to the west there were fences; to the east there was a road frontage and to the north was Dolphin Place with nothing to separate the plot from it. From about 1967 the previous owners of Dolphin Place had maintained the plot and treated it as part of their garden; they had mowed the grass and trimmed the hedges. In 1971 Dolphin Place was conveyed to the defendant 'together with ... all such estate right title and interest as the vendors may have in or over (the plot)'. The vendors made a statutory declaration to the effect that since 1967 they had cultivated the plot and from time to time parked a horse-box there and that no-one had challenged their right to occupy it. They further declared that their permission had been sought to lay an electric cable across the plot. The plaintiffs sought possession of the plot and the defendant claimed that they had been dispossessed by him more than 12 years before they instituted the proceedings. The judge found that the plaintiffs had never discontinued their possession of the plot and that finding was not now challenged. Nevertheless, he declared that the defendant was the freehold owner of the plot: the plaintiffs appealed.

Held

The appeal would be dismissed: the defendant had shown both factual possession and the requisite intention to possess.

Slade LJ:

'Under the Limitation Act 1980, as under the previous law, the person claiming a possessory title had to show either discontinuance by the paper owner followed by possession or dispossession (or, as it was sometimes called, "ouster") of the paper owner ...

If the law was to attribute possession of land to a peson who could establish no paper title to possession, he must be shown to have both factual possession and the requisite intention to possess (animus possidendi). A person claiming to have "dispossessed" another similarly had to fulfil both those requirements.

However, a further requirement which the alleged dispossessor claiming the benefit of the Limitation Act 1980 had to satisfy was to show that his possession had been "adverse" within the meaning of paragraph 8 of Schedule 1 to the Act.

The crucial question was whether Mr Moran was in adverse possession of the plot on 28 October 1973 ...

On the evidence it would appear clear that by 28 October 1973, Mr Moran had acquired complete and exclusive physical control of the plot. He had secured a complete enclosure of the plot and its annexation to Dolphin Place.

Any intruder could have gained access to the plot only by way of Dolphin Place, unless he was prepared to climb the locked gate fronting the highway or to scramble through one or other of the hedges bordering the plot.

Mr Moran had put a new lock and chain on the gate and had fastened it.

He and his mother had been dealing with the plot as any occupying owners might have been expected to deal with it. They had incorporated it into the garden of Dolphin Place.

The more difficult question was whether Mr Moran had the necessary *animus possidendi* ... the *animus possidendi* involved the intention, in one's own name and on one's own behalf, to exclude the world at large, including the owner with the paper tile, so far as was reasonably practicable and so far as the process of the law would allow.

The placing of the new lock and chain and gate did amount to a final unequivocal demonstration of Mr Moran's intention to possess the land.'

Morrice v *Evans* (1989) The Times 27 February Court of Appeal

Facts

In 1974 Mr and Mrs Evans purchased a property from Mrs Dummett; adjoining the property was the plot in question. The plot was overgrown and neglected; it was owned by Mrs Dummett but it was not included in the conveyance to the Evans. The only access to the plot was via the Evans' garden and there was no marked boundary separating the two pieces of land. At all times the Evans used the plot as part of their garden, but in 1975 Mrs Dummett's son-in-law and agent, Mr Morrice, told Mr Evans to stop using the greenhouse on the plot and he had done so.

Mrs Dummett died in 1985 and by 1986 the plot was vested in her daughter, Mrs Morrice. On 18 September 1987 she commenced proceedings seeking a declaration that she was the freehold owner of the plot and entitled to possession of it. The declaration was made and the Evans appealed, relying on s15(1) of the Limitation Act 1980.

Held

The appeal would be dismissed.

Balcombe LJ:

'Paragraphs 1 and 8 of Schedule 1 to [the 1980] Act (relating to the time that a right of action was to be treated as accruing) made it clear that for Mr and Mrs Evans to succeed in their claim to title to the plot by adverse possession, they had to establish that before 18 September 1975 - that is, 12 years before the date of the commencement of action:

i) that Mrs Dummett was dispossessed or discontinued her possession of the plot; and

ii) that since that date Mr and Mrs Evans had been in adverse possession of it ...

The law on adverse possession had been recently clarified by the Court of Appeal's decision in *Buckinghamshire County Council* v *Moran* [1989] 2 All ER 225 where adverse possession of a plot treated as a garden was held to be established so as to entitle the possessor to a declaration that he was the freehold owner of it.

On whether the necessary animus possidendi existed in that case, Slade LJ had cited what he himself had stated in *Powell* v *McFarlane* (1977) 38 P & CR 452, 471-2, that 'the *animus possidendi* involves the intention, in one's own name and on one's own behalf to exclude the world at large, including the owner with the paper title ... so far as was reasonably practicable and so far as the process of the law would allow.'

Mr Evans' evidence had been that 'if Mr Morrice told me not to do something, I accepted that I was not to do it'. That evidence, together with the facts of the case, showed that the judge was clearly right to conclude that Mr Evans had not the necessary *animus possidendi* to establish the relevant adverse possession of the plot.'

It must be shown that the claimant has accepted the assertion of the right by the paper owner and the mere assertion alone by the true, paper, owner of a claim to possession in land contained in a letter sent to the squatter is not sufficient to prevent the squatter obtaining title by adverse possession: *Mount Carmel Investments Ltd* v *Peter Thurlow Ltd* [1988] 3 All ER 129.

11.4 Analysis of questions

The questions do appear in their own right and have even looked at the fundamental reason for its existence by asking: 'Why do we need adverse possession?' The answer will be found in an article of the same title by Martin Dockray in the *Conveyancer and Property Lawyer* for July/August 1985 at p 272.

Other questions may use the registered land aspects and the overriding interest under s70(1)(f) and the full effect of s75 LRA 1925 must be understood. Finally, the different treatment of leases in registered and unregistered land must also be appreciated.

11.5 Questions

Question 1

a) Explain the circumstances in which a register of title kept under the Land Registration Act 1925, as amended, may be rectified against the interests of the registered proprietor in possession.

When is a person suffering loss by reason of rectification entitled to be indemnified?

b) For 20 years, X has adversely possessed a strip of land which is included in Y's registered title. Recently X has allowed the fences to deteriorate so that the bounary is indistinct. Last week Y transferred his title to Z.

Discuss X's right to require rectification of the register. In the event of rectification being ordered, has Z any right to an indemnity?

University of London LLB Examination
(for External Students) Land Law June 1981 Q9

General comment

Part (a) illustrates the importance of reading the question with care. This is not an invitation to write all you know about rectification of the register but is limited to rectification 'against the interests of the registered proprietor in possession'. The answer requires the amendments made by the Administration of Justice Act 1977 to be considered in full.

Part (b) is a good practical question linking the question of overriding interest to rectification and the possible claim for indemnity for any loss suffered due to rectification.

Skeleton solution

a)   i)   Rectification. Consider s82 LRA 1925

    ii) Note s82(3) as to rectification to give effect to an overriding interest - amendments of s24 AJA 1977 to be considered

    iii) Indemnity - s83 LRA 1925

    iv) Only compensation if loss is due to rectification. No compensation for a general loss due to poor conveyancing. *Re Chowood's Registered Land* (1933).

b) X has adversely possessed a strip of land for 20 years. As a result X has an overriding interest against Y under s70(1)(f) LRA 1925 as a 'right acquired ... under the Limitation Acts ...'˙ or s70(1)(g) LRA 1925 as a 'right of every person in actual occupation of the land ...'

Only practical problem is whether deterioration of fences makes the proof of adverse possession or actual occupation of the particular land more difficult.

Epps v *Esso Petroleum Co Ltd* (1973) - parking car on unidentified strip of land forming part of garage not actual occupation.

Here there does appear to be an overriding interest. If so - rectification of the register against Z is possible under s82(3) LRA 1925 'for the purpose of giving effect to an overriding interest'. It is possible to obtain rectification in favour of a squatter: *Chowood Ltd v Lyall* (1930). This right is valid against a subsequent registered proprietor: *Blacklocks* v *J B Developments (Godalming) Ltd* (1982).

If Z suffers loss by reason of rectification he is entitled to an indemnity - s83(1).

Any loss suffered must be shown to have been directly due to rectification.

Here the loss is not due to rectification but because of the purchase of an interest which was no longer in Y. In *Re Chowood's Registered Land* in similar circumstances it was held the loss to the new proprietor was due to paying the vendor for a strip of land to which the vendor could no longer make title because of adverse possession by another the adverse possessor having acquired the benefit of overriding interests (as above s70(1)(f) and s70(1)(g) LRA 1925) before the new proprietor purchased. See Clauson J in *Re Chowood's Registered Land* (1933): 'In these circumstances I must hold that Chowood have suffered no loss by reason of the rectification of the register.'

Similarly Z also suffered no loss as a direct result of rectification but because he bought land to which Y did not have title.

Suggested solution

a) Rectification demonstrates that even an apparent absolute title may be at risk if someone can establish a better right to the property. It is s82 of the Land Registration Act 1925 which gives the registrar or the court jurisdiction to rectify the register. The occasions when this may occur include where any entry has been obtained by fraud, where a legal estate has been registered in the name of a person who, if the land had not been registered, would not have been the estate owner or where 'by reason of any error or omission in the register ... it may be deemed just to rectify the register.'

The proprietor in possession is, however, protected against rectification with the exceptions set out in s82(3) of the Land Registration Act 1925 as amended by the Administration of Justice Act 1977. Thus rectification may only take place against the proprietor in possession:

i)   to give effect to an overriding interest, or an order of the court;

ii) where he has caused or substantially contributed to the error or omission by fraud or lack of proper care (s82(3)(a)); or

iii) where it would be unjust not to rectify (s82(3)(c)).

It should be noted that s24 of the Administration of Justice Act 1977 substantially amended s82(3) of the 1925 Act by providing that the register can be rectified so as to affect the title of a proprietor in possession to give effect to an order of the court; previously this could only be done to give effect to an overriding interest unless the additional grounds in s82(3)(a)-(c) could be shown. The 1977 Act also introduced a new s82(3)(a) whereby that ground for rectification against a proprietor in possession was changed to the above wording that the proprietor has 'caused or substantially contributed to the error or omission by fraud or lack of proper care', whereas previously this ground was based on the act, neglect or default of the proprietor. The effect of this amendment is to reduce the ground for rectification by bringing it into line with the payment of compensation under s83 of the 1925 Act. The former paragraph 82(3)(b) - rectification against a proprietor registered as a result of a void disposition to himself or a predecessor through whom he claims as a volunteer - was repealed by the 1977 Act.

The general effect of s82 is that a purchaser who buys registered land and who goes into and remains in possession is guaranteed this possession. Rectification will not be ordered against him except to give effect to an overriding interest or an order of court. A recent illustration is *Blacklocks v J B Developments (Godalming) Ltd* (1982) where rectification was ordered of the register in respect of a title to land which had been mistakenly transferred by a vendor to the purchaser, who was still unaware of the mistake, and sold it to a third party. It was held that the right to rectification is an equity ancillary to an interest in land which may be transmissible and of a character enduring through different ownerships of the land. Where such a right is accompanied at all times by actual occupation of the land by the party claiming the right, this right to rectify is an overriding interest within the meaning of s70(1)(g) of the LRA 1925. This association of the right to rectify with actual occupation is the reason why it constitutes such an overriding interest.

Where the proprietor in possession has contributed to the error by fraud or lack of proper care, rectification may be ordered against him. Such a contribution would be where the description of the property in an application leads to other property being included and to which the applicant then becomes registered as first proprietor. There is a discretion in the exercise of this jurisdiction.

Under s83 of the Land Registration Act 1925 a number of grounds for compensation are provided including loss by reason of rectification, or non-rectification of the register. Compensation is only paid when a person suffers loss by reason of a rectification, or because of a mistake made on the register which is not rectified. This is illustrated by *Re Chowood's Registered Land* (1933).

A purchaser bought registered land, including certain woodlands, to which a third party, without the knowledge of either the vendor or purchaser, had obtained a possessory title by adverse possession. Rectification was ordered because this right was an overriding interest under s70(1)(f) LRA 1925. In a subsequent action, reported as above, the purchaser was unable to obtain an indemnity because the loss was not 'by reason of the rectification', but had resulted from the purchase itself. He had purchased land from a vendor against whom a squatter had already obtained title so that the rectification made him no worse off than before rectification. In the circumstances no loss was suffered and so there was no entitlement to indemnity.

By s83(4) of the Land Registration Act 1925 if the proprietor of registered land claims in good faith under a disposition which is forged and the register is rectified against him, he is deemed to have suffered loss by reason of the rectification.

No indemnity is payable if the applicant or a person from whom he derives title 'has caused or substantially contributed to the loss by fraud or lack of proper care': s83(5)(a) of the 1925 Act (as amended).

The liability to pay indemnity is a simple contract debt and is barred after six years although time does not begin to run until the claimant knows of the existence of the claim or, but for his own default, might have known: *Epps* v *Esso Petroleum Co Ltd* (1973).

b) Although X has adversely possessed a strip of land which is included in Y's registered title he has taken no steps to have this interest registered with a possessory title. He can, however, attempt to claim against Z that he has overriding interests within either or both s70(1)(f) and (g) of the Land Registration Act 1925, which provides:

'70(1) All registered land shall, unless under the provisions of this Act the contrary is expressed on the register, be deemed to be subject to such of the following overriding interests as may be for the time being subsisting in reference thereto, and such interests shall not be treated as incumbrances within the meaning of this Act, (that is to say) ...

(f) ... rights acquired or in course of being acquired under the Limitation Acts; ...

(g) The rights of every person in actual occupation of the land or in receipt of the rents and profits thereof, save where enquiry is made of such person and the rights are not disclosed ...'

It would appear that X had overriding interests against Y and the question is: Do these continue to apply against Z? Where the right of actual occupation is substantiated as an overriding interest under s70(1)(g) there is recent authority to support the contention that any right of rectification derived from this right of actual occupation itself becomes part of that overriding interest: *Blacklocks* v *J B Developments (Godalming) Ltd* (1982).

The facts were that Brickwall Farm was sold by Blacklocks' uncle in 1969 to Godden. The sale included a parcel of other land not part of the original title. Neither party appreciated it had been transferred to Mr Godden and both agreed that Blacklocks had marked the boundary wrongly on a map. Mr Godden never used the land which was at all times occupied by Blacklocks and who built a Dutch barn on it. Thus a right to rectification existed in favour of B. In 1972 G sold the land to J B Developments (Godalming) under this same mistake, and B continued to occupy the land and use the farm. The mistake was only discovered in 1975 when J B made a planning application. The court had to consider whether at the time of the transfer to J B the right of B to rectify as against G amounted to an overriding interest in the land under s70(1)(g) of the 1925 Act to which the transfer was subject. The court held that the right to rectify was of an enduring character. B had an equity ancillary to an interest in land that was transmissible. He had a right within s70(1)(g) which was not itself an overriding interest but it had been accompanied at all times by actual occupation. The association of the right with actual occupation constituted an overriding interest that was binding on the land which was now in the hands of J B. An order for rectification of the register was granted.

This decision should be contrasted with *Epps* v *Esso Petroleum Co Ltd* (1973) where the parking of a car on an unidentified strip of land forming part of certain garage premises was held not to be an assertion of actual occupation. Rectification would not be ordered against the registered proprietors of the strip of land.

In the problem itself it may well be difficult to establish whether Z is in possession of the land in question because the deterioration of the fences has made the boundary indistinct.

If the land is not capable of ready identification or if X cannot establish that he is in actual occupation of any part of the land then on the basis of *Epps* v *Esso Petroleum Co Ltd* case no rectification will be ordered.

On the other hand, if X can show a clear area of land of which he is now in actual occupation and has been so for 20 years then it is necessary to consider *Chowood Ltd* v *Lyall* (1930) where the register was rectified in favour of a squatter who had acquired title by adverse possession to part of the land registered in the name of the proprietor. In addition, on the basis of *Blacklocks* v *J B Developments (Godalming) Ltd* (1982), this right is valid against a subsequent registered proprietor and is binding on him as an overriding interest.

If this is so then X could seek rectification of the register against Z on the basis of s82(3) of the 1925 Act (as amended) which provides:

'(3) The register shall not be rectified, except for the purpose of giving effect to an overriding interest or an order of the court, so as to affect the title of the proprietor who is in possession.'

As to whether Z has a right to indemnity under s83 of the 1925 Act, it is necessary to consider whether he has suffered loss by reason of the rectification itself or for some other reason. The questions to exercise Z are first whether he had a prima facie right to compensation and then whether he can distinguish the decision in *Re Chowood's Registered Land* (1933).

Section 83(1) of the Land Registration Act 1925 provides:

'(1) ... any person suffering loss by reason of any rectification of the register under this Act shall be entitled to be indemnified.'

To establish a claim for such an indemnity any loss suffered by Z must be shown to have been directly due to the rectification. On the facts this may not be easy if X proves he has either an overriding interest or a title by adverse possession. In either case any loss by Z will not be due to the rectification but because of the purchase itself. At the time of his purchase X already had a title against Y so the rectification itself would not cause Z any loss. In conclusion, a further consideration of the *Chowood* decisions will reveal the problems that Z faces.

Chowood Limited bought some freehold land purporting to include certain strips of woodland. First registration was applied for which gave Chowood an absolute freehold title. It was not known at that time that a Mrs Lyall, who owned adjoining land, had acquired a title to the strips of woodland by adverse possession. In an action reported as *Chowood Ltd v Lyall* (1930), Mrs Lyall obtained an order from the court for the rectification of the register by the removal therefrom of the strips of woodland.

In a subsequent action reported as *Re Chowood's Registered Land* (1933), Chowood Ltd applied to be indemnified for the loss they alleged they had suffered as a result of the rectification of the register in respect of the woodland. Mrs Lyall had acquired the benefit of overriding interests under both s70(1)(f) and (g) before Chowood Ltd purchased. Their purchase was, therefore, subject to both overriding interests. Clauson J held that Chowood Ltd had suffered no loss by reason of the rectification ordered by the court. They were, therefore, not entitled to any indemnity since their title was at all times subject to the overriding interests held by Mrs Lyall. The rectification of the register merely recognised the existing position and put Chowood Ltd in no worse position than they were before. The overriding interests had existed all along and the land was taken subject to them and any loss was because Chowood Ltd had failed to ascertain, at the time of their purchase, that Mrs Lyall was in possession under circumstances which prevented the vendor from making a title to the woodland. The loss was due to Chowood Ltd paying the vendor for a strip to which he could not make title.

Clauson J concluded thus:

'In these circumstances I must hold that Chowood have suffered no loss by reason of the rectification of the register.'

This is the problem which faces Z and a similar conclusion may well be appropriate in these circumstances.

Tutorial comments

a) Consider the particular cases where rectification is available under LRA 1925.

b) The effect of rectification on the mirror principle should be noted.

c) Consider s70(1)(f) LRA 1925.

Question 2

In 1968 Widgets Ltd were estate owners in fee simple of their factory, which adjoined a warehouse which Toppletoys Ltd held on a long lease from Littleton Ltd. In 1973, Toppletoys ceased to use the warehouse, boarding up the windows and padlocking the doors; they announced that they would re-open when trade improved. However, vandals soon broke open the windows and door and for a time squatters lived there. In 1976, Widgets Ltd finding the warehouse an increasing nuisance, took control; they repaired the windows and door, included the warehouse in the area patrolled by their night watchman, and stored goods there. This situation, which had been valuable to Widgets, has continued, but on 1 January Toppletoys were taken over by Bettertoys Ltd, and Widgets fear they may want to use the warehouse again.

Advise Widgets:

a) if the title to the warehouse is unregistered;

b) if the title to the warehouse is registered with good leasehold title under the Land Registration Act 1925.

University of London LLB Examination
(for External Students) Land Law June 1983 Q5

General comment

This is an interesting question which explores some of the more complex aspects of adverse possession in both unregistered and registered land. This combination of adverse possession and registration is a popular way of examining the rules of adverse possession.

Skeleton solution

Section 15 Limitation Act 1980: no action can be brought to recover any land after 12 years from date on which right of action accrued.

Crucial date 1976 - W took control by repairs and patrol. - burden of proof: *Treloar* v *Nute* (1977) and *Powell* v *McFarlane* (1977)

Prima facie - evidence to support adverse possession - *Buckinghamshire County Council* v *Moran* (1989) - effect:

a) Title to warehouse *not* registered. T had a long lease. B acquired residue of this leasehold interest. Then W's adverse possession will bar B from re-possession. Does not destroy the lease and rights of re-entry remain.

Fairweather v St Marylebone Property Co Ltd (1963)

Thus L could accept a surrender from B and grant new lease to exclude W. But if W continues after lease expires - in time could claim against L also.

b) Title to warehouse registered. Good leasehold - under LRA 1925

Main distinction - if proved, then proprietor holds on trust for adverse possessor (s75)

If W becomes registered proprietor of leasehold interest - registrar could close B's title to prevent L and B combining to defeat W's possessory title. In registered land consider if it is a breach of the s75 trust if B attempts to surrender his leasehold interest to L.

Spectrum Investment Co v Holmes (1981)

W should proceed as quickly as possible to become registered proprietor - until then L and B can combine to defeat him. If L purported to sell the freehold W would be protected by an overriding interest - s70(1)(f) LRA 1925.

W could seek rectification of the title: s82(3) LRA 1925

Chowood Ltd v Lyall (1930)

Purchaser from L would not be entitled to indemnity under s83 LRA 1925 because has only bought a title which has already been lost due to adverse possession. Hence nothing to indemnify.

Re Chowood's Registered Land (1933).

Suggested solution

Section 15(1) of the Limitation Act 1980 provides that no action can be brought to recover any land after the expiration of twelve years from the date on which the right of action accrued to the plaintiff. If Widgets Ltd are advised to take any steps in this matter it will be essential to look at 1976 as the date when Widgets Ltd took control of the warehouse and at the year in which any action which is found to exist accrued in favour of Widgets Ltd. See s15(6) of and Schedule 1, para 1 to the Limitation Act 1980.

It is then necessary to establish why 1976 is the base date for any potential action. The cessation of use by Toppletoys Ltd in 1973 is not sufficient because any claim that Widgets Ltd may have depends upon more than mere dispossession of the existing occupier. It was only in 1976 that Widgets Ltd 'took control' in that 'they repaired the windows and door, included the warehouse in the area patrolled by their night watchman, and stored goods there.' The fact that some of this involved acts of trespass by or on behalf of Widgets Ltd must also be taken into account. On the question of proof the words of Sir John Pennycuick in *Treloar v Nute* (1977) should be noted:

'The person claiming by possession must show either (1) discontinuance by the paper owner followed by possession or (2) dispossession ... of the paper owner ...'

In addition Widgets Ltd must show the intention to exclude the owner as well as other people and the facts from the question set out above are the basis of any such claim. As to the burden of this proof, see the words of Slade J in *Powell* v *McFarlane* (1977):

' ... the question is whether a trespasser has acquired possession. In such a situation the courts will ... require clear and affirmative evidence that the trespasser, claiming that he has acquired possession, not only had the requisite intention to possess, but made such intention clear to the world. If his acts are open to more than one interpretation and he has not made it perfectly plain to the world at large by his actions or works that he has intended to exclude the owner as best he can, the courts will treat him as not having had the requisite *animus possidendi* and consequently as not having dispossessed the owner.'

These words have now been given Court of Appeal approval by Slade LJ in *Buckinghamshire County Council* v *Moran* (1989).

The actions of Widgets might together be construed as sufficient animus possidendi although an alternative interpretation could be self-interest in securing the premises and patrols by the night watchman to ensure no risk is created to their own adjoining factory. On the basis that the facts provide prima facie evidence of adverse possession it is now necessary to consider the question as to alternative titles.

a) *If the title to the warehouse is unregistered*

The original tenants, Toppletoys, had 'a long lease' and it is assumed that when taken over Bettertoys Ltd acquired the residue of this long leasehold interest. If Widgets Ltd are able to establish twelve years' adverse possession this will simply bar Bettertoys Ltd from seeking the remedy of re-possession by legal proceedings. This is identified by s17 of the Limitation Act 1980:

' ... at the expiration of the period prescribed by this Act for any person to bring an action to recover land ... the title of that person to the land shall be extinguished.'

In the case of a lease this has the following consequences. The dispossession of Toppletoys Ltd does not destroy the lease and the landlord is entitled to sue the lessee on the covenants and may re-enter the land if the adverse possessor commits an act of forfeiture, provided the lease contains a forfeiture clause.

The title acquired by Widgets is against Toppletoys Ltd in that they, and in turn Bettertoys Ltd, have lost the right to sue for possession.

On this point the decision in *Fairweather* v *St Marylebone Property Co Ltd* (1963) must be noted.

The conclusion from this decision is that Widgets Ltd would be vulnerable to a combined remedy in the hands of Littleton Ltd and Bettertoys Ltd. If Littleton Ltd accepted a surrender of the term now in Bettertoys Ltd then Littleton Ltd would be in the position to grant a new lease thereby excluding Widgets Ltd whose adverse possession is against the tenant alone. In addition Littleton Ltd could claim the lease had disappeared into their freehold and this freehold gave them the right to immediate possession of the warehouse. The warning was expressed by Lord Radcliffe in *Fairweather* v *St Marylebone Property Co Ltd.*

'He (Widgets Ltd) is not at any stage of his possession a successor to the title of the man he has dispossessed. He comes in and remains in always by right of possession, which in due course becomes incapable of disturbance as time exhausts the one or more periods allowed by statute for successful intervention. His title, therefore, is never derived through but arises always in spite of the dispossessed owner.'

The only assistance to Widgets is that if they continue in possession after the long lease has expired and Littleton Ltd take no action, then, after a further period from the expiry of the original lease, the freeholders, in turn, will lose their remedies against Widgets Ltd.

b) *If the title to the warehouse is registered with good leasehold title under the Land Registration Act 1925*

The Limitation Act 1980 does apply where the title to the land is registered and much of the previous information as to detail if adverse possession continues to apply. There is, however, one major distinction which is well summarised by Cheshire and Burn:

'When a squatter acquires a legal title to unregistered land by adverse possession, the former owner's estate is automatically extinguished. With registered land, however, there is no automatic extinction of the proprietor's title but it is deemed to be held by the proprietor on trust for the squatter, though without prejudice to the rights of any other person interested in the land whose estate or interest is not extinguished by the Act of 1980.'

From this we can see that any adverse title against Bettertoys Ltd will have no direct impact on the title to the freehold reversion in Littleton Ltd. Cheshire and Burn goes on to say:

'Anyone claiming to have acquired a title to registered land under the Limitation Act may apply to be registered as proprietor and he may be registered with an absolute, good leasehold, qualified or possessory title, as the claim may be, but his estate will be a completely new one and the registration will be treated as that of a first proprietor.'

We saw in the case of unregistered land that Littleton Ltd and Bettertoys Ltd could together defeat Widgets Ltd by a surrender of the lease. The same effect would not arise in registered land: if Widgets Ltd applied for and obtained registration as proprietor of the leasehold interest with possessory title then the Registrar could close the good leasehold title of Bettertoys Ltd. If this did take place it would no longer be possible for Bettertoys to surrender the lease to Littleton Ltd to enable the latter to obtain possession.

This was the effective decision in *Spectrum Investment Co v Holmes* (1981) where Browne-Wilkinson J held that the decision in *Fairweather v St Marylebone Property Co Ltd* did not apply to registered land. If the title of Bettertoys Ltd was closed they would no longer be the registered proprietors with good leasehold title and so had no lease to surrender. The *Spectrum Investment Co v Holmes* case also highlighted the need that any surrender by Bettertoys Ltd would have to be made by a registered disposition and could not simply be a surrender inter se (between themselves) and Littleton Ltd.

The importance of this to Widgets Ltd is that they proceed as quickly as possible to have their possessory title entered on the register. Littleton Ltd and Bettertoys Ltd could defeat the potential title of Widgets Ltd by surrender before the latter obtains registration of the possessory title. Once Widgets Ltd have the title registered then the distinction between part (a) and part (b) of the question becomes apparent in the light of the decision in *Spectrum Investment Co v Holmes* (1981).

In the case of unregistered land we also considered the rights against Littleton Ltd, the owners of the freehold reversion.

If Littleton Ltd purported to sell their freehold interest then the rights of Widgets Ltd would be protected as an overriding interest under s70(1)(f) of the Land Registration Act 1925 if adverse possession against the freehold title could be shown. Thus any purchaser would take subject to the rights of Widgets Ltd. The right of rectification would be available in favour of Widgets Ltd and the purchaser from Littleton Ltd would not be entitled to an indemnity, the reason being that such a purchaser loses very little because he had a title already barred by the adverse possession of Widgets Ltd. A similar argument would prevail in the case of Bettertoys Ltd in that Widgets Ltd have an overriding interest against the good leasehold title of Toppletoys Ltd and any rectification of the leasehold title to give effect to that overriding interest would mean no loss to Bettertoys Ltd.

Re Chowood's Registered Land (1933).

Tutorial comments

a) How does the question of adverse possession against the landlord when the tenant has already lost possession vary between registered and unregistered land?

b) How difficult is the proof of intention in adverse possession?

c) Why is the question of indemnity a problem if rectification is available in the case of s70(1)(f) LRA 1925?

Question 3

Peter owned a house at No 12 Church Street and Quentin owned the neighbouring house at No 14 Church Street. The titles to both properties were registered under the Land Registration Acts. In 1975 Peter erected a tool-shed partly on his own garden and partly on a strip of the garden of No 14 without Quentin's consent. In 1985 Peter sold No 12 to James who continued to use the shed and in 1990 Quentin sold No 14 to Henry. Henry now wants James to remove the shed.

Advise James. How would your advice differ if the land was unregistered?

University of London LLB Examination
(for External Students) Land Law June 1991 Q6

General comment

This was probably not a very welcome question to many students as adverse possession is an area of the syllabus which is often omitted in revision and the rules on rectification of the register are sometimes glossed over by those who regard registered land as being solely about overriding interests and in particular s70(1)(g) of the Land Registration Act 1925.

Skeleton solution

Time period for adverse possession - Aggregation of periods of adverse possession by different owners? - Does the register provide a guarantee of title - Squatters rights or overriding interests? - Compensation for rectification? No loss due to overriding interests not rectification - Position on unregistered land.

Suggested solution

The Limitation Act 1980 sets a 12 year period for the recovery of land and the issue in this case is to establish whether Henry may still recover possession of the part of his garden on which the tool-shed has been erected, or whether his right of action has been barred by lapse of time since it is more than 12 years since the tool-shed was erected.

The tool-shed was erected on the garden of No 14 in 1975 and time begins to run as soon as the rightful owner has been dispossessed. Adverse possession is a matter of fact, but in this case it seems clear that Peter's acts are inconsistent with Quentin's ownership. Peter had not established title against Quentin when he sold No 12 in 1985, as only ten years had passed, but it is well-established that the period taking the squatter's interest can add the squatter's period of possession to his own. Thus James may aggregate his own and Peter's periods of occupation. There are various situations in which a longer period of occupation is required or when the date from which time begins to run is postponed but there seems no indication that any of these apply in this case.

When he bought No 14 Henry was registered with freehold absolute and the register will show him as the proprietor of the garden including the part with the tool-shed on it. The register is said to provide a state guarantee of title. However this state guarantee is not comprehensive and if James can show that he has acquired title under the Limitation Act, he will be entitled to have the register rectified under s82 Land Registration Act 1925. When Henry purchased No 14 in 1990 he purchased subject to any overriding interests, and rights acquired or in the course of being acquired under the Limitation Acts are overriding interests under s70(1)(f) LRA 1925. Once title has been acquired by adverse possession the registered proprietor holds on trust for the squatter. James may apply for registration as proprietor and will be registered with an absolute or possessory title as appropriate. His estate is a new one and not a transfer of an existing one and will be treated as a first registration.

Although the LRA 1925 does provide for compensation to be paid to any person suffering loss by reason of rectification of the register under s83, it seems that Henry will not be entitled to compensation here. In *Re Chowood* (1933) C was registered as proprietor with title absolute to land, but previously L had acquired title to part of that

241

land by adverse possession. The register was rectified against C and C was held not entitled to compensation because C had always bought subject to any overriding interests and C's loss was due not to the rectification but to failing to ascertain the existence of the overriding interest before he purchased. In this case Henry's loss is not due to the rectification but to paying Quentin for land to which Quentin could not make title.

If this were unregistered land James would still be able to claim title by adverse possession but there will be no transfer of title to James from Henry. James's title depends on his possession and the title of Henry is automatically extinguished under s17 Limitation Act 1980.

12 UNIVERSITY OF LONDON LLB (EXTERNAL) 1993 QUESTIONS AND SUGGESTED SOLUTIONS

UNIVERSITY OF LONDON
LLB EXAMINATIONS 1993
for External Students
Part I EXAMINATION (Scheme A) and
SECOND AND THIRD YEAR EXAMINATIONS (Scheme B)

LAND LAW

Tuesday, 8 June: 10.00am to 1.00pm

Answer *FOUR* of the following EIGHT questions

1   In 1980 John suggested to Mary, his mother, who was old and in poor health, that they should buy a house together. Mary agreed and, knowing that John had little money, offered to pay £50,000 towards the purchase price. The house, which was unregistered land, was conveyed into John's sole name. The purchase price of the house was £100,000 and the remaining £50,000 was raised by means of a building society mortgage for which John was solely responsible. Mary knew nothing of the mortgage. A few years later John obtained, again without Mary's knowledge, a loan of £70,000 from Quickloans Ltd, at a relatively high rate of interest, secured by a charge on the house in his sole name. Although Quickloans Ltd knew that Mary was living in the house, they made no inquiries of her. John used part of the £70,000 to redeem the first mortgage, pocketed the rest and disappeared. Quickloans subsequently sought possession of the house from Mary because the loan instalments have not been paid.

Advise Mary.

2   'No one by the light of nature ever understood an English mortgage of real estate.'

Outline the main criticisms that can be made of the English law of mortgages and suggest ways in which the law could be reformed to meet those criticisms.

3   Jim was the registered owner of Blackacre and in 1990 he orally agreed to sell a part of the land to his friend, Ben, for £20,000. Ben did not pay anything, but he built a house on the part he had agreed to purchase and went into occupation. In 1922 Jim sold the whole of Blackacre to Victor and Victor was registered as the new owner. Victor has now told Ben to leave the land.

Advise Ben.

Would your advice be different if either (a) the agreement between Jim and Ben had been in writing, or (b) Blackacre had been sold to Victor expressly 'subject to Ben's rights'?

4   Consider the effect of

a)   a lease of Redacre at a rent to Alf until he marries;

b)   a lease of Pinkacre at a rent to Bill for five years which contains a covenant to renew on the same terms;

c)   a lease of Greenacre at a yearly rent to Cal until the landlord requires the land for development, Cal goes into possession and pays rent yearly.

5   Jake owned a baker's shop and a yard behind the shop which served as a carpark for his customers. Jake also owned the track that led from the highway along the side of the shop to the yard. On the other side of the track was Sid's carpentry shop and in 1965 Jake executed a deed granting Sid a 'licence' to use the track and to park his van in the carpark. This made it possible for Sid to deliver timber to the back of his shop and he therefore built a rear extension to the shop for the purpose of storing the timber. In 1991 Sid sold his shop to William, who has since expanded the carpentry business. Not only does William park his van in Jake's carpark, but William's two young apprentices also park their motorcycles there. Jake has now written to William demanding that he cease to use the track and the carpark and informing William of his intention to convert the carpark into a cafe for his customers.

Advise William.

6   When Stella decided to buy a farm, she invited her lover, Paul, to come and live with her and help her run the farm. Stella paid the whole purchase price and the farm was conveyed into her sole name. When Paul asked why it had not been conveyed into their joint names, Stella told him that there was no need for him to worry as he would get a half-share when they got married and as she was going to leave him her London apartment in her will anyway. Stella and Paul never married but they worked hard on the farm for several years, sharing the profits equally, and as a result the value of the farm doubled. Recently Stella has died leaving all her estate to her mother. Paul now claims both the farm and the London apartment.

Advise Stella's mother.

7   In 1989 Leslie granted Alice a lease of Redstone House (unregistered land) for 20 years, Alice covenanting, *inter alia*, to pay a yearly rent of £10,000, to keep the house in a good state of repair and not to use the house for immoral purposes. In 1990 Alice assigned her lease to Bert and in 1993 Bert granted a sublease to Chris for five years. In 1993 Leslie assigned his reversion to Rachel. No rent has been paid since 1991, the house is in serious need of repair and Chris has recently been convicted to keeping a brothel.

Who has remedies against whom in respect of these breaches of covenant?

8   'The 1925 legislation has endowed trusts for sale with all the advantages of settled land. Little would be lost if all settlements were made to take effect as trusts for sale.'

Discuss.

Question 1

In 1980 John suggested to Mary, his mother, who was old and in poor health, that they should buy a house together. Mary agreed and, knowing that John had little money, offered to pay £50,000 towards the purchase price. The house, which was unregistered land, was conveyed into John's sole name. The purchase price of the house was £100,000 and the remaining £50,000 was raised by means of a building society mortgage for which John was solely responsible. Mary knew nothing of the mortgage. A few years later John obtained, again without Mary's knowledge, a loan of £70,000 from Quickloans Ltd, at a relatively high rate of interest, secured by a charge on the house in his sole name. Although Quickloans Ltd knew that Mary was living in the house, they made no inquiries of her. John used part of the £70,000 to redeem the first mortgage, pocketed the rest and disappeared. Quickloans subsequently sought possession of the house from Mary because the loan instalments have not been paid.

Advise Mary.

University of London LLB Examination
(for External Students) Land Law June 1993 Q1

General comment

A fairly standard question on the acquisition and protection of an equitable interest in land, except that a good understanding and application of the principles relating to a party's implied consent to a mortgage is essential to a good answer.

Skeleton solution

- Resulting trust.
- Overreaching.
- Notice.
- *Caunce* v *Caunce* (1969).
- *Kingsnorth Finance* v *Tizard* (1986).
- Implied consent.
- *Paddington Building Society* v *Mendelsohn* (1985).
- *Equity & Law Home Loans* v *Prestidge* (1992).

Suggested solution

The first issue is whether Mary has an interest in the house. As the house is conveyed into John's sole name, it is clear that Mary does not have a legal interest in it, therefore any interest she has must be equitable. There is no suggestion that the conveyance spells out any trust in favour of Mary, so she cannot rely on *Goodman* v *Gallant* (1986).

However, Mary has contributed £50,000 towards the purchase of the house costing £100,000, and as there is nothing to indicate that she intended this as a gift or loan, she will acquire a beneficial interest in the house under a resulting trust. Consequently, there is a co-ownership situation which finds expression in an implied or statutory trust for sale (ss34-36 Law of Property Act (LPA) 1925). John holds the house on trust for sale for himself and Mary in proportion to their respective contributions.

As the house stands in an area of land governed by the Land Charges Act 1925, Mary cannot protect her beneficial interest by registering a land charge (classes A-F). As her interest arises behind a trust it is a non-registrable but overreachable one. That being so, Quickloans could take free of it if they have overreached it according to s2 Law of Property Act 1925. However, it appears that Quickloans only ever dealt with John (the sole legal owner), and as such, they have not dealt with or paid two trustees and have not overreached.

Despite the fact that Quickloans have not overreached, they will only be bound by Mary's interest if it can be shown that they had notice of it and that Mary did not impliedly consent to the mortgage.

As far as notice goes, a non-registrable but overreachable interest which has not been overreached, is binding on everyone except the purchaser without notice - actual, constructive or imputed. Quickloans does not have personal knowledge of Mary's interest and thus does not have actual notice. They may, however, have constructive or imputed notice. Constructive notice exists where the purchaser would have discovered the existence of the equitable interest if he had investigated properly or at all. Imputed notice is simply constructive notice of an agent.

According to *Caunce* v *Caunce* (1969), a purchaser of property vested in the sole legal title of a husband does not have notice of a wife's equitable interest by virtue of her actual occupation. In such cases the wife's presence is said to be wholly consistent with the sole legal title offered by the husband. By analogy it could be said that even if Quickloans were aware of Mary's presence in the house that could be explained on the basis that she was there simply because she was John's mother - in other words that her presence was wholly consistent with the sole legal title offered by John. On this basis Quickloans would take free of Mary's interest.

On the other hand, according to *Kingsnorth Finance* v *Tizard* (1986), where a purchaser is aware that some other person is in occupation of the premises he should undertake further investigations to see whether that person has an interest. Failure to do so will mean that the purchaser is subject to all equitable interests he would have discovered if he had investigated properly or at all. On the facts, as Quickloans knew that Mary was living in the house they should have made further enquiries to see whether she had an interest. Their failure to do so would mean that they were subject to her interest unless it can be shown that Mary impliedly consented to the mortgage.

When the house was first purchased, Mary was well aware that John had little money, but it is not clear whether she knew what the value of the house was. If she did, it could be argued that she must have realised that a mortgage was necessary in order to purchase the house, and, therefore could be said to have impliedly consented to the building society mortgage (see *Paddington Building Society* v *Mendelsohn* (1985)). If that is the case, then when John took the mortgage from Quickloans and used it to pay off the first building society, Mary's implied consent to the amount of the first mortgage is deemed to be an implied consent to that amount of the Quickloans mortgage (*Equity & Law Home Loans Ltd* v *Prestidge* (1992)).

Therefore, should Quickloans succeed in obtaining possession of the property and selling it, unless Prestidge applies in their favour, Mary would have an interest which takes priority over theirs and which must be defrayed out of the expenses of sale before the mortgage monies are recovered.

Question 2

'No one by the light of nature ever understood an English mortgage of real estate.'

Outline the main criticisms that can be made of the English law of mortgages and suggest ways in which the law could be reformed to meet those criticisms.

University of London LLB Examination
(for External Students) Land Law June 1993 Q2

General comment

Not a write all you know about mortgages question! The question demands a critique of the law of mortgages, and therefore a knowledge of the Law Commission's proposals is essential to a good answer.

Skeleton solution

- Definition.
- Methods of creation.
- Priorities.
- Postponing redemption.
- Collateral advantages.
- Consumer Credit Act 1974.

Suggested solution

A mortgage is simply security for a loan redeemable upon repayment of the loan. However, unlike the definition, the realities and practicalities of mortgages are very complex, and as Lord MacNaghten noted in *Samuel* v *Jarrah Timber and Wood Paving Corporation Ltd* (1904) 'No one ever understood an English mortgage of real estate'.

Criticisms of the English mortgage can be made across the board form creation to priorities, including mortgagees' rights. Although the method of creating mortgages has simplified since the 1925 property legislation, the whole process is still cumbersome. Legal mortgages no longer involve a conveyance of the fee simple but instead are created by a demise for a term of years absolute or by legal charge - the latter being simpler and the preferred option. However, English law does recognise the creation of equitable mortgages which, under the Law of Property (Miscellaneous Provisions) Act 1989, must be created by a written contract containing all of the relevant terms and signed by both parties. It is readily apparent, that the law of mortgages suffers from the same defects which were apparent in land law prior to the 1925 legislation, namely a plethora of interests both legal and equitable which can exist in the same piece of land. To remedy this the Law Commission recommended in its report on Land Mortgages No 99, that all the existing methods of creating mortgages be abolished and replaced by a Formal Land Mortgage created by statute.

The logical consequence of the recognition of legal and equitable mortgages is the operation of two different schemes of protection and complex rules for determining priorities of mortgages. Legal mortgagees either protect themselves by taking title deeds, registering legal charges or puisne mortgagees (Ci land charge), whereas equitable mortgagees have to register general equitable charges (Ciii). Where registration is required for protection, the normal rules apply making a mortgage void against a subsequent purchaser for want of registration. The adoption of a single form of statutory mortgage would render the differing forms and methods of protection unnecessary.

Because of the different types of mortgage, complex rules have evolved governing the determination of priorities between competing mortgages. Generally speaking, legal mortgages prevail over equitable, and the first in time has priority. However, a prior mortgagee who has taken the title deeds for protection can lose that priority through fraud estoppel or gross negligence (*Hewitt* v *Loosemore* (1851); *Agra Bank* v *Barry* (1874)). As far as equitable mortgages are concerned they are governed by the rule in *Dearle* v *Hall* (1828) (as amended by s138 and s139 Law of Property Act 1925), which provides that priority deeds in the order in which notice of the mortgage is received by the owner of the legal estate. Again the adoption of a single statutory mortgage which must be registered would eradicate this problem.

Although the law will not allow a mortgage which is irredeemable (*Fairclough* v *Swan Brewery Co Ltd* (1912)), a term in a mortgage which postpones redemption until the end of the mortgage can be valid if it is not oppressive or unconscionable (*Knightsbridge Estates Trust Ltd* v *Byrne* (1939)). This means that the mortgagor is prevented from redeeming until the end of the mortgage and must continue to pay interest on the loan for the whole of that period. In the meantime his dealing with the land will always be against the backdrop of the mortgage and subject to, (in most cases), the mortgagee's legal charge - a situation which makes it difficult to use the land as collateral and which does not promote alienability of the land, one of the reasons for the 1925 legislation. Mortgages governed by the Consumer Credit Act 1974 are prohibited from containing such a term by s94 of the Act which gives the debtor (mortgagor) a statutory right of early redemption. The Law Commission considered that a similar provision could be adopted for all mortgages, which would effectively render postponement impossible.

Other problems arise in the context of collateral advantages - terms in a mortgage which are designed to give the mortgagee something more than his security and interest. The relevant principles can be stated as follows: a collateral advantage which exists until redemption can be valid, but will be void if it is oppressive or unconscionable; a collateral advantage which exists beyond redemption is void unless it exists as an independent transaction (see eg *Noakes* v *Rice* (1902); *Biggs* v *Hodinott* (1898)). Where valid, the existence of a collateral advantage has two major consequences. Firstly, the mortgagor may find that he is 'tied-in' to the mortgagee in a business sense (for example, that during the course of the mortgage he has to buy all his stock from the mortgagee), a situation which could actually last for the whole of the mortgage if the right to redeem has been effectively postponed. Secondly, the mortgage then becomes a valuable asset for the mortgagee, even more so if the right to redeem has been postponed. These problems could be eradicated, to a greater or lesser extent, by the enactment of a statute similar to the Consumer Credit Act which prohibits any term designed to recover more than security and interest, and/or by making the mortgagee's assignment of the mortgage dependent on the consent of the mortgagor.

Additionally, criticism may be levelled at rates of interest imposed in mortgages. Obviously, if an exceptionally high rate of interest is imposed or is disguised as a collateral advantage, then if it is found to be oppressive and unconscionable it will be struck down (*Cityland & Property (Holdings) Ltd* v *Dabrah* (1968)). In the case of Consumer Credit Act mortgages, if the rate of interest is found to be extortinate the court has the power to re-open and re-write the agreement. Although a similar statutory power would (arguably), be more appropriate than the existing common law approach, it must be borne in mind that as currently drafted the Consumer Credit Act does recognise a creditor's right to charge high rates of interest (see *Ketley* v *Scott* (1981) - 48% APR was valid).

As far as the mortgagee's remedies go, the main criticism lies in the existence of the right to foreclose. The courts have shown themselves extremely reluctant to allow a mortgagee to foreclose, preferring instead to order sale (which at least means that any excess capital monies after paying off expenses and mortgage go to the mortgagor). In the circumstances the time may well have come for this remedy to be abolished - again a matter considered by the Law Commission.

Similarly, when a mortgagee goes into possession either as a prelude to sale or as a means of recovering interest, with the exception of the principle of wilful default, the mortgagor has no effective means of controlling the mortgagee or of making him account for any benefit he receives. As before the adoption of a statutory requirement of accountability would go some way to cure this defect.

Given the criticisms that could be levelled at the law of mortgages, essential reforms would appear to be required in respect of creation and registration of mortgages as well as the content of the agreement. This would probably best be achieved by the enactment of a single act drawing upon some of the principles enshrined in the Consumer Credit Act 1974.

Question 3

Jim was the registered owner of Blackacre and in 1990 he orally agreed to sell a part of the land to his friend, Ben, for £20,000. Ben did not pay anything, but he built a house on the part he had agreed to purchase and went into occupation. In 1922 Jim sold the whole of Blackacre to Victor and Victor was registered as the new owner. Victor has now told Ben to leave the land.

Advise Ben.

Would your advice be different if either (a) the agreement between Jim and Ben had been in writing, or (b) Blackacre had been sold to Victor expressly 'subject to Ben's rights'?

University of London LLB Examination
(for External Students) Land Law June 1993 Q3

General comment

Formalities for a contract of sale are at the heart of this question. It is therefore necessary to deal with s2 Law of Property (Miscellaneous Provisions) Act 1989. Thereafter this is a straightforward question on estoppel, registration and notice.

Skeleton solution

- Law of Property (Miscellaneous Provisions) Act 1989.

- Estoppel.

- Section 70(1)(g) Land Registration Act 1925.

- *Lyus* v *Prowsa* (1982).

- *Peffer* v *Rigg* (1978).

- *Binions* v *Evans* (1972).

Suggested solution

In order for there to be a valid contract of sale in respect of Blackacre there must be compliance with s2 Law of Property (Miscellaneous Provisions) Act 1989. That Act requires the contract to be in writing, contain all the relevant terms and be signed by both parties. If not the contract is void. As the contract between Jim and Ben is oral only, it is void and no action can be brought on it. It follows that as the contract is void it cannot form the basis of an estate contract and be registered as a minor interest under the Land Registration Act 1925.

Nonetheless Ben has, with the knowledge of Jim, gone onto the land and built a house on it. As Jim has, apparently, stood back and allowed or tacitly encouraged Ben to spend money on his (Jim's) land, it could be argued that a proprietary estoppel arises in Ben's favour (see *Willmott* v *Barber* (1880); *Taylor Fashions* v *Liverpool Victoria Trustees* (1982)). If an estoppel arises in favour of Ben being of a proprietary nature, he could have protected it against subsequent purchasers by entering on a minor interest (in the form of a notice, caution or restriction). There is nothing to say that Ben has

251

done so and consequently it would be void against Victor as a subsequent purchaser (s20, s59(6) Land Registration Act 1925).

However, Ben may be able to argue that he has an overriding interest in the land under s70(1)(g) Land Registration Act 1925. He is in occupation of the land prior to the sale to Victor and he has a proprietary interest in the land by virtue of the estoppel. Therefore, provided Victor has not asked Ben whether he has an interest which he (Ben) deliberately concealed, all the elements of s70(1)(g) would appear to be present. In these circumstances Victor would be bound by the interest unless he took the conveyance from, and paid the capital monies to two trustees (s2 Law of Property Act 1925 - *Williams and Glyn's Bank* v *Boland* (1981), *City of London Building Society* v *Flegg* (1988)).

a) *If the agreement were in writing*

If the agreement were in writing it would comply with s2 Law of Property (Miscellaneous Provisions) Act 1989, and form the basis of a registrable estate contract. It could be protected by entering on a minor interest. Failure to do so would, as discussed above, make it void against Victor, but Ben may be able to rely on s70(1)(g).

b) *'Subject to Ben's rights'*

If the land had been sold expressly subject to Ben's rights, due to his knowledge Victor may be held to be a constructive trustee of the land for Ben even if Ben has not entered on a minor interest (see *Lyus* v *Prowsa Developments Ltd* (1982); *Peffer* v *Rigg* (1977) and *Binions* v *Evans* (1972)). This outcome has been the subject of much criticism especially as it runs counter to the clear wording of s20 and s59(6) Land Registration Act 1925.

Question 4

Consider the effect of

a) a lease of Redacre at a rent to Alf until he marries;

b) a lease of Pinkacre at a rent to Bill for five years which contains a covenant to renew on the same terms;

c) a lease of Greenacre at a yearly rent to Cal until the landlord requires the land for development, Cal goes into possession and pays rent yearly.

University of London LLB Examination
(for External Students) Land Law June 1993 Q4

General comment

A variation on the usual kind of question dealing with types of leases. The question centres on the relationship between s149(6) Law of Property Act 1925, s145 Law of Property Act 1922 and certainty of duration.

Skeleton solution

- Characterisation of a lease.

- Section 149(6) Law of Property Act 1925.

- Section 145 Law of Property Act 1922.

- *Parkus* v *Greenwood* (1950).

- *Marjorie Burnett* v *Barclay* (1980).

- Certainty of duration.

- Periodic leases.

- *Lace* v *Chantler* (1944).

- *Prudential Assurance Co Ltd* v *London Residuary Body* (1992).

Suggested solution

For a valid lease or tenancy to exist four things must be satisfied. Firstly, the premises must be sufficiently defined; secondly, exclusive possession must have been granted; thirdly, the term or duration must be certain; and fourthly, leases in excess of three years must be granted by deed, whereas periodic tenancies can come into existence without the need for writing at all. Periodic tenancies come into existence through the acts of taking possession and paying rent - the period of the tenancy being determined by the period over which rent is calculated.

a) By virtue of s149(6) Law of Property Act 1925, leases at a rent for life or lives or until the marriage of the lessee (as in Albert's case) are converted into leases for a term of 90 years. Albert therefore has a lease for 90 years which can be determined after his marriage by either party giving one month's written notice to expire on one of the quarter days.

b) A lease for five years with a covenant to renew on the same terms could be a perpetually renewable lease under s145 Law of Property Act 1922. It is a question of construction whether there is a perpetually renewable lease, with the courts tending to lean against such a finding. Basically, if the covenant for renewal is part of a separate obligation then there is no perpetually renewable lease (see *Marjorie Burnett* v *Barclay* (1980)), but if the lease is to be renewed on the existing terms 'including the covenant for renewal', then there will be a perpetually renewable lease (*Parkus* v *Greenwood* (1950)).

If, on construction, Bill is found to have a perpetually renewable lease, then under s145 of the Act it will be converted into a term of 2,000 years, which can only be determined by the tenant by giving 10 days' notice to expire on the date on which, but for the operation of the statute, the lease would have determined. In other words by Bill giving 10 days' notice to expire at the end of the five year term.

Moreover, if it is found to be perpetually renewable, Bill could, of course assign it provided the assignment is registered with the landlord within six months of it taking place. However, unlike other leases, upon assignment the assignee (Bill) ceases to be liable even in contract for breaches committed after the assignment by the assignor.

c) The problem for Cal here is to establish that there is certainty of duration. In order for a lease for a fixed term to be valid it must have a certain duration (see *Lace* v *Chantler* (1944) - where a lease for the duration of the war was void). This principle was reaffirmed in *Prudential Assurance Co Ltd* v *London Residuary Body* (1992), where the House of Lords said that the principle in *Lace* applied to all leases and tenancy agreements, and that a lease 'until the land was required for widening the road' was void because the period was uncertain. Therefore, following *Prudential* Cal could not claim to have a lease for a fixed term, as a lease 'until the land is required for development' is equally uncertain.

However, Cal has gone into possession and pays rent yearly, the combined effect of which is to establish a periodic tenancy in his favour - the period being determined by reference to which the rent is calculated. In Cal's case the rent is assessed yearly and hence there would appear to be a yearly periodic tenancy. Generally speaking yearly leases can be determined by such notice as the parties agree, failing which a half year's notice to expire on one of the normal quarter days is required.

Unfortunately for Cal, the House of Lords also held in *Prudential* that a grant for an uncertain term which takes the form of a yearly tenancy which cannot be determined by the landlord, does not create a lease. In that case although the plaintiffs had gone into possession paying a yearly rent, there could only be a yearly tenancy if the terms of the agreement were such that both the landlord and tenant could give half a year's notice, and that the term preventing the landlord giving notice until the land was required for road widening was inconsistent with a yearly tenancy. On the facts Cal would be in the same position, and his lease would be determinable upon six months' notice.

Question 5

Jake owned a baker's shop and a yard behind the shop which served as a carpark for his customers. Jake also owned the track that led from the highway along the side of the shop to the yard. On the other side of the track was Sid's carpentry shop and in 1965 Jake executed a deed granting Sid a 'licence' to use the track and to park his van in the carpark. This made it possible for Sid to deliver timber to the back of his shop and he therefore built a rear extension to the shop for the purpose of storing the timber. In 1991 Sid sold his shop to William, who has since expanded the carpentry business. Not only does William park his van in Jake's carpark, but William's two young apprentices also park their motorcycles there. Jake has now written to William demanding that he cease to use the track and the carpark and informing William of his intention to convert the carpark into a cafe for his customers.

Advise William.

University of London LLB Examination
(for External Students) Land Law June 1993 Q5

General comment

A question which requires the candidate to distinguish between easements and licences. The principles relating to the acquisition of leases are important. Candidates should not try to put square pegs into round holes - (if it is not an easement do not try to make it one).

Skeleton solution

* *Re Ellenborough Park* (1956).

* Accommodation.

* Exclusive possession.

* *Newman* v *Jones* (1982).

* *London & Blenheim Estates Ltd* v *Ladbroke Retail Parks Ltd* (1993).

* Acquisition.

* Express grant.

* Section 62 Law of Property Act 1925.

* Licences.

* Estoppel.

* *Ashburn* v *Arnold* (1988).

Suggested solution

An easement is a right in or over the land of another. In order to be an easement the right in question must satisfy the characteristics in *Re Ellenborough Park* (1951), and must be properly acquired as an easement.

In this case William's continued use of the track and car park will depend on whether he can establish an easement in his favour. In the first place *Re Ellenborough* must be satisfied.

On the facts Jake's land would be the servient land and William's land the dominant, hence the first requirement of *Ellenborough* is satisfied. Secondly, the right of way and of parking must accommodate William's land. In other words, the rights must be more than personal - they must be of a proprietary nature (see *Hill* v *Tupper* (1863), contra *Moody* v *Steggles* (1879)). In so far as the rights in question are connected to the running of the business from the dominant land they may be said to be proprietary. Equally, they could be said to make the dominant land a better or more convenient property and to increase its value, factors which were recognised in *Ellenborough* itself as amounting to accommodation of the dominant land. Thirdly, as both pieces of land are not owned and occupied by the same person the third element of *Ellenborough* is satisfied.

Finally, the rights claimed must be capable of forming the subject matter of grant - they could have been granted by deed. There appears to have been a capable grantor

(Jake) and grantee (Sid), rights of way and parking are recognised as being sufficiently definite to be easements and, finally, the right to use the track (which is essentially a right of way) is undoubtedly in the nature of recognised easements. As far as the parking goes, easements to park have been recognised (see *Newman* v *Jones* (1982), *London & Blenheim Estates Ltd* v *Ladbroke Retail Parks Ltd* (1993)) despite the fact that the law is generally wary about recognising as easements rights which amount to a claim to exclusive or joint possession of all or part of the servient land (see *Copeland* v *Greenhalf* (1952)).

Subject to the exclusive possession point, it appears that both the rights in question have the characteristics of an easement.

In terms of acquisition, although Jake granted Sid a licence, he did not expressly grant him an easement (*IDC Group Ltd* v *Clark* (1992)). Neither is there any evidence of the need to imply an easement of necessity or common intention. Section 62 Law of Property Act is not applicable as there has never, according to the facts, been a conveyance by Jake to Sid, and therefore Sid has nothing which he can pass on to William (*Quicke* v *Chapman* (1903)). Similarly, *Wheeldon* v *Burrows* (1879) is inapplicable as there is nothing to suggest that Jake ever owned both dominant and servient land. Prescription cannot apply, not least because there is not a long enough period of user and the use has been with permission.

In the circumstances, whilst the rights in question have the characteristics of an easement, they do not appear to have been acquired as such.

It would appear then that what Sid had was a licence to use the track and car park. It could be that Sid had merely a bare licence, and in so far as Jake allowed William the same right of access he too had the same. If so, the licence would be revocable at any time and William and employees would become trespassers upon expiry of a reasonable time. Alternatively, it could be argued that there was a contractual licence with the deed forming the consideration. If this was the case, the better view is that such licences are personal only and would only operate in favour of the contracting parties (Jake and Sid), so that William would acquire no rights under it (see *King* v *David Allen & Sons Billposting Ltd* (1916); *Clore* v *Theatrical Properties Limited* (1936); and *Ashburn Anstalt* v *Arnold* (1983)).

Alternatively, Sid may be able to argue that he has an estoppel licence by virtue of the fact that he has extended his shop in order to store timber and Jake stood by and tacitly allowed or encouraged him to do so. In other words, if Sid can show that Jake's conduct was such as to make it inequitable for him to deny the existence of the right to use the path and to park (*Taylor Fashions* v *Liverpool Victoria Trustees* (1982)). If the estoppel arises then it can operate in favour of William, who may be able to use the same argument himself given that he has expanded the business. The court would, of course, have to decide how best to satisfy any estoppel which may mean that William will be entitled to continue to use the path and park.

Question 6

When Stella decided to buy a farm, she invited her lover, Paul, to come and live with her and help her run the farm. Stella paid the whole purchase price and the farm was conveyed into her sole name. When Paul asked why it had not been conveyed into their joint names, Stella told him that there was no need for him to worry as he would get a half-share when they got married and as she was going to leave him her London apartment in her will anyway. Stella and Paul never married but they worked hard on the farm for several years, sharing the profits equally, and as a result the value of the farm doubled. Recently Stella has died leaving all her estate to her mother. Paul now claims both the farm and the London apartment.

Advise Stella's mother.

University of London LLB Examination
(for External Students) Land Law June 1993 Q6

General comment

A standard question on the acquisition of interests in land dealing with resulting trusts, constructive trusts and proprietary estoppel. A knowledge of the decision in *Hammond* v *Mitchell* (1992) would be useful.

Skeleton solution

- Conveyance.
- *Goodman* v *Gallant* (1986).
- Resulting trust.
- *Gissing* v *Gissing* (1971).
- Constructive trust.
- Informal agreement.
- *Lloyds Bank* v *Rosset* (1990).
- *Eves* v *Eves* (1975).
- Detriment.
- *Hammond* v *Mitchell* (1992).
- Estoppel.
- *Re Basham* (1986).
- *Grant* v *Edwards* (1986).

Suggested solution

The main issue here is whether Paul has any interest in the farm or London apartment.

As both the farm and apartment were vested in Stella's sole name, clearly Paul has no legal interest in them. Furthermore, there is no evidence to suggest that conveyances contained a trust in favour of Paul (contra: *Goodman* v *Gallant* (1986)). In the circumstances, if Paul is to have an interest he must have acquired it by way of resulting or constructive trust or by way of proprietary estoppel.

Farm

As regards the farm, Stella paid the whole of the purchase price thus ruling out any form of direct financial contribution by Paul to its acquisition. Furthermore, there is no evidence of Paul making any form of indirect contribution which would entitle him to an interest under a resulting trust (*Pettitt* v *Pettitt* (1970); *Gissing* v *Gissing* (1971)).

In order to claim an interest under a constructive trust Paul would have to argue that there was either an express informal agreement between the parties which he acted upon to his detriment, or that an agreement should be imputed between them giving him an interest (see Lord Bridge in *Lloyds Bank* v *Rosset* (1990)).

As for the former, it might be argued that Stella's excuse for not putting the farm into joint names was evidence of an agreement between the parties that he should have an interest, in much the same way as in *Eves* v *Eves* (1975), *Cooke* v *Head* (1972) and *Grant* v *Edwards* (1986). It does not matter that such an agreement came into existence after the acquisition of the farm, for as Lord Bridge stated in *Rosset*, in exceptional cases the agreement could come into existence at a later date. In any event Paul would have to produce cogent evidence of the agreement. If Paul can establish the existence of the agreement he also needs to show that he has acted to his detriment in reliance upon it. Clearly, Paul participated fully in the farm business and it may be argued that his involvement in the commercial venture was enough to give him an interest in the land (see *Hammond* v *Mitchell* (1992)). Alternatively, it could be said that there was no agreement that he should have an interest and the share of the profits was his only reward.

As regards the latter, the court would analyse the subsequent conduct of the parties to see whether they are sufficient to spell out some presumed intention on the part of the parties. Clearly, Paul's hard work would indicate that he should have some share, but, it could be argued, that should be limited to a share in the profits only. If a constructive trust arises in favour of Paul, his actual occupation coupled with the interest under the trust would give him an overriding interest in land under s70(1)(g) Land Registration Act 1925, which would be binding on Stella's mother (*Williams & Glyn's Bank* v *Boland* (1981)).

If Paul's claim to an interest under a constructive trust were to fail, he could rely on estoppel as in *Grant* v *Edwards* (1986). In order to do so, he would have to show the existence of a representation and reliance as in the case of a constructive trust (indeed in *Lloyds Bank* v *Rosset* they were recognised as being very similar doctrines). As described above, Stella's statement to Paul could be seen as the representation. As in the case of the constructive trust, Paul's wholehearted participation in the commercial activities on the farm could be seen as a detriment and evidence that he had acted consistently with the representation (*Hammond*).

If an estoppel arises in favour of Paul, the task for the court will be how best to satisfy it, and the court will do the minimum necessary to do justice to the estopel (*Crabb* v *Arun District Council* (1976)). The precise remedy appears largely to depend on the representation in that the applicant gets what he has been promised, be that the transfer of fee simple (*Pascoe* v *Turner* (1979)) or a life interest (*Inwards* v *Baker* (1965)). On this basis, if the representation is that Paul will get a one share that is what the court will award.

Apartment

The same principles as discussed above in relation to the farm are relevant when considering the claims to the apartment. As in the case of the farm, Paul has made no direct financial contributions which would justify an interest by way of resulting trust.

Furthermore, such acts as he has done to his detriment appear to relate exclusively to the acquisition of an interest in the farm and not the apartment. Those activities were not of a nature which would justify the inference of an intended proprietary interest in his favour in the apartment (see *Hammond*).

As far as proprietary estoppel is concerned, whilst it is possible for a promise of a future interest to found an estoppel (see *Re Basham* (1986)), the problem for Paul here is largely the same as that connected with constructive trusts, viz, his acts are acts of detriment connected to the farm not the apartment (*Hammond*).

In the circumstances, it appears that Paul will have a better prospect of claiming an interest in the farm, be it by constructive trust or proprietary estoppel, than he will in the apartment.

Question 7

In 1989 Leslie granted Alice a lease of Redstone House (unregistered land) for 20 years, Alice covenanting, *inter alia*, to pay a yearly rent of £10,000, to keep the house in a good state of repair and not to use the house for immoral purposes. In 1990 Alice assigned her lease to Bert and in 1993 Bert granted a sublease to Chris for five years. In 1993 Leslie assigned his reversion to Rachel. No rent has been paid since 1991, the house is in serious need of repair and Chris has recently been convicted to keeping a brothel.

Who has remedies against whom in respect of these breaches of covenant?

University of London LLB Examination
(for External Students) Land Law June 1993 Q7

General comment

A typical question on leasehold covenants. The question requires an exposition of the rules relating to the transmissibility of leasehold covenants and not an answer devoted wholly, or mainly, to remedies.

Skeleton solution

• Privity of estate.

• Privity of contract.

• *Spencer's Case* (1583).

• *Tulk* v *Moxhay* (1848).

- Sections 141 and 142 Law of Property Act 1925.
- Forfeiture.
- Section 146 Law of Property Act 1925.
- Landlord and Tenant Act 1927.
- Distress.
- Arrears.

Suggested solution

Leslie and Alice

In 1989 when Leslie granted Alice a lease for 20 years, there existed between the parties a contract (the lease being simply a form of contract) and privity of estate (a relationship of landlord and tenant with Leslie being the landlord). Between Leslie and Alice the covenants in the lease, whether expressed (repairs and user) or implied (payment of rent), are enforceable in contract, and their contractual liability is a continuing one lasting for the whole period of the lease even though in the interim they may have assigned their interests (*Celsteel* v *Alton House Holdings (No 2)* (1986)).

Alice assigns to Bert

In 1990 Alice assigned her lease to Bert, thereby ceasing to be tenant and destroying privity of estate with Leslie. Alice does, of course, remain liable to Leslie in contract. The effect of the assignment is that Bert steps into Alice's shoes provided the principles in *Spencer's Case* (1583) are satisfied. Firstly, the assignment must be by deed, and, secondly, there must be a complete assignment of the whole term. If these are satisfied then the benefit and burden of all covenants touching and concerning the land run to the assignee (Bert). Covenants which affect the landlord as landlord and the tenant as tenant touch and concern the land; personal covenants do not. In the present case all three covenants could touch and concern the land, so that under *Spencer's Case* the benefit and burden of them will run to Bert. At this stage there exists privity of estate between Leslie and Bert (a relationship of landlord and tenant) but not privity of contract.

Bert sub-leases to Chris

A sub-lease differs from an assignment in that the sub-lessor (Bert) retains a reversionary interest in the lease. Therefore at this stage, Leslie is the landlord, Bert is the tenant and Chris the sub-tenant. As between Leslie and Chris there exists neither privity of contract nor estate. The burden of the covenants cannot have run to Chris as there has been no assignment and he will only be bound by them if they have run under the doctrine in *Tulk* v *Moxhay* (1848) which requires the covenants to be negative in nature (*Haywood* v *Brunswick Permanent Benefit Building Society* (1881) - of the three covenants only the user covenant is negative in nature).

As between Bert and Chris there exists both privity of contract and estate - Bert is Chris's immediate landlord. Therefore, if Bert had inserted the same covenants in his lease with Chris as exist in the head lease, Chris will be bound by them.

As mentioned above, between Leslie and Bert there already exists privity of estate.

Leslie assigns reversion to Rachel

For there to be a valid assignment of the reversion it must be by deed, and provided this is satisfied s141 and s142 Law of Property Act 1925 have the effect of passing to the assignee the benefit of burden of all covenants which have reference to the subject matter of the lease (which is little more than a statutory formulation of touch and concern the land). Consequently, Rachel steps into the shoes of Leslie and can sue in respect of breaches committed prior to the assignment of the reversion provided they have not been expressly or impliedly waived by Leslie.

By 1993, Rachel is the landlord, Bert the tenant and Chris the sub-tenant. There exists between Rachel and Bert privity of estate just as existed between Leslie and Bert; between Rachel and Chris neither privity of estate nor contract, and between Bert and Chris privity of estate and contract.

Clearly the covenants have been breached, and according to the basic provisions of enforceability, Rachel can commence an action against anyone with whom she had privity of estate even for breaches committed prior to the assignment of the reversion to her.

Rachel v Bert

Accordingly, Rachel's primary cause of action will lie against Bert (subject to any waiver). In respect of the breach of the rent covenant she has several possible remedies, namely, an action for arrears, distress or an action for possession. There is no need for her to issue a formal demand under the Common Law Procedure Act 1852 as the arrears exceed six months.

Provided there is a forfeiture clause, Rachel could forfeit the lease against Bert. To do so for breach of the user clause she would have to issue a notice under s146 Law of Property Act 1925. As the premises would be tainted with immorality (*Rugby School v Tannahill* (1934)) the breach would not be capable of remedy and it is extremely unlikely that relief from forfeiture would be granted.

As for the breach of the repairing covenant, Rachel's initial remedy against Bert would be a claim for damages under the Landlord and Tenant Act 1927 - the measure being the fall in the value of the reversion. Failing that, she could forfeit the lease (if there was a forfeiture clause) by issuing a s146 notice suitably amended to inform Bert of his rights under the Leasehold Property (Repairs) Act 1938.

In any of the cases, if Rachel applies for forfeiture, Bert could apply for relief from forfeiture, as could Chris as sub-tenant. If relief is refused Chris's sub-lease, being a lesser interest, would fold with Bert's lease.

Bert v Chris

As Rachel's primary cause of action is against Bert, he in turn may have certain rights against Chris. Firstly, Bert may be able to rely on an implied indemnity whereby Chris indemnifies him for any breaches committed by him (Chris). Secondly, Bert may be able to rely on an express indemnity if he has inserted such a clause in his lease with Chris (s77 Law of Property Act 1925).

261

Rachel v Chris

Although Rachel cannot sue Chris directly due to lack of privity, she will be able to obtain an injunction (mandatory) to prevent the premises being used as a brothel because the burden of the user covenant will have run with the land to Chris under the doctrine in *Tulk* v *Moxhay*. For this to happen the covenant must be negative in substance (which this clearly is), and there must be an intention that the burden should run (s79 Law of Property Act 1925).

Leslie v Alice

As mentioned above, Alice remains liable to Leslie in contract throughout the term of the lease. Consequently, she could be sued on this basis, but may well be able to rely on an express or implied indemnity.

Question 8

'The 1925 legislation has endowed trusts for sale with all the advantages of settled land. Little would be lost if all settlements were made to take effect as trusts for sale.'

Discuss.

University of London LLB Examination
(for External Students) Land Law June 1993 Q8

General comment

This is not a write everything you know about settlements and trusts for sale, or a general comparison between the two. What is required is an analysis of the position of the tenant for life and trustees of the settlement with that of the trustees for sale.

Skeleton solution

- Settled Land Act 1925.
- Law of Property Act 1925.
- Section 19 Settled Land Act.
- Tenant for life's powers.
- *Wheelwright* v *Walker* (1883).
- Limitation.
- Section 106 Settled Land Act.
- *Re Trenchard* (1902).
- *Re Orlebar* (1936).
- Role of trustees of settlement.
- Powers of trustees for sale.
- Section 28 Law of Property Act 1925.
- Section 25 Law of Property Act.
- *Re Inns* (1947).

Suggested solution

The 1925 property legislation recognised two ways of settling land which have certain similarities but which, arguably, were intended to achieve different things. Traditional thinking has it that strict settlements (governed by the Settled Land Act 1925), are designed to keep property in the family whereas trusts for sale (governed by the Law of Property Act 1925), are to be used as a vehicle to ensure easier alienability of land.

The essence of the strict settlement is that the tenant for life - a beneficiary of full age and immediately entitled to possession of the land - holds the legal title to the property as well as his own beneficial interest. The tenant for life has a number of powers in respect of the legal estate. For instance, he can sell the settled estate although as a fiduciary for the remaindermen he must get the best price reasonably obtainable (*Wheelwright* v *Walker* (1883)). He can also exchange or lease the land, and, as in the case of sale, he is under an obligation to get the best rent reasonably obtainable. Additionally, the tenant for life can grant options over the land and mortgage or charge it for limited purposes, the golden rule being that the land can only be mortgaged for the benefit of the settled land.

As well as these powers the tenant for life has a host of minor powers, eg to cut and sell timber, to sell the principal mansion house and to compromise claims. The Act provides that the powers of the tenant for life cannot be curtailed in any way (s106 Settled Land Act 1925), so that any term in the settlement which is designed to prevent him from exercising his powers is void (*Re Trenchard* (1902); *Re Orlebar* (1936)), with the result that the tenant for life could validly sell the land thus defeating the supposed object of keeping it in the family. The corollary of s106 is s104 which provides that a tenant for life cannot assign, release or contract not to exercise his powers.

As for the role of the trustees of the settlement, that is peripheral. Their main task is to receive and hold capital monies following overreaching and to invest it at the direction of the tenant for life. In addition they are to receive notification from the tenant for life that he intends to exercise his powers and give consent where appropriate.

Although the trust for sale was, theoretically, designed to operate in a different way to the settlement, in fact it can achieve all that the settlement can. For a start, the trustees for sale, who may also be the beneficiaries, are given all the powers of a tenant for life and the trustees of the settlement under s28 Law of Property Act (LPA) 1925.

Moreover, in some respects much would be achieved by converting settlements into trusts. The trust for sale has several advantages over the settlement; for instance, it is simpler to create - it is not necessary to have two documents as in the case of a settlement and ss34-36 LPA 1925 brings trusts for sale into existence automatically in cases of co-ownership. Secondly, unlike the tenant for life, the trustees can delegate their powers to a person of full age who is beneficially entitled (s29 LPA 1925). Thirdly, and paradoxically, the trust for sale is a much better device for keeping land in the family if that is what is desired. It can be achieved either by the trustees exercising their power to postpone sale (s25 LPA 1925), or by making sale dependent on the consent of a named person (*Re Inns* (1947)). Fourthly, strict settlements only apply to realty, whereas trusts for sale can be used for both personalty and realty. Consequently, the settlor can deal with both in the one trust whereas if he wishes to create a strict settlement that must be done under a separate trust from the trust of personalty. Fifthly, Trusts for Sale are a much better way of giving concurrent interest to beneficiaries.

Clearly, there are undoubted benefits in replacing settlements with trusts for sale as the Law Commission recognised in their report on trusts of land. The Commission recommended that all settlements should be established behind a trust unless a settlement were expressly and specifically created.